Chinese St. Louis

From Enclave to Cultural Community

Huping Ling is Professor of History at Truman State University and the author of *Surviving on the Gold Mountain: A History of Chinese American Women and Their Lives.*

Chinese St. Louis

*From Enclave to
Cultural Community*

HUPING LING

TEMPLE UNIVERSITY PRESS
Philadelphia

To My Family—
Sami, William, and Isaac

Temple University Press
1601 North Broad Street
Philadelphia PA 19122
www.temple.edu/tempress

Copyright © 2004 by Temple University

All rights reserved

Published 2004

Printed in the United States of America

∞ The paper used in this publication meets the requirements of the
American National Standard for Information Sciences—Permanence
of Paper for Printed Library Materials, ANSI Z39.48-1984

LIBRARY OF CONGRESS CATALOGING-IN-PUBLICATION DATA

Ling, Huping,1956–
   Chinese St. Louis : from enclave to cultural community /
Huping Ling.
      p. cm.
   Includes bibliographical references (p.) and index.
   ISBN 1-59213-038-0 (cloth : alk. paper) – ISBN 1-59213-039-9
(pbk. : alk. paper)
1. Chinese Americans–Missouri–Saint Louis–History.
2. Chinese Americans–Missouri–Saint Louis–Social conditions.
3. Chinese Americans–Cultural assimilation–Missouri–Saint
Louis. 4. Chinese Americans–Missouri–Saint Louis–Societies, etc.
5. Ethnic neighborhoods–Missouri–Saint Louis–History.
6. Community life–Missouri–Saint Louis–History. 7. Saint Louis
(Mo.)–Ethnic relations. 8. Saint Louis (Mo.)–Social conditions.
I. Title: Chinese Saint Louis. II. Title.
   F474.S29C5 2004
   977.8′6600451–dc22

2004044017

2 4 6 8 9 7 5 3 1

Contents

Acknowledgments

THE CHINESE SAYING *"Yin shui si yuan"* (One should appreciate the origins of a river when drinking its water) well expresses my feelings now that I have finished this book. As I hold the thick manuscript in my hands and remember the long, challenging intellectual quest, I am keenly aware of the debt I owe the following people and institutions for their kindness, generosity, and selfless support.

My gratitude goes first to the many Chinese Americans in St. Louis. From the very beginning of this project they supported me with enthusiasm and in every possible way. The city's two Chinese-language newspapers, the *St. Louis Chinese American News* and the *St. Louis Chinese Journal*, supplied me with their weekly issues. Hundreds of Chinese St. Louisans provided me with useful information. More than sixty individuals welcomed me warmly into their homes, businesses, and offices and contributed their time and their memories. My heartfelt thanks to Lillie Hong, Annie Leong, Ann Ko, and Don Ko, all former residents of Hop Alley, without whose participation the project could never have been completed; to Richard Ho, a veteran of the St. Louis Chinatown now residing elsewhere, who sought me out after reading a news item about this project in the newsletter of the Chinese Historical Society of America, and who corresponded with me through the mail despite his ailment and advanced age; and to Hong Sit, another former Hop Alley resident, now living in Houston, Texas, who offered me his life history and a published autobiography. I am especially grateful to Doris Bounds, Haiyan Cai, Kin Cai, James Chi, Patti Chi, Edwin Chiu, Jean Chiu, Mi Chou, Miller Chow, Anna Crosslin, Ngoc Doan, Hung-Gay Fong, Tony Gao, Melissa Henry, Mu-lien Hsueh, Eric Huang, Wen Hwang, Xinsheng Jiang, Lily Ko, Walter Ko, Yee M. Kwong, Harold Law, Hong L. Le, Susanne LeLaurin, Chung Kok Li, Jerry Li, Zhihai Liang, Sherwin Liou, Grace Shen Lo, Grace Yin Lo,

Andrew Lu, Chris Lu, Jenny Lu, Karman Mak, Ed. Moncada, Samuel Pan, Dachung Pat Peng, Tzy C. Peng, Eliot F. Porter Jr., Yuan-sheng Sui, Mrs. Siu, Bin Sun, Ching-Ling Tai, William K. Y. Tao, Tong Wang, Nelson Wu, Hsinyi Yang, James Yeh, Patricia L. Yeh, Grace Chen Yin, Guanzheng Yu, Francis Yueh, May Yueh, James Zhang, Peter Zhang, Anning Zhu, and Wubing Zong. Many other Chinese St. Louisans who have made significant contributions to the Chinese community and to the broader society deserve to be mentioned here, but space does not permit. Yet I am certain they will find it easy to identify with the collective experience of Chinese St. Louisans reflected in the book.

A number of colleagues offered advice and constructive suggestions over the years I worked on this project. I am indebted to Allan M. Winkler and David Robinson for their thorough editing of the entire manuscript. I am also deeply grateful to Louise C. Wade, Sue Fawn Chung, and Tony Peffer for their candid criticisms and important suggestions. I am especially grateful to Yong Chen, Roger Daniels, Timothy P. Fong, Madeline Y. Hue, Peter S. Li, Wei Li, Him Mark Lai, Thomas Spencer, Henry Shih-shan Tsai, John Kuo Wei Tchen, Philip Yang, Renqiu Yu, and Min Zhou, who read the manuscript in whole or in part and offered constructive advice. Yen Le Espirito, Karen Leong, Shehong Chen, and other colleagues at the annual conferences of the Association for Asian American Studies also offered helpful suggestions for improving the manuscript. I would also like to thank the two anonymous reviewers, who endorsed the manuscript enthusiastically while making useful suggestions. Tim Barcus, the photographer at Truman State University, provided vital assistance, and Winston Vanderhoof, the university's graphic designer, created the maps for the book. I am deeply grateful to Janet M. Francendese, the editor-in-chief at Temple University Press, whose persistence, efficiency, and specific suggestions enabled the publication of the book. I am also grateful to the other staff members at Temple University Press for their dedication, professionalism, and hard work.

Truman State University generously supported my research through its summer faculty research grants and sabbatical grant and by providing travel and conference funds. The Department of History at Washington University extended me a visiting professorship, which enabled me to begin researching and then writing this book. My thanks also go to the staff at the Missouri Historical Society Library and Research Center, the Mercantile

Library, the Olin Library, the West Campus Library at Washington University, the St. Louis Public Library, the Recorder of Deeds at St. Louis City Hall, the St. Louis Art Museum, the National Archive–Central Plains Region, Kansas City, Missouri, the International Institute of Metro St. Louis, and Valhalla Cemetery. All of these people offered me selfless support and advice.

My family was constantly and directly affected by this undertaking and shared my restlessness and frustrations as well as my joys. To them I dedicate this book.

1 Introduction

In 1857, ALLA LEE, a twenty-four-year-old native of Ningbo, China, seeking a better life, came to St. Louis, where he opened a small shop on North Tenth Street selling tea and coffee. As the first Chinese in St. Louis—and probably the only one for some time—he mingled mainly with immigrants from Northern Ireland; in fact, he eventually married an Irish woman.[1] Within a decade he had been joined by several hundred of his countrymen from San Francisco and New York, who came seeking work in the mines and factories in and around St. Louis. Most of them lived in boarding houses along or near a small street called Hop Alley. In time, Chinese hand laundries, dry goods stores, herb dispensaries, restaurants, and clan association headquarters sprang up in that neighborhood. In St. Louis, Hop Alley became synonymous with Chinatown.

Local records indicate that Chinese businesses—especially hand laundries—attracted a wide clientele. As a consequence the businesses run by Chinese immigrants contributed disproportionately to the city's economy. In the late nineteenth and early twentieth centuries the Chinese provided 60 percent of the laundry services for the city, even though they comprised less than 0.1 percent of the population.[2] St. Louisans willingly patronized these businesses but did not welcome the Chinese themselves, regarding them as "peculiar" creatures. Hop Alley was perceived as an exotic part of town and as a hotbed of criminal activities such as murder, tong wars, and the opium trade (manufacturing, smuggling, and smoking). Despite frequent police raids and the biases of many white St. Louisans, Hop Alley showed remarkable resilience and energy until 1966, when bulldozers of urban renewal leveled the area to make a parking lot for Busch Stadium.

The old Chinese settlement around Hop Alley disappeared. However, by then a new, suburban Chinese American community was quietly yet rapidly emerging. Over the next few decades the city's ethnographic distribution changed considerably; more and more Chinese were residing in St. Louis County—specifically, in the suburban municipalities to the south and west of the city. The U.S. censuses indicate that in the St. Louis area, the number of suburban Chinese Americans increased from 106 (30 percent of the total Chinese in the St. Louis area) in 1960, to 461 (80 percent of the total) in 1970, to 1,894 (78 percent of the total) in 1980, to 3,873 (83 percent of the total) in 1990.[3] Since 1990 the Chinese population of Greater St. Louis has been increasing rapidly—to 9,120 according to the U.S. census of 2000.[4] Various unofficial estimates, however, give the figure as between 15,000 and 20,000, with the great majority scattered through suburban communities and constituting 1 percent of the total suburban population of Metropolitan St. Louis.[5]

The Chinese population of St. Louis has grown substantially. There is no easily discernable commercial or residential Chinese district; even so, evidence of a Chinese American presence is visible enough. A Chinese American engineering consulting firm, William Tao & Associates, has helped design more than half the city's buildings and structures. Two weekly Chinese-language newspapers serve the community. Three Chinese-language schools offer classes in Chinese language, arts, and culture. A dozen Chinese religious institutions are heavily attended. More than forty community organizations sponsor—independently or jointly—a wide variety of community activities ranging from cultural gatherings to the annual Chinese Culture Days. The latter are held in the Missouri Botanical Gardens and attract more than ten thousand visitors each year. More than three hundred Chinese restaurants cater to St. Louisans, who clearly enjoy the ethnic cuisine.

How are we to understand this phenomenon of a not quite visible yet highly active and productive Chinese American community? How did that community evolve, and how is it unique? After I settled in Kirksville, Missouri, in 1991 to teach at Truman State University, I found myself intrigued by these questions whenever I visited St. Louis for business or pleasure. Longing for answers, I conducted a series of oral history projects among Midwestern Chinese Americans, in both metropolitan areas and small towns. I spent my sabbatical year 1998–99 in St. Louis researching the city's Chinese American community. For more than a decade, I have had ample opportunity to observe and participate in this community, to interact with its members in many activities, and to research its history. My work has taken me to libraries and archives, to public and private agencies, to Chinese burial grounds, to Chinese restaurants, grocery stores, bakeries, and florists, and to Chinese law firms and acupuncture clinics, as well as into Chinese homes. I hope this book will show the process by which St. Louis's Chinatown gave way to a suburb-based Chinese American community. To explain this transformation, I propose a "cultural community" model that will define St. Louis's experience since the 1960s and place it in the context of other multiethnic and multicultural American communities.

THE CHINESE COMMUNITY IN ST. LOUIS FROM THE PERSPECTIVE OF MIGRATION AND ASSIMILATION THEORIES

Among American academics, interest in migration and assimilation is nearly as old as the country itself. The literature on this topic is vast. Scholars have developed countless theories to explain how these processes have shaped the American character and how that character can account for the experience of various groups in their efforts to become part of American society.

As urbanization and immigration came to dominate American life, academics expanded their purview to include immigration and cultural assimilation. Robert E. Park, the University of Chicago sociologist, in his essay "Human Migration and the Marginal Man," argued that a migrant inevitably tried to live in two different cultural groups. This condition produced a "marginal man," and in the mind of the marginal man these conflicting cultures met and fused.[6] Park's writings strengthened the influence of the "melting-pot" theory. This theory—which was popularized by a play, *The Melting Pot*, written by Jewish writer Israel Zangwill and presented on Broadway in 1908—emphasizes the idea that as different ethnic groups interact, different groups of immigrants blend together, thereby creating "Americans" with American characteristics.[7] To test his hypothesis, Park launched a massive project, the Survey of Race Relations, on the West Coast. It ran from 1925 to 1927 and provided abundant data for later research on race relations and Asian American studies.

A postwar incarnation of the melting-pot theory is the "assimilation" theory developed by Milton Gordon in his classic work *Assimilation in American Life*. Gordon suggested that assimilation in America has typically involved seven stages: cultural assimilation, structural assimilation, marital assimilation, identificational assimilation, attitude receptional assimilation, behavioral receptional assimilation, and civic assimilation.[8] However, there is no single model of the assimilation theory, as Jon Gjerde noted in his book-length study of important problems in American immigration and ethnic history.[9] Oscar Handlin portrayed immigration as an experience characterized by uprootedness—by sadness, death, and disaster.[10] Unlike Handlin, John Bodnar looked at transplantation as a dominant feature of immigration. When confronting capitalism, individual immigrants "had to sort out options, listened to all the prophets, and arrive at decisions of their own in the best manner they could."[11]

Since the 1990s the "whiteness" of European Americans has been emerging as a controversial subfield of assimilation studies. David R. Roediger's *The Wages of Whiteness* was one of the first historical works on whiteness. Roediger discussed how white workers in the antebellum United States came to identify themselves as white. He argued that in a racist republic in which slaveholding was legal, white workers identified themselves by what they were not: blacks and slaves. In another important study of whiteness, *Whiteness of a Difference Color*, Matthew Frye Jacobson declared that race ought to be recognized "as an ideological, political deployment rather than as a neutral, biologically determined element of nature."[12]

Scholarship on Chinese immigration has focused largely on the causes and effects of the Chinese exclusion laws during the exclusion era. Most European immigrants assimilated into the "white" American culture after generations of hard work and sacrifice; in contrast, the Chinese—along with the Japanese and Koreans—were perceived by the public as members of a peculiar and debased race and therefore as "unassimilable." For this reason the study of the peculiarity of the East Asians was long categorized as the "oriental problem."[13] Perceptions that the Chinese were "nonassimilable" contributed to the Chinese Exclusion Act of 1882, which barred Chinese laborers from the United States. This law was not repealed until 1943.[14] Mary Coolidge's *Chinese Immigration*, the first important study of this subject, attributed the enactment of the Chinese exclusion laws to antiforeign sentiment in California[15]—an explanation later supported by Stuart Creighton Miller.[16] More recently, Lucy E. Salyer has written about how, as soon as it was passed, the Chinese fought doggedly to overturn the Chinese Exclusion Act.[17] Andrew Gyory regards the Chinese Exclusion Act as the precursor of the more far-reaching exclusion laws against Japanese, Koreans, and other Asians in the early 1900s, and against Europeans in the 1920s.[18]

Paul C. P. Siu was perhaps the first Chinese American scholar to propose the controversial "sojourner" hypothesis.[19] Gunther Barth similarly claims that the Chinese immigrated only to accumulate wealth and return home; thus they lacked the motivation to involve themselves in the mainstream culture.[20] In the 1960s the sojourner theory became the basis for most American scholarship on Chinese exclusion.[21]

Two decades later, scholars challenged the sojourner theory with evidence that the Chinese had been settlers from the very beginning—that in both Hawaii[22] and the continental United States they established permanent settlements and integrated into host societies. Scholars have documented that in the late nineteenth and early twentieth centuries, the Chinese settled around Monterey Bay, in the Sacramento–San Joaquin Delta, in the Rocky Mountains, and in Midwestern cities.[23]

In the postwar era, Chinese settlements have been overwhelmingly family-oriented. In the 1970s, after a century of imbalance, the male/female ratio of the Chinese American community finally achieved balance.[24] Moreover, inspired by the civil rights movement, millions of ethnic Americans began reassessing their cultural heritage and demanding that their cultures be represented more fairly in mainstream America. Academics have reflected on the demographic and social changes and have begun incorporating family and community issues into their scholarship. Rose Hum Lee studied Chinese family organization and social institutions in Chinese communities of the Rocky Mountains.[25] Stanford M. Lyman has examined family, marriage, and the community organizations among Chinese Americans.[26] One of my own studies has examined the changing roles of Chinese immigrant women in the context of marriage.[27]

Recent studies of Chinese immigrant communities have renewed interest in nationalism and ethnic identity, focusing on the impact of political, cultural, social, and economic conditions in the sending countries and on immigration and settlement patterns. Some anthropologists note that immigrants have lived their lives across geographical borders and maintained close ties to home; the term "transnationalism" has been used to describe such cross-national, cross-cultural phenomena.[28] A number of historians have endorsed this idea in their monographs;[29] among these, Adam McKeown's recent work is exemplary.[30] Ling-chi Wang's study classifies five types of Chinese identity in the United States, all epitomized in the following Chinese phrases: (1) *luoye guigen* (the sojourner mentality), (2) *zhancao-chugen* (total assimilation), (3) *luodi shenggen* (accommodation), (4) *xungen wenzu* (ethnic pride and consciousness), and (5) *shigen qunzu* (the uprooted).[31]

Meanwhile, Asian scholars and American sinologists have associated the identity of Chinese overseas with their host countries. Wang Gungwu notes that the postwar Chinese overseas preferred to see themselves as "descendants of Chinese (*huayi* or *huaren*)" rather than as "sojourners" (*huaqiao*), and their communities as "new kinds of local-born communities."[32] Harvard scholar Tu Wei-ming proposes a broad and tripartite division of China as "cultural China," including not only "societies populated predominantly by ethnic and cultural Chinese"—Mainland China, Taiwan, Hong Kong, and Singapore—but also the 36 million Chinese in diaspora as well as "individual Chinese men and women . . . who try to understand China intellectually and bring their conception of China to their own linguistic community."[33]

How does the Chinese community in St. Louis fit the above models? Transnationalism emphasizes two-way or multidirectional movements of migrants; in this context, the Chinese community in St. Louis seems to stay mainly within its own social boundaries. The diasporic paradigm and the idea of cultural China remain as workable methodologies, yet they lack specificity and precision in defining a Chinese community that has integrated economically into the larger society while clinging culturally to Chinese heritage. So it is clear that we must develop a new theoretical model to interpret the Chinese American community in St. Louis since the 1960s.

THE CHINESE COMMUNITY IN ST. LOUIS IN THE CONTEXTS OF CHINESE URBAN COMMUNITIES AND URBAN STUDIES

The preceding discussion of migration and assimilation theories points to the need for a new approach to examining the Chinese American community in St. Louis since the 1960s; a scrutiny of that community in the context of Chinese urban communities and urban studies underscores the need for a new theory.

Since the early twentieth century, Chinese immigration to the United States has been a mainly urban phenomenon. Table 1.1 shows that in 1930, 64 percent of the 74,954 Chinese in the United States resided in urban centers. A decade later the Chinese population was 77,504 and 71 percent lived in large American cities. By 1950 over 90 percent of the Chinese population resided in cities,[34] and the trend continues upward. Obviously, then, Chinese American studies must have a large urban-studies component, and scholars across all disciplines now realize it.

Like other immigrant groups, Chinese immigrants settled mainly in entry ports and major urban centers. In these urban settings they established their communities, known as Chinatowns. Chinatowns have evolved as integral components of the North American urban socioeconomic and cultural landscape, yet scholars have not been able to define "Chinatown" precisely. Historians and sociologists have studied Chinatowns in terms of their socioeconomic and cultural functions. When discussing the San Francisco Chinatown as it existed in 1909, historian Mary Coolidge described it as a "quarter" of the city established by the Chinese to "protect themselves and to make themselves at home."[35] Sociologist Rose Hum Lee offered a similar description of Chinatown: an area organized by Chinese "sojourners for

TABLE 1.1 Percentage of Chinese population in the United States by urban and rural residence, 1930–2000

Year	Total	Urban	Rural	Percentage of Urban
1930	74,954	47,970	26,984	64
1940	77,504	55,028	22,476	71
1950	117,140	109,036	8,104	90.5
1960	236,048	225,527	10,557	95.5
1970	431,583	417,032	14,551	96.6
1980	812,178	787,548	24,630	97.0
1990	1,648,696	1,605,841	39,631	97.6
2000	2,432,585	2,375,871	56,714	97.7

Source: Figures of 1930 and 1940 are computed according to Shih-shan Henry Tsai, *The Chinese Experience in America*, 105. The rest of the table is tabulated according to the U.S. Census, 1940–2000.

mutual aid and protection as well as to retain their cultural heritage."[36] In another study she described them as "ghetto-like formations resulting from the migration and settlement of persons with culture, religion, language, ideology, or race different from those of members of the dominant groups."[37] Anthropologist Bernard P. Wong has examined Chinatown in terms of racial discourse and views it as a racially closed community. Geographer Kay Anderson interprets Chinatown as "a European creation."[38] By far the most comprehensive scholarly conceptualization of Chinatown was probably made by geographer David Lai: "Chinatown in North America is characterized by a concentration of Chinese people and economic activities in one or more city blocks which forms a unique component of the urban fabric. It is basically an idiosyncratic oriental community amidst an occidental urban environment."[39] Lai's definition of Chinatown holds for St. Louis before 1966 but cannot account for the dispersed Chinese American community since the 1960s.

To contextualize the model of "cultural community" that I develop in this book, I will turn to a historiographic examination of how Chinatowns throughout America have been mapped.

TYPES OF CHINATOWNS

According to Rose Hum Lee, by 1940 Chinese Americans had established Chinatowns across the country in twenty-eight cities. San Francisco, New York, and Los Angeles were the largest, in that order. Of the country's 77,504 Chinese, 69 percent or 53,497 were congregated in these three Chinatowns.[40] Although Lee omitted St. Louis from this list of Chinatowns, a separate study by her suggests that St. Louis, with a Chinese population of 236 in 1940, would have been ranked twenty-second at the time, between Newark (259) and New Orleans (230).[41] To situate the Chinese American community of St. Louis in the context of Chinese American urban history, and to help readers understand the broader phenomenon of the Chinese American urban development in North America, I have categorized the studies of Chinatowns by geographical division and characteristic divisions.

Geographical Division

Chinatowns can be categorized by geographic location. Chinese American settlement has been an urban phenomenon across the country; that said, scholarly studies of Chinatowns in America have long limited themselves to the three main Chinese urban communities: San Francisco, New York, and Los Angeles.

The following are exemplary studies of San Francisco Chinatown. Victor G. and Brett de Bery Nee interviewed residents and on the basis of that work compiled *Longtime Californ'*, which explores the forces that created San Francisco Chinatown and that continue to account for its resilience and cohesiveness as an ethnic community.[42] Thomas W. Chinn's *Bridging the Pacific* chronicles the history of San Francisco Chinatown through its social structure and the people who helped shape its history.[43] Chalsa M. Loo's *Chinatown: Most Time, Hard Time* is an empirical study that provides "an understanding of the life problems, concerns, perceptions, and needs" of the Chinatown residents.[44] Yong Chen's *Chinese San Francisco, 1850–1943*, depicts the cultural and social transformation of the Chinese in San Francisco over a century.[45] Nayan Shah's *Contagious Divides: Epidemics and Race in San Francisco's Chinatown* offers fresh insights into complex issues of public health and race in the city.[46]

There is also a rich literature on New York Chinatown. Anthropologist Bernard P. Wong alone has written three books about it. In these he analyzes the dynamics of the interpersonal relationships of the Chinese and their contributions to the economic well-being and social life of the community,[47] investigates the adaptation of the Chinese in New York,[48] and examines how the patronage and brokerage systems developed and have been manipulated.[49] Similarly, two studies by Peter Kwong examine the social structure of New York Chinatown.[50] New York Chinatown may look cohesive; in fact, it is a polarized community: the "Uptown Chinese," professionals and business leaders, are engaged in property speculation, while the "Downtown Chinese," manual laborers and service workers, must work in Chinatown and rent tenement apartments there.[51] Sociologist Min Zhou studies and writes about social and economic life in New York Chinatown, challenges past notions that Chinatown is an urban ghetto plagued by urban problems, and describes Chinatown as an immigrant enclave with strong socioeconomic potential.[52]

Scholarship on New York makes note of alternative settlement models to Chinatown. Hsiang-shui Chen's work on the post-1965 Taiwanese immigrant neighborhoods of Flushing and Elmhurst in Queens asserts that these communities are no longer Chinatowns; their residents are beginning to scatter and to mix with other ethnic groups.[53] Jan Lin's study presents New York Chinatown as a global town.[54] Scholarly literature has also looked into the work-force of New York Chinatown, with particular regard to unioniza-tion among hand laundrymen (such as Renqiu Yu's study) and Chinese women garment workers (such as Xiaolan Bao's study).[55] Some writers (such as Xinyang Wang) have begun utilizing a comparative approach.[56]

The Chinatowns of Los Angeles have also begun attracting the attention of scholars. Timothy P. Fong in *The First Suburban Chinatown* uses ethnographic observation, archival research, oral history interviews, and sociological imagination to present the experiences of the multiethnic residents of Monterey Park and their reactions to change in the community.[57] John Horton's work views the multiethnic diversity of Monterey Park as the key to understanding the middle-class city in an era of rapid economic globalization.[58] Similarly, Yen-Fen Tseng asserts that the Chinese ethnic economy in Los Angeles has formed multinuclear con-centrations in suburban communities in the San Gabriel Valley. The inflow of capital and entrepreneurs from the Chinese diaspora has strongly integrated the valley's economy with that of the Pacific Rim.[59] Leland T. Saito's study also examines Monterey Park, with special attention to Asian Americans' participation in local political campaigns.[60] Geographer Wei Li proposes a new model of ethnic settlement in Los Angeles: *ethnoburbs* (ethnic suburbs), that is, suburban ethnic clusters of residential areas and business districts in large metropolitan areas that are intertwined with the global, national, and place-specific conditions.[61]

Characterizational Divisions

Chinatown studies have also looked at social structures, socioe-conomic functions, and ethnic composition and physical space. In terms of the social structure of Chinatowns, scholars are debating whether Chinatowns are communities of ethnic cohesion or ethnic class cleavage. Earlier studies perceived Chinatowns as communities of order and harmony; more recent studies by Peter Kwong, Chalsa Loo, and Jan Lin have viewed Chinatowns as oppressive and polarized communities in which ethnic capitalists and a political elite have exploited those with less education, money, skills, and knowledge of English—albeit not without challenges from this group.

In terms of the socioeconomic functions of Chinatowns, researchers disagree as to whether Chinatowns have impeded

assimilation. Some scholars focus on the social and economic problems of ethnic communities; others see Chinatowns as dynamic
and economically successful. The former view, represented by Rose
Hum Lee, Peter Kwong, and Chalsa Loo, sees the residents of Chinatowns as caught in a world that works against social mobility
and cultural assimilation. In contrast, Min Zhou's work emphasizes
that Chinatown economies offer jobs to new immigrants and that
as a consequence of these opportunities, the second and third generations find social and cultural integration an easier task.

In terms of the ethnic composition and physical space of
Chinatowns, the differences relate to whether Chinatowns are
isolated and homogenous urban ghettos or multiethnic suburban
communities. The former position, found in most works dealing
with Chinatowns, treats Chinatowns as urban ghettos or enclaves
consisting of mainly Chinese immigrants. The latter argument,
represented by Hsiang-shui Chen, Timothy P. Fong, Yen-Fen Tseng,
Jan Lin, and Wei Li, asserts that with the diverse socioeconomic
backgrounds of new immigrants since the mid-1960s, Chinese
communities are no longer homogenous and strongly urban;
rather, the Chinese are mixing with other ethnic groups and are
increasingly suburban.

It is generally understood that every settlement includes two
basic elements: physical space and social space. The physical
space establishes the geographical boundaries within which the
settlement is defined and its members interact in a multitude of
ways: economically, socially, culturally. The physical space is
easy to recognize; however, the social space of a community is
not necessarily confined by its physical space and can extend
beyond the physical boundaries of the settlement.

Most of the above-noted studies focused on the physical space of
a given Chinese community, be it urban or suburban; thus
they overlooked its social space. Before the appearance of suburban
Chinese communities, there was no problem to interpret Chinatowns with physical spatial boundaries. The traditional Chinatowns in San Francisco, New York City, Chicago, and many other
urban centers—including the old Chinatown of St. Louis—were
unquestionably urban ethnic ghettos or enclaves. Yet ever since the
emergence of suburban Chinese communities, such as the ones in
Oakland, New York (Flushing), and Los Angeles (Monterey Park),
scholars have struggled to interpret them accurately. Timothy P.
Fong sees a continuity between urban ethnic enclaves and the

suburban Chinese communities. However, Wei Li's "ethnoburb" model notes the contrast between traditional urban Chinese settlements and ethnoburbs.[62] Yen-Fen Tseng contends that in Los Angeles the strong expansion of upper-class professional jobs and service/petty-manufacturing jobs has created dual cities.[63] Similarly, Jan Lin argues that inner-city congestion has driven the development of "satellite Chinatowns" in the suburbs.[64] Yet all of these models focus on the geographical parameters of the new Chinese suburban settlements and thus fail to explain how there can be an ethnic community without a geographical concentration.

Clearly, unless we consider the social space of a Chinese settlement, we will find it difficult to explain why new suburban Chinese communities have emerged, have scattered, and have blended with other ethnic groups. The physical definition of a community is not adequate to explain these dispersed suburban settlements. This is why we must study the socioeconomic structures of the suburban Chinese communities not only in terms their physical parameters, but also in terms of their social dimensions.

DEFINING CULTURAL COMMUNITY AND ITS SIGNIFICANCE

Defining Cultural Community

Resting on the framework of social space, this study proposes a new model of the Chinese American community in St. Louis as a "cultural community." A cultural community does not necessarily have particular physical boundaries; instead it is defined by the common cultural practices and beliefs of its members. A cultural community is constituted by its language schools, religious institutions, community organizations, cultural agencies, and political coalitions or ad hoc committees, and by the broad range of cultural celebrations and activities facilitated by the aforementioned agencies and groups. Since the 1960s the St. Louis Chinese community has been a typical cultural community. Its members live everywhere in the city and its suburbs; there are no substantial business and residential concentrations or clusters that would constitute a "Chinatown" or a "suburban Chinatown." Yet the Chinese St. Louisans have nurtured their community through various cultural activities organized by community groups and cultural institutions. They have preserved their cultural heritage and achieved ethnic solidarity without a recognizable physical community. Such a community is better understood as a cultural community.

A cultural community can also be identified by its economy, demography, and geography. In economic terms, the great majority of Chinese Americans in St. Louis have been professionally integrated into the larger society; as a consequence, the economy within their community does not significantly affect the well-being of its members and the community as a whole. In demographic terms, the Chinese American cultural community in St. Louis includes a large proportion of professionals and self-employed entrepreneurs; one consequence is that their economic well-being depends more heavily on the larger economy than on the Chinese American "ethnic" economy. The professionals are employed mainly by firms in the larger society; the entrepreneurs, although self-employed, also depend on the general population for their economic success. Only a small portion of Chinese Americans in St. Louis can be categorized as working-class. In geographic terms, a cultural community is more likely to be found in a hinterland or remote area, where the transnational economy has only limited penetration.

In the Chinese suburban communities in Flushing and Monterey Park—and in Vancouver and Toronto, in Canada—Chinese Americans/Canadians have invested heavily in the banking, manufacturing, real estate, and service sectors. In contrast, the Chinese Americans in St. Louis tend mainly to be professionals in the employ of mainstream companies and agencies.[65] It follows that economic self-interest is less likely to be the driving force behind the St. Louis Chinese community. In St. Louis the Chinese are more likely to congregate at cultural institutions such as language schools, churches, and temples, or at cultural activities organized by community groups. Moreover, the Chinese American community in St. Louis has no clearly defined physical boundaries, either in the inner city or in the suburbs.

SIGNIFICANCE OF THE CULTURAL COMMUNITY MODEL

The cultural community model can do more than simply help us interpret the St. Louis Chinese American community. First, the idea of cultural community can serve as a new model for understanding other Chinese American communities—that is, those in which Chinese professionals have assimilated into the broader society and their work is not tightly linked with the Chinese ethnic community. This model can be applied to places where there are not enough Chinese to constitute a large physical ethnic concentration, but there are enough that social communities can

form, with or without physical boundaries. In such circumstances, the cultural community model is yet another avenue for
understanding the complexities of contemporary Chinese American
communities.

Second, the cultural community model can help us better
understand issues of cultural identity. A cultural community does
not form to meet economic needs (i.e., for mutual aid); rather, it
forms to meet people's psychological needs (i.e., for a cultural
and ethnic identity). When the Chinese Americans are scattered
throughout middle-class or upper-middle-class neighborhoods, it
is difficult and less practical for them to establish a physical
Chinese ethnic concentration. Their desire to share, maintain,
and preserve their cultural heritage encourages them to develop
cultural communities complete with language schools, churches,
community organizations, cultural agencies, political long-term or
ad hoc committees, and cultural celebrations and social gatherings.
On these occasions the presence of other Chinese Americans
makes it easy for them to recognize their cultural and ethnic
identity. Cultural identity and ethnic solidarity thus provide
comfort to those Chinese who do not have significant ethnic
surroundings in daily life.

Third, the cultural community model reminds ethnic groups
that they have reached a certain stage of assimilation and acculturation. History tells us that an immigrant or ethnic group's
advancement in America generally follows three stages: physical
concentration for economic survival; cultural congregation for
ethnic identity; and political participation or coalition for a sense
of democracy and justice.[66]

Most immigrant or ethnic groups, once they arrive in America,
must before anything else find a way to survive. Inevitably,
survival in an alien and often hostile environment relies heavily
on strategies of mutual aid; this is why ethnic groups form physical
communities. These ethnic communities have historically been
identified as "ghettos" or "enclaves," as ethnic settlements such
as "Germantown," "Jewishtown," or "Chinatown," or as replicas
of an ethnic group's original culture, as in "Little Tokyo" or
"Little Saigon." During this stage a physical ethnic settlement is
essential to the group's survival.

Once an ethnic group has economically integrated itself
into the larger society, mutual aid matters less; this explains
why physical ethnic settlements are soon enough abandoned.[67]

The economically integrated and geographically dispersed ethnic group now focuses on maintaining and preserving its cultural heritage without a physical ethnic settlement to make this easier.

European immigrants up to the 1960s had mostly constituted the earlier and larger ethnic components of America. By that decade most of the European ethnic groups had moved out of their ethnic communities and merged with mainstream, "white" society. Yet even these economically assimilated European ethnic groups—especially the smaller ones such as the Jews—still felt a pressing need to preserve their ethnic and religious heritage and to identify themselves by where their ancestors came from. Jews have met this need by developing faith communities complete with synagogues, schools, theaters, and cultural and social organizations.[68] Asian immigrants have demonstrated similar patterns in preserving their ethnic identity. Stephen S. Fujita and David J. O'Brien's study explains how Japanese Americans have succeeded in staying heavily involved in their ethnic community even though the vast majority of them have been structurally assimilated into mainstream American life. They have done so through their ability to perceive all members of their ethnic group as "quasi kin."[69] Kyeyoung Park documents the importance of Christian churches, community organizations, and other cultural institutions in stabilizing the Korean American communities in New York.[70] Linda Trinh Võ and Rick Bonus extend the contemporary Asian American communities to include those of "less territory-centered" and more "fluid" spaces.[71] Similarly, since the 1960s Chinese Americans in St. Louis have been forming a cultural community. During this stage, cultural and social spaces rather than physical space constitute the ethnic community.

Once an ethnic group has achieved economic security, it begins to participate in mainstream politics and social activism. The best example at hand is the Organization of Chinese Americans, which was organized in 1973 and ever since has fought against discrimination and social injustice directed toward Chinese Americans. The "Committee of 100," formed after the Tiananmen Incident of 1989 and consisting of one hundred prominent Chinese Americans, has lobbied hard to promote positive relations between the United States and China.[72] Since the 1990s, Asian Americans have become more involved in local and national politics with the goal of protecting their freedoms and civil rights.

During this stage, political manifestations of an ethnic community are more visible.

In summary, during its survival stage an ethnic community has no choice but to concentrate in ghettos or enclaves. Later on, this physical concentration gives way to community structures such as cultural facilities, social organizations, political groups, and even cyber-communities, all of which are less bound by geography. These rather than the original enclave constitute the group's cultural community.

SCOPE AND METHODOLOGY

The Chinese Americans in St. Louis have transformed themselves from a Chinatown into cultural community. In this process, significant questions have emerged. What forces—social, economic, cultural, geographic—attracted Chinese immigrants to the region? What have been the Chinese American experiences in the Midwest? What do those experiences tell us about Chinese American society as a whole, and in particular, what can they tell us about the Chinese on the East and West Coasts? Does the ethnic adaptation theory explain the settlement patterns of Chinese Americans in St. Louis?

The transformation of Chinese St. Louisans from Chinatown residents to a Chinese American cultural community coincided with the historical development of Chinese American society in the United States. The St. Louis Chinatown, "Hop Alley," which existed from 1869 to 1966, was a physical manifestation of ethnic solidarity and cultural gravitation; it was also the product of racial and cultural prejudice institutionalized by the Chinese exclusion laws. Hop Alley, like other Chinese communities, reminds us how adaptable and culturally resilient Chinese immigrants are. As more and more Chinese Americans entered the professions after World War II, and as a Chinese cultural community emerged in the 1960s, Chinese Americans showed how upwardly mobile they could be, both socially and economically. The 1965 immigration reforms, which brought more professionals to the United States, accelerated this upward mobility. The development of the cultural community since the 1990s is evidence of the potential socioeconomic and political influence of the new Chinese immigrants from Mainland China.

Chinese St. Louisans share a history with other Chinese Americans, but they also have their own unique history. Chinese settlement in St. Louis has been exceptional in a number of ways. Many Chinese came to St. Louis from already established Chinatowns on the East and West Coasts, but many others, from the very beginning, came to St. Louis directly from China. As happened in other American cities, the Chinese in St. Louis formed an ethnic enclave. Hop Alley was more than a place to eat Chinese food and see exotic sights—it was also a cultural institution that transplanted traditional elements from the homeland and absorbed new ideas from the adopted land.

As in other American cities, the first Chinese in St. Louis worked mainly in laundries, groceries, and restaurants. This occupational segregation was a product of racism and discrimination; however, it was also a reflection of the adaptability of the newcomers, who were seeking out niches that would enable them to survive in the New World. After World War II, and especially beginning in the 1960s, this pattern was broken when Chinese immigrants with better education and more fluency in English broke this occupational segregation and began entering the professions—medicine, engineering, computer science, and academia. The absence of a Chinatown after 1966 made it difficult for newcomers to St. Louis to survive without marketable skills and fluency in English. All of this explains why most Chinese St. Louisans today are professionals and entrepreneurs. By 1990, 80 percent of the Chinese in the St. Louis region who were working were either professionals or entrepreneurs; they were employed in the banking, insurance, real estate, business, and repair sectors. Also by that time, 83 percent of the Chinese in the region were living in the suburbs.[73] This high concentration of Chinese professionals and business owners is not something present in the major Chinese communities of San Francisco or New York. More importantly, Chinese St. Louisans today constitute a cultural more than an economic community. Chinese St. Louisans are more likely to gather at schools, churches, and cultural events than in Chinese business districts.

To highlight the transformation of the Chinese community in St. Louis from a Chinatown to a representative cultural community and to underscore the unique experiences of Chinese St. Louisans, this book includes nine chapters, which are divided into two parts—

"'Hop Alley,' A Community for Survival, 1860s–1966" and "Building a Cultural Community, 1960s to 2000s." This introductory chapter has defined the concept of cultural community and its significance in the broader contexts of the studies of immigration and ethnicity and urban history, by means of a historiographical discussion. It examines the influential theoretical approaches and methodologies, and compares and contrasts the significant literature in American immigration history and the Chinese urban studies.

Chapters 2 through 5 within Part I reconstruct the historical St. Louis Chinatown, "Hop Alley" that existed from the 1860s to 1966. Each of the four chapters investigates closely an aspect of the Chinese St. Louisans' experiences—the effort to build a self-defensive and self-reliant community, the attempts to assimilate into American culture, the self-governing mechanism of the community, and the dwindling and the final extinct of the Chinatown under the urban renewal campaign. Part I hails the triumph of ordinary Chinese men and women in the city despite hardship and adversity.

Chapter 2, "Building 'Hop Alley,'" portrays the effort of the early Chinese in St. Louis in building a community for their economic survival in an alienating environment. This chapter emphasizes the substantial contribution the Chinese made to the city in its overall industrial and urban development. Chapter 3, "Living in 'Hop Alley,'" examines the residential lives of the Chinese community from living quarters to final resting places in cemeteries, focusing on the fundamental issues of ethnic studies—class, gender, sexuality, interracial relations, assimilation, and ethnic identity.

Chapter 4, "Governing 'Hop Alley,'" chronicles the rise and the decline of the On Leong Chinese Merchants and Laborers Association, organized to cope with the discriminatory environment the Chinese merchants faced on the East Coast and in Midwest America. Although tainted with stereotypical imaging of criminal acts of tong-fighting and drug-smuggling, the St. Louis On Leong arduously worked to protect the commercial interests and legal rights of the Chinatown residents. Chapter 5, "Dwindling 'Hop Alley,'" examines the forces that limited the growth and contributed to the extinction of the St. Louis Chinatown.

Chapters 6, 7, 8, and 9 constitute Part II, which portrays a new type of Chinese American community—a cultural community—through its emergence and development. These four chapters define the nature and scope of the model of cultural community through chronological and thematic treatment, and pinpoint the significance and applicability of the model to other Chinese American settlements in the country.

Chapter 6, "Emerging Suburban Chinese American Communities," analyzes the factors in the formation of a cultural community. Continued urban renewal efforts repeatedly halted the attempts of the Chinese to rebuild a Chinatown. The newly arrived Chinese professionals had limited incentive to recreate a Chinatown. Meanwhile, the dispersion of the Chinese restaurant businesses made it difficult and impractical to form a new Chinatown.

Chapter 7, "Building a Cultural Community," defines the model of cultural community in terms of its nature, scope, and characteristics. The perspective of a cultural community concentrates on the social-spatial parameter of a community. A wide array of community organizations, ethnic language schools, ethnic religious institutions, cultural agencies, and a variety of cultural celebrations and gatherings constitute a cultural community.

Chapter 8, "Development of the Cultural Community," depicts the more recent expansion and development of the cultural community in St. Louis since the 1990s. Students and professionals from Mainland China have joined Chinese American professionals in St. Louis. During this period, the Chinese ethnic economy has become more diversified. Meanwhile, the Chinese Americans in St. Louis have also displayed a higher level of political participation in electoral and coalition politics.

Chapter 9, "Cultural Community in Retrospect and Prospect," finds the local variants of a cultural community among other ethnic minority groups and Chinese Americans in other areas. It views cultural community as an alternative model for understanding the ever-changing multifaceted American society.

This work is a useful addition to studies of regional history, urban history, Asian American history, and urban policy, for at least three reasons. First, it is difficult to understand St. Louis without understanding its population's multiethnic character—many St. Louisans are foreign-born. More than two hundred works have been published already to depict the multicultural and multiethnic nature of St. Louisans; these works have greatly increased our understanding of the region as a multicultural metropolis from the moment it was founded. Yet only a few of these works have dealt with the Chinese in the region, and most of these are merely compilations of data.[74] The underrepresentation of Chinese in scholarly works reflects the marginalized existence of Chinese in the past and the present lack of recognition of their significance to the region. Chinese Americans constitute only a little over 1 percent of St. Louisans today. Their social and economic contributions to the area have been far greater than that figure would indicate. For instance, the 1990 census found that 60 percent of the Chinese families in St. Louis had two or more workers, that 64 percent of Chinese St. Louisans older than sixteen were participating in the labor force, and that 78 percent of Chinese St. Louisans between eighteen and twenty-four were enrolled in college; in each of these categories the figures for the Chinese were higher than for the population of St. Louis as a whole.[75] Chinese St. Louisans are growing in number, and their visibility in the region is increasing, so it is important for scholars to study their history to get a better idea of the city's multiethnic and multicultural development.

Second, a study of the Chinese in the Midwest is needed for a more complete understanding of the Asian Americans. Most Asian Americans still live in the great coastal cities; however, the demographics have been changing in this regard since the 1950s. Asian American populations have been growing rapidly in the midwestern states. In Missouri, for instance, the Asian and Pacific Islander population has been doubling or tripling every decade since 1940. That year it was only 408 (0.01 percent of general population); by 2000 it was 60,000 (1.7 percent). These demographic changes have motivated scholars to expand the frontiers of Asian American studies. This study contributes directly to that expansion by focusing on a Chinese community in the Midwest, far from either coast.

Third, a thorough understanding of the circumstances of Chinese American communities will help governments at all levels formulate and implement urban policies as they relate to new immigrants and ethnic communities. The poignant history of Chinese St. Louisans undoubtedly has valuable lessons and insights to offer urban policymakers.

The sources employed in this study fall into two broad categories: American government records and pubic media, and evidence from the Chinese community. Chinese communities in America have long been perceived as byproducts of American public policies—most obviously, the immigration legislation and other laws affecting Chinese immigrants and Chinese Americans. To gain a comprehensive understanding of American public policies and their practical effects, I gathered national, regional, and municipal records. Immigration files in the National Archives in Washington, D.C., and Chinese Exclusion Act Cases in the Pacific Sierra Regional Archives at San Bruno provided copious information on the nationwide practice of the Chinese Exclusion Act. At the regional level, the Chinese Exclusion Cases Habeas Corpus Petitions (1857–1965), and the Records of U.S. District Court for the East District of Missouri from the National Archives–Central Plains Region, Kansas City, Missouri, offered valuable data on the early Chinese immigrants in Missouri.

At the local level, I searched manuscripts and data from St. Louis City Hall, the St. Louis Police Department, and various public and private libraries and archives, including the Mercantile Library, the Missouri Historical Society Library and Research Center, the Olin Library and West Campus Library at Washington University, the St. Louis City Public Library, and the St. Louis County Public Library. Regarding municipal records, the St. Louis Recorder of Deeds, the Annual Report of the Board of St. Louis Police Commissioner, and St. Louis Directories (to name only a few) told me a great deal about the lives of the Chinese in St. Louis at different points in history.

The U.S. Census and the annual reports of the Immigration and Naturalization Service provided a tremendous amount of data. In addition, American public media sources offered me a great deal of information about public perceptions of the Chinese and their communities. From these sources I collected many articles relating to the Chinese in St. Louis.

Chinese St. Louisans have not been merely passive victims of institutionalized exclusion and discrimination, of public prejudice and racial profiling. Rather, they have been active agents and both collectively and individually have shaped their communities and their history. For this study I developed a standardized oral history interview questionnaire that touched on the following: immigration background, education, employment, marriage, family, and sociopolitical activities. The interviews I conducted averaged two hours in length. By the end of this project I had interviewed more than two hundred Chinese Americans in the Midwest, including more than sixty from the St. Louis area. I located the interviewees through business and commercial directories and through public and private agencies. I selected the subjects so as to ensure as much diversity of perspectives as possible. I place great value in oral histories but am also keenly aware of their limitations; for example, memories are often selective, and biases are often unconscious. This is why when using oral history records, I always incorporate census data and archival documents. Also, in this study I never use information from oral history interviews without corroboration.

From a broader, collective perspective, the two local Chinese-language newspapers—*St. Louis Chinese American News* and *St. Louis Chinese American Journal*, established in 1990 and 1996 respectively—constitute a strong voice for Chinese St. Louisans.

I have also kept in mind that the history of Chinese St. Louisans cannot be separated from the history of St. Louis, of Chinese Americans, of American ethnicity and immigration, and of American urban development. For this reason, I have placed this case study of Chinese St. Louisans within the broader framework of St. Louis history, Chinese American studies, American ethnicity and immigration studies, and American urban studies. In this, I have consulted with both primary and secondary sources, as indicated in the classified bibliography.

I. "HOP ALLEY,"
A COMMUNITY FOR
SURVIVAL, 1860S–1960S

2 Building "Hop Alley"

Myth and Reality, 1860s–1930s

Meet me in St. Louis,
Meet me at the Fair.
Don't tell me the lights are shining
anywhere but there.

—*Meet Me in St. Louis* (1904)

SINCE THE MID-nineteenth century, immigrants from Germany, Greece, Ireland, Italy, Poland, Russia, and the American South had been coming to the booming city of St. Louis, Missouri. In the streets, peddlers of different nationalities sold coal, wood, and ice from dilapidated carts, giving the city a worldly appearance. Around this time, Chinese began arriving in St. Louis. By the end of the century the Chinese community had grown to about three hundred; for most of them, life centered on "Hop Alley." Along Seventh, Eighth, Market, and Walnut Streets, Chinese hand laundries, dry goods stores, groceries, restaurants, and tea shops served Chinese residents and the rest of the ethnically diverse city of St. Louis, which at the time was the fourth-largest city in the United States.

In this chapter I discuss how the Chinese came to St. Louis, what life was like in Hop Alley, and how other St. Louisans perceived the Chinese. I will describe the efforts made by the first Chinese in St. Louis to build a community that would enable them to survive in an alien environment. These pioneers faced much the same prejudice and discrimination as Chinese in other American cities and engaged in similar economic activities—hand laundries, restaurants, grocery stores, tea shops, and opium parlors. Their financial success and their disproportionate contribution to the city's economy did little to allay the suspicions of other residents. In this regard as well, their experience mirrored that of Chinese elsewhere in the United States.

EARLY ARRIVALS: FROM THE GOLDEN STATE TO THE MOUND CITY

Alla Lee was the first Chinese to settle in St. Louis. According to scarce records, he was born in Ningbo, a city near Shanghai, in 1833. He came to America in his early twenties with a missionary of the Episcopal Church, who intended to minister to the Chinese working in California's gold and silver mines and agricultural fields, with Alla Lee as his interpreter. With the help of church and business networks, Lee traveled to the East Coast. In 1857 he arrived in St. Louis, where he started a tea shop on North Tenth Street that brought him a modest income.[1] Alla Lee associated mostly with Irish immigrants in the area. Within a year he married a young Irishwoman, Sarah Graham, in the Second Presbyterian Church.[2] Their union produced several children.[3]

Regarding his unusual first name "Alla," one speculation holds that Alla is the first-person singular pronoun in the Ningbo dialect. When responding to a request for a family name, a Ningbo native would say, "alla [I am] Lee." Alla Lee chose "Alla" as his first name because it was easy for non-Chinese to pronounce and because the sound of it reminded him of his identity.[4] It is more likely that when he entered the United States on the West Coast, he responded to the immigration officer's question, "What is your name?" by saying, "Alla Lee [I am Lee]." His response was officially recorded as his name, and thus he became Alla Lee. There is no way to verify this speculation; however, the frequent alteration of foreign names into more familiar Western ones (e.g., "Smith" from "Schmidt" and "Yanni" from "Mastroianni" at entry ports has been well documented).[5]

Alla Lee kept a fairly low profile until 1869, when around 250 Chinese came to St. Louis from San Francisco in search of work. Many stayed in the city to toil in the local factories and mines. The Chinese immediately became objects of curiosity, and other St. Louisans flocked to Market Street to catch a glimpse of them. The Chinese were just as astonished at the reaction they generated among St. Louisans.[6] To satisfy local curiosity, several reporters visited Alla Lee, the resident expert. In this way more details about him entered the public record.

According to the news reports, Alla Lee was "quite a fine, intelligent looking Celestial" with "rather more than the usual height." He was "a thrifty Chinaman" "with a frank, open face, eyes that indicated a man pretty wide awake to most things." The papers described his Irish wife Sarah Graham as a "handsome Irish lady," a "buxom Irish lass," and a "Celtic beauty."[7] Apparently the couple won the newspapers' approval. Alla Lee answered reporters' questions about the customs of the "Celestials" with temperate and insightful information and explained why Chinese men wore the queue—it was a sign of submission to the non-Chinese Manchu rulers.[8]

A few weeks later, in January 1870, another group of Chinese arrived in St. Louis from New York. According to reports, they were procured by an F. A. Rozier & Company, a Missouri coal-mining company, and adapted well. Among the new arrivals were some Chinese women, who took charge of the boarding houses for the Chinese men.[9]

These accounts make an important point about the early Chinese presence in St. Louis: many new arrivals were "re-migrants" seeking new opportunities after their situations deteriorated elsewhere in the country. In the rather hostile social and economic climate of the United States, these immigrants had to keep moving to survive. Their paths to the Mound City—St. Louis's nickname (the early Native Americans had built many enormous burial mounds nearby)—were determined largely by religious connections, kinship networks, and the recruitment efforts of factory and mine owners.

The stories of Alla Lee and the Chinese workers in St. Louis are not unusual. Individual Chinese had been immigrating to America since 1785.[10] Then the discovery of gold in California in 1849 brought a wave of them. In the following three decades about 300,000 Chinese entered the United States, mainly to work as gold miners, laundry and grocery operators in urban communities, farm laborers in agricultural areas, or fishermen in coastal villages in California.[11] Although California continued to hold the majority of Chinese in the United States, the proportion of Chinese in California's total population slowly and steadily declined from 9.2 percent in 1860, to 8.7 percent in 1880, and to 3.1 percent in 1900.[12]

The anti-Chinese movement on the West Coast, which was given extra impetus by economic depression in the final decades of the nineteenth century, contributed to the redistribution of Chinese immigrants. Economic discrimination in the form of special taxes and levies targeted the Chinese. For example, in the 1850s a tax on foreign miners discouraged Chinese in particular,[13] and an 1870 San Francisco ordinance taxed laundrymen who did not use horses for their delivery wagon (i.e., Chinese with small operations).[14] Anti-Chinese sentiment also subjected immigrants and their businesses to physical attacks and abuse.[15]

The completion of the Transcontinental Railroad in 1869 also contributed to the dispersion of Chinese laborers. During the last stages of the construction of the Central Pacific Railroad, 90 percent of the workforce of 12,000 was Chinese. The availability of so many Chinese laborers heightened the competition between them and European Americans. Although most of the discharged railroad workers found jobs in agriculture in California, many others migrated south and east, to work on southern plantations or in new boomtowns such as St. Louis.[16] The *Missouri Republican*, a local newspaper, reported that approximately 250 Chinese railroad veterans visited St. Louis on 30 December 1869, and that curious residents swarmed Market Street to glimpse these "John Chinamen."[17] Many of these former railroad workers stayed in St. Louis to work for a wire factory.[18]

After the 1882 Chinese Exclusion Act banned the immigration of laborers, a few Chinese resorted to trafficking in human beings. The profits for smugglers were very high. How Chun Pong, a Cantonese immigrant, first landed in Vancouver, Canada, in 1899. He worked as a laundryman for four years and then was smuggled to New York City by train. Later he moved to St. Louis, where he ran a hand laundry until he was arrested in 1913 for the allegedly smoking and selling opium. In his testimony, he described his illegal entry to Harry C. Allen, the United States Immigration Inspector:

> I boarded the train with a white man at Montreal. It was quite dark, and when I got in the car there was no one there except the white man and myself, when the train run about several hours until daylight and then the train stopped I don't know the name of the station. I was put in a small room on the train first and then I was brought out in the car where there [were] other passengers. And I left the train at New York City . . . [I paid] $130 to the Chinese smuggler [in Montreal] and he paid the white man.[19]

The Chinese on the West Coast were attracted to those American cities that were undergoing rapid industrial expansion. By the end of the nineteenth century, the country was producing three times as many manufactured goods as in 1860; every major American city was growing rapidly. The 1870 census shows that the population of St. Louis had reached 310,864, making it the

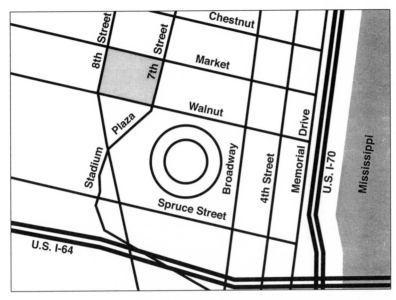

MAP 2.1 "Hop Alley" (shaded), St. Louis Chinatown, 1870s–1966 (created by Winston Vanderhoof, Truman State University Publications).

fourth-largest city in the United States, behind New York, Philadelphia, and Brooklyn.[20] Ambitious boosters like Logan Reavis, the owner of a local newspaper, *St. Louis Daily Press*, even started a campaign to move the national capital to St. Louis and published a book, *St. Louis: The Future Great City of the World*, which was widely distributed in Europe.[21] Although the effects of such efforts cannot be traced, they clearly were aimed at promoting the city's reputation and growth.

During the last decades of the nineteenth century, St. Louis became a city of rich ethnic diversity. Immigrants from other continents comprised one-third of the city's population.[22] Most of the ethnic communities were crammed into the north and south sections by the river and surrounding the city's business district. In the north, Biddle Street, which ran for twenty-six blocks from the river on the east to Jefferson Avenue on the West, was home to German, Irish, Jewish, and Italian immigrants as well as African Americans.[23] In the south the Chinese had formed Hop Alley, a commercial, residential, and recreational center with a population of three to four hundred (see Table 2.1).

Table 2.1 Chinese population in St. Louis (city) in comparison
with total population, 1870–1930

Year	Total Population	Chinese Total	Chinese Male	Chinese Female
1870	310,864	1	1	—
1880	350,518	91	91	—
1890	451,770	170	164	6
1900	575,238	312	310	2
1910	687,029	423	—	Several
1920	772,897	328	—	—
1930	820,960	350	—	—

Sources: Compiled according to the U.S. Census and *St. Louis Globe-Democrat*.
Note: Dash "—" in the table indicates no data available.

MYTH OF "HOP VALLEY" AND THE INSTITUTIONALIZED DISCRIMINATION

Hop Alley, a small back street running between Walnut and
Market Streets, was lined with boarding houses and apartment
buildings that were mostly occupied by Chinese residents. The
origins of its name are obscure. "Hop" sometimes refers to drug
use ("hop" means opium, thus "hop-heads" or "hopped up"). It
might be related to the American pronunciation of Cantonese
names such as Hop Sing. Some Chinese settlements in Nevada
and California were also called "Hop Alley."[24] Whatever its
source, the name for St. Louis's Chinatown apparently reflected
the cultural and racial biases of the larger society, and it was
eventually used for the entire Chinese quarter beyond the original
alley. Hop Alley first appeared in public records in 1896, in the
St. Louis Police Department annual report.[25] After the turn of the
century it was widely used in newspaper stories and other
accounts to represent the Chinese business district in downtown
St. Louis where Chinese hand laundries, general stores, grocery
stores, herb shops, restaurants, and clan association headquarters
were located.

Hop Alley, like many Chinese communities in other parts of
the country, was generally considered mysterious and dangerous
and was associated with opium dens, tong wars, and murders.
Most news stories about Chinatown in the St. Louis papers
were sensational stories of horror. In 1875 the *St. Louis Globe-
Democrat*, a major daily newspaper in St. Louis, reported that

"police throughout the nation were alerted for renewal of war-
fare between Chinese 'tongs'—secret fraternal and commercial
societies. A six-month truce ended with the murder of a Boston
man who set up a restaurant in a rival tong's area. Within hours,
shooting erupted in several cities, including St. Louis, where the
'king' of Chinatown was shot down by six gunmen."[26]

In 1883 the so-called "Highbinder Murder Case" took place in
St. Louis Chinatown. An African American man named Johnson
was killed in "an alley between the Seventh and Eighth and
Market and Walnut Streets" (namely, Hop Alley), and later his
head was found in a basket of rice. The local police believed that
a conflict between the African American man and a Chinese gam-
bler who was connected with the Highbinders was the cause of
the murder.[27] The Highbinders were the Chinese secret societies
allegedly associated with many murders in large Chinese communities. Though there were no witnesses, the police arrested six
Chinese men from Hop Alley as suspects in the murder. The
Chinese men were prosecuted vigorously, but due to lack of
evidence the court was unable to convict them.[28] Not only were
the local police quick to suspect Chinese as criminals, but the news
media regarded all Chinese in St. Louis as Highbinders. The *St. Louis
Globe-Democrat* estimated in 1892 that there were "about three
hundred Highbinders in St. Louis." That was practically the entire
Chinese population of St. Louis at the time.[29]

Aroused by the sensationalized media reports and guided by the
Chinese exclusion mentality,[30] St. Louis law enforcement agencies
assumed there were many illegal laborers and criminals among
the Chinese in the city and relentlessly targeted the entire
Chinese population. Figure 2.1 indicates that the years 1895 and
1905 to 1911 were the peaks for police arrests of Chinese. Unsurprisingly, the heightened police harassment of Chinese coincided
with the renewals of the Chinese Exclusion Law in 1892, 1902,
and 1904. Media reports confirmed the arrest data. According to
the *St. Louis Globe-Democrat*, on 25 August 1897, St. Louis
police rounded up all 314 Chinese in the city at the request of
a government agent who was investigating reports that illegal
Chinese immigrants had been smuggled into the city. Thirteen
Chinese men were found without proper documents and were
arrested to await deportation.[31] In the first two decades of the
twentieth century the St. Louis police repeatedly raided Hop
Alley and apprehended scores of Chinese individuals, charging
them with smuggling, manufacturing, and selling opium.[32] Immi-

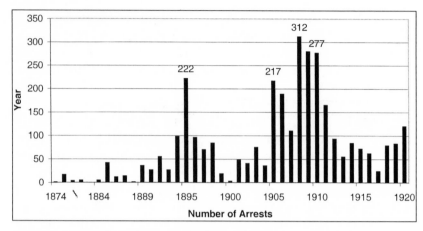

FIGURE 2.1. Number of arrests of Chinese by St. Louis Police Department, 1874–1920

gration authorities launched a nationwide roundup to identify illegal Chinese. The data for St. Louis from the 1890s to 1910s are worth comparing to those for Boston, Massachusetts, in 1903, when the police and the Immigration Bureau jointly searched Boston Chinatown for the tong murderers who had allegedly killed a member of a rival tong, and for Cleveland in 1925, when police arrested every Chinese in the city following a series of Chinatown murders.[33]

The negative media reports and the institutionalized legal actions that followed in their wake effectively demonized Chinatown and alienated its residents. One local resident recalled, "When I was a boy it was a great stunt for the older boys to tell the younger ones 'tall' stories about 'Hop Alley' and display their bravery by escorting them through the forbidden passageway."[34]

REALITY IN HOP ALLEY: BUSINESSES

What was life really like in Hop Alley? The absence of first-hand written records by Chinese residents has made it difficult for scholars. However, oral histories and critical readings of media reports and archival manuscripts enable us to develop a realistic picture of life in Hop Alley in the late nineteenth and early twentieth centuries.

In 1894, Theodore Dreiser, soon to be a famous novelist (*Sister Carrie*), was a twenty-three-year-old reporter for the

St. Louis Republic. He went to Hop Alley to write a sensational and somewhat biased story about the Chinese in St. Louis:

> Within the confines of St. Louis at present there are about 1,000 Chinese. Within the same confines there are nearly half as many laundries operated by Chinamen. The public is familiar with the Chinese laundry and the Chinese method of labor. It knows how they toil, is fully aware of their manner of clothing themselves and has read endless accounts of what they eat or are supposed to eat. Dissertations on social life in China, like that on the discovery of roast pig by Lamb, are common library familiarities, and the movements of the Chinatown at the Golden Gate have been recorded and re-recorded.
>
> St. Louis has no Chinatown and no specific Chinese quarters. The red and white signs one can stumble across almost anywhere between De Hodiamont and East St. Louis. She has no high-class opium-joint abominations and no progressive Chinese emporium to which upper tendom [sic] pays homage and money at one and the same time. She has, however, what it is difficult elsewhere to find—a Chinese rendezvous. In this rendezvous, restaurants, lounging and smoking rooms, a few Chinese families and general sociability prevail; and more, this rendezvous has the patronage and good will of the entire Chinese element in this city.
>
> When a St. Louis Chinaman wishes to "blow himself" he takes the requisite cash and saunters down that portion of South Eighth street lying between Walnut and Market streets. Here he finds every opportunity to dispose of his week's wages or profits, or, perhaps, his laundry— for laundries have been lost and won in this block. Sundays and Mondays are days off in the laundry business. At noon Sundays all the laundries in the city are closed for the day, and in a short time the different car lines begin dropping Chinamen by ones and twos in the vicinity of Eighth and Market streets. Some straggle around on foot, and by 2 o'clock, it is safe to say, there are several hundred Mongolians in this block enjoying themselves in a way peculiarly Chinese. The crowd shifts and changes all afternoon and evening, but never grows less. As far as one sporty John "goes broke" at the game of fan-tan another takes his place, and the broken one stoically gazes on while the winner keeps on winning and the loser drops out.
>
> The more pretentious of the resorts in this neighborhood have restaurants as side issues, a meal partaken at one of which will form the subject of a later discussion. The more pretentious keepers of these more pretentious resorts have wives and oblique-eyed babies, who are occasionally permitted to disport themselves, clad in the tiniest little blue frocks, on the front steps of the paternal dwelling. It is usually when the morning sun is streaming its genial rays into Eighth street that these little codgers may be seen, and then for a not over-length [sic] period. John has discovered "lat Melicans" are deeply interested in these queer little babies and are entirely too fond of stopping to enjoy their company.[35]

Dreiser's story about the Chinese in St. Louis points to the economic significance of Hop Alley as a unique component of an ethnically diverse city. It also reveals a strong curiosity (and bias as well) about the Chinese among St. Louisans generally. Once we discard words like "Celestials," "Mongolians," "Chinaman," and "heathen"—popular terms referring to Chinese, widely used by writers of Victorian era—a great deal of information remains, which offers a starting point for the following discussion.

Hand Laundries

Dreiser's report was the first known to describe the Chinese laundries in St. Louis. Certainly, Chinese hand laundries were ubiquitous in the city in the late nineteenth and early twentieth centuries. The hand laundry was the primary trade for the Chinese in St. Louis, as in many other cities. It is, however, unlikely that the Chinese population had reached one thousand by the end of nineteenth century, as Dreiser claimed in his story, or that about five hundred Chinese were operating laundries. Other sources indicate that more than three hundred Chinese were residing in the Chinatown area and that most of them were working in Chinese hand laundries in and around Hop Alley.[36] Court records further note that laundry was the primary trade for the Chinese in St. Louis until the 1930s. In the first decades of the twentieth century, St. Louis police raided Chinatown often and arrested Chinese laborers without Certificates of Residence. Most of these Chinese laborers worked in Chinese laundries.[37] The census also offers information about the Chinese laundrymen. The 1890 census recorded that a Chinese man named Amon Donn was running a Chinese hand laundry in the St. Louis downtown.[38]

The above sources provide only sketchy or anecdotal information about the Chinese hand laundrymen. Fortunately, *Gould's St. Louis Directories* provide more systematic and significant data on the Chinese hand laundry business in St. Louis. Chinese hand laundries first appeared in *Gould's St. Louis Directories* in 1873. That year, six Chinese laundries were listed among the total of thirty laundries in the city: Ah Wah at 810 and 811 Pine Street; Hap Kee at 511 Market; Lee Yee at 623 Locust; Sing Chang at 12 South Sixth Street; Wah Lee at 320 Chestnut Street; and Yet Sing at 112 North Seventh Street.[39] The following year, ten Chinese laundries were listed among the city's thirty-six laundries.[40] The number of Chinese laundries continued to increase until 1888, when seventy-three Chinese laundries were listed; then, starting in 1889, for reasons unknown, Chinese laundries suddenly disappeared from the directory.[41]

According to *Gould's St. Louis Directory* (see Table 2.2), the sixteen years from 1873 to 1889 constituted the initial stage of

TABLE 2.2 Chinese Hand Laundries in St. Louis, 1873–1944

Year	Chinese Laundries	All Laundries	Year	Chinese Laundries	All Laundries
1873	6	30	1916	108	150
1874	10	36	1917	102	246
1875	4	45	1918	112	206
1876	12	62	1919	102	189
1977	11	65	1920	98	—
1878	9	90	1921	100	186
1879	10	85	1922	91	201
1880	13	131	1923	96	200
1881	22	118	1924	114	220
1882	28	118	1925	140	256
1883	36	138	1926	148	258
1884	44	153	1927	149	267
1885	50	159	1928	143	337
1886	70	170	1929	165	278
1887	59	128	1930	161	278
1888	76	173	1931	155	231
1889	0	89	1932	128	221
1890	0	89	1933	123	—
1891	0	84	1934	123	—
1892*	0	90	1935	104	214
1911	36	—	1936	123	269
1912	56	153	1939	89	173
1913	53	164	1941	78	169
1914	83	194	1944	48	63
1915	97	—			

Source: Tabulated according to *Gould's St. Louis Directory for 1873–1944.*
* From 1893 to 1910, the total numbers of laundries were not tallied, as no Chinese laundries were listed during this period.
Note: A dash "—" in the table indicates no data available.

the Chinese hand laundry business in St. Louis. During this period, Chinese laundries grew in number and spread beyond the boundaries of Hop Alley. Between 1873 and 1879 all Chinese laundries were located in Chinatown, mainly clustering along Sixth, Seventh, Eighth, Market, Chestnut, Pine, Locust, and Elm streets. After 1880 a few laundries opened on Chinatown's periphery, for example, on Washington and Chouteau avenues.[42]

Chinese hand laundries started to reappear in *Gould's St. Louis Directory* in 1911, and the laundry business continued to be the primary occupation of the Chinese until the end of the 1930s. These three decades were the heyday of the Chinese hand laundry business. During this period, that business had two distinctive characteristics: clan domination and geographical dispersion. The surnames Kee, Lee, Leong, Sing, Wah, and Wing were the ones that appeared in the directories most frequently.[43] The Lee, Lung, Sing, and Wah clans were predominant in the 1910s, and were joined in the 1920s by the Kee, Leong, Lum, Wing, and Yee clans. After 1927, *Gould's St. Louis Directory* began listing Chinese hand laundries under a separate heading as Chinese laundries. By that year they accounted for over 60 percent of all the laundries in the city. In the listings, Lee and Sing were the two most frequent surnames. The predominance of certain clans in the Chinese laundry business suggests at least two important implications regarding patterns of immigration and urban ethnic adaptation. First, many Chinese laundrymen came to America as links in a migration chain; common surnames are clear indicators of blood ties, or lineage among the Chinese laundrymen, although they could also indicate the practice of sponsoring "paper sons." Basically, this involved sponsoring an immigrant by falsely claiming a blood relationship and thereby end-running the Chinese exclusion laws. Second, it points to the vital importance of ethnic networking in initiating and operating a business (as will be illustrated later in the cases of the Gee brothers and Lum Hey).

Geographical dispersion was also evident among the Chinese hand laundries from the 1910s to 1930s. In the earliest stages of the Chinese laundry business, laundries were concentrated in the Chinese business district; now the Chinese laundries were scattered throughout the city. The geographical dispersion was partly a result of self-governance—that is, of the Chinese community taking steps to prevent competition among the laundries. The On Leong Merchants and Laborers Association, the most important Chinese business organization, founded in 1909, was the de facto Chinese government in St. Louis. It ruled: "One Chinese laundry within the perimeter of a mile." Any Chinese who violated this edict could encounter unexpected catastrophe if not death.[44] Intimidated by On Leong's power, Chinese laundrymen abided by the order. More importantly, the Chinese laundrymen followed the fundamental rule of economics of supply and demand; they would open a laundry wherever there was a demand or wherever a Chinese laundry did not yet exist. Since non-Chinese were the main clientele, it was natural for Chinese laundries to spread out across the city to meet the demand. The same pattern was found in other urban communities such as San Francisco, New York, Chicago, and Milwaukee.[45]

That laundry was a hallmark trade among the Chinese in St. Louis also reflected the occupational segregation the Chinese encountered across the United States. In San Francisco, Chicago, and New York, laundry was a vitally important business for them, as documented by Victor G. Nee and Brett de Bary Nee, Paul Chan Pang Siu, and Renqiu Yu.[46] This occupational segregation was largely a result of socioeconomic barriers confronting Chinese immigrants in the late nineteenth and early twentieth centuries. Most Chinese immigrants came from villages in Guangdong province, China. Few could speak English before immigrating, and few possessed any industrial skills. Without these skills they were practically excluded from the mainstream labor market and could only find jobs that mainstream laborers were unwilling to embrace. Laundry seemed to be such a trade. Washing clothes was tedious, arduous, and time-consuming labor, and only working-class housewives endured the drudgery. Furthermore, laundry required few skills and little capital. All a laundryman needed to start a business was a tub, a scrub board, some soap, an iron, and an ironing board. Chinese laundrymen could canvas a neighborhood, pinpoint a low-rent location, and open a business.

The central importance of hand laundries for the Chinese of St. Louis was also a result of immigration and settlement patterns. Most of the city's Chinese came from much larger Chinese American communities—San Francisco, New York, Chicago—and maintained ethnic ties with these cities through business networks and social and family contacts.[47] Chinese immigrants fleeing the social prejudice and economic competition of the larger cities brought their capital and past work experience with them to the city of their new destination.

As a consequence, Chinese hand laundries in St. Louis functioned in much the same way as those in other Chinese communities across the country. According to Siu, the typical Chinese laundry had four sections. (1) The front section, which usually occupied one-third of the house, served as an office and workshop. Here the laundryman ironed, labeled laundry, and waited on his customers. Here he kept the ironing board, the abacus, the laundry shelves, the lock counter, and the secret cash drawer. (2) In the center of the house immediately behind a curtained doorway (which was usually between two laundry shelves) were the living quarters. (3) In the center or rear part of the house was the drying room, which held an old-fashioned coal stove for drying the wet laundry. About a dozen strong wires were strung across in parallel lines to put up the wet laundry. (4) In the rear section were found almost all the laundryman's machines—the washing machine, washing sink, and steam boiler.[48]

Sam Wah Laundry in St. Louis was almost a replica of the Chinese laundry described by Siu. A Chinese man named Sam Wah opened the laundry in 1887 at 329 Market Street. He seemed to do well in the business; after 1912 he opened two laundries at 1408 North Jefferson Avenue and 4298B Finney Avenue, and after 1915 he was running four or five laundries simultaneously, including one at 4381 Laclede Avenue, which survived until 1986. In 1922 the aging Sam Wah brought his two nephews, Gee Kee One (also know as Gee Sam Wah) and Gee Hong, from Canton, China, to join him. Gee Kee One and Gee Hong disembarked at San Francisco, where they stopped to learn the laundry business. Then they went to Chicago to open a laundry. Unaccustomed to the cold weather in Chicago, they came to St. Louis to join their uncle.[49] They worked for him first in the laundry at 4381 Laclede Avenue and later inherited the laundry after Sam Wah passed away. The brothers operated the laundry under the same name using more or less the same techniques until 1986, when both proprietors passed away.[50] A story about the laundry in the *St. Louis Post-Dispatch* of 12 November 1978 provides a graphic picture of the laundry.

> The Sam Wah Laundry is on Laclede Avenue, a few hundred feet east of Newstead and a turn north through a door into St. Louis, a half century ago.
>
> Inside—after passing under a rubber tree plant that grows westward along a system of ceiling hooks and jerry-built supports, a plant that soars out of its pot near the wall and achieves the form of a dragon— is the shop of the brothers Gee Sam Wah and Gee Hong, long out of Canton, China. Wah is 88 years old, Gee is 86.

PHOTOGRAPH 2.1 Sam Wah reaches into an ancient drier, *St. Louis Post-Dispatch*, 12 November 1978. Photo by Robert C. Holt III. Courtesy of *St. Louis Post-Dispatch*.

With its worn wooden washtubs, its drum dryer powered by a noisy and archaic direct current motor, its naked light bulbs and sagging wooden floors, the Sam Wah Laundry seems ready to stand for a spot in the Smithsonian Institution, or at least the Museum of Westward Expansion, this paint-peeling and dusty memorial to a part of the Chinese role in American history. . . .

. . . the Gee brothers live and work in Spartan quarters. They apparently sleep on mats near an old stove. The walls of the laundry are adorned in places by an odd mixture of pictures and photographs—religious art, mostly Jesus Christ at various ages, a newspaper photo of Chairman Mao and former President Gerald R. Ford shaking hands, 1962 calendars from the Canton Market and the Wing Sing Chong Co., Inc., both of San Francisco, and a glossy photo of a standing room hockey crowd at the Checkerdome. There are numerous snapshots of weddings and assembled families.

Gee Sam Wah still uses an antique hand atomizer when he irons shirts. He has had the atomizer since his days in Canton, which probably means at least 80 years or more. Despite the appearance of disorganization, regular customers do not need a ticket, said Wah. The launderers have a system of numbering the bundles and remembering the faces. They do not forget regular customers, and no one, apparently, has had reason to complain. Not-so-regular customers get a ticket. Everything is lettered in Chinese.

Gee Hong and Gee Wah, by western standards, are certifiable workaholics. Even in their 80s, the two are up ironing and washing early in the morning and are at it still late at night, say longtime customers.

They had a television set, presumably for relaxation, but it has been broken and unused for some time. There is also a sickly-looking radio on the premises. . . .[51]

Like the Gee brothers, Lum Hey came to St. Louis in the 1920s to help a Chinese "uncle" in his laundry. Lum Hey came to America from China at the age of twenty to join his father, who was running a "westerner's" grocery store in Mississippi. He landed in Seattle, Washington, where he waited for a month to go through a lengthy interrogation by immigration officers, who cross-checked the answers from Lum Hey with those from his father in Mississippi. Once released, Lum Hey took a train to Chicago and then to Mississippi to help in his father's grocery business. Three years later, Lum Hey and his wife, whom he had since brought over from China as a dependent of a merchant, relocated in St. Louis to help a Chinese "uncle" in his laundry. They stayed for a few months, living in a small room and earning minimal wages. Then they decided to go into the laundry business themselves and bought a downtown laundry for $1,000 from an "old Chinese man."[52]

By the last decades of the nineteenth century, the washing machine had already been invented and was beginning to appear in middle-class homes. Even so, Chinese hand laundries had a reputation for costing little and for making clothes last longer, so they still had many patrons. In the 1920s, Sam Wah Laundry charged fifteen cents for men's shirts and twenty cents for women's shirt-waists.[53] In the early 1930s, J. H. Lee Laundry, a Chinese hand laundry run by Jung Chooey and his uncle, charged only ten cents to launder a shirt. J. H. Lee charged less than many Chinese laundries due to its location in an African American neighborhood.[54]

Mainstream businesses sought customers largely through advertising, which had been recognized as a key to business success since the early twentieth century. Chinese laundries maintained and expanded their clientele mainly through the quality of their services and through word of mouth. Few Chinese laundries listed in the Business Directory and Mercantile Register from 1903 to 1910.[55]

The Chinese laundries could charge low prices because their owners lived extremely frugally. To minimize their living expenses, they lived in the back of their laundries. Mrs. Lillie Hong, one of the few surviving residents of Hop Alley, came to St. Louis in 1924 from Canton, China, at the age of five with her mother and spent most of her working years in the family laundry after her marriage in 1935. She recalled her life in the laundry: "We did the ironing in the front, and in the back part, we had a couple of bedrooms . . . and the kitchen was in the back."[56] Tak Jung, another old-timer, left Canton in 1930, when he was nine. He joined his father, who was running a laundry at the corner of Academy and Delmar. Like the Hongs, Jung's family lived in the back of their business. Using bunk beds, they squeezed a family of eight—Tak Jung's parents and six children—into two back rooms.[57] In large families the teenage children often slept in the laundry. James Leong, a contemporary of Hong and Jung, was born into his family laundry at 4360 Lee Avenue in 1924. During his high school years he slept on a cot in the laundry that was extremely hot and humid in summer and freezing cold in winter: "I usually stretch the army cot out. . . . In the summertime, didn't have to put nothin' on there except the sheets, but in the wintertime, had to throw a mattress on top of the army cot. . . . In the morning, I get up six o'clock and light up the boiler and let the steam come up, let it hot, and then I start work about an hour. And about the time eight o'clock, grab a little bit to eat and take the bus to go to school."[58]

Many laundry operators without families simply combined their living quarters with the laundry. The back of the laundry was living quarters for the Gee brothers throughout their long, hard working lives; they slept on mats near a gas stove and cooked in the back part of the laundry.[59]

Chinese laundry workers had to work hard to increase profit margins; hence, laundry work was characterized by long hours and hard and monotonous toil. Most Chinese laundry operators worked from early morning until late at night on the repetitive tasks. The hardships of laundry work were publicly recognized: "Work in laundry is so arduous that two or three times each year the laundryman is compelled to knock off for a couple of weeks."[60] The family histories of some Hop Alley residents further testify to the drudgery of laundry work. Lillie Hong recalled her typical working day:

> We got up at six o'clock to do washing. We had an old washing machine made of wood. We had to hang up clothes on wires and let them dry in one room. We heated iron in a stove. If it was too hot, we ducked it in a bucket of water. We worked from six or seven in the morning till late night with no rest, no break. You were on your feet all day long.[61]

Tak Jung described similar experiences. He worked at his father's laundry as a teenager in the 1930s:

> We had a machine for washing, but ironing had to be done by hand. . . . The irons are cast irons heated up and then you have a handle as a grip so you won't burn your hands. Then they ironed clothes. When the iron cools, they put it back on the stove and heat it again and take the hot one, so there's a lot of walking back and forth from ironing board to the heating . . . a lot of elbow grease put into ironing.[62]

Tak Jung's Family worked the year round without taking any vacations. They maintained a constant workload and took only half-days off on Sundays.

As these accounts make clear, Chinese hand laundries were family ventures. The low prices for their services and the hard work required a collective effort. Both parents and children of all ages participated in the laundry work. Lillie Hong's nine children all worked in the family laundry during their childhood: "After school, my children came back to home and they all helped in the laundry. They iron front and back of sleeves, and front and back of shirts. I then folded them."[63]

James Leong started working in the family laundry at the age of seven, starching the detachable white collars that men wore with their dress shirts in those days:

> We used to have thousands of those collars. . . . They starched it. Then you had to smooth them out. And the little boys, you know, four or five years old—they had a great big, long board to put it on the table. . . . The collars all starched already, but they are in bundles. You have to separate it. Smooth 'em out with your hand and stack 'em up. . . . Each one was on a hook—a great big, long pole, and you hang that pole up on a wire and let it dry. . . . And then they wet it again and then they used a machine to iron it out, and it makes it real hard, real white.[64]

Other Businesses: Grocery Stores, Restaurants, Tea Shops, Opium Shops, and Barber Shops

Although Dreiser's story failed to mention Chinese grocery stores, they had already emerged as another important Chinese business in St. Louis. They provided ingredients for Chinese cooking and laundry supplies for hand laundries. *Gould's St. Louis Directory* listed two Chinese grocers in 1888: Lung Wah at 813 South Market Street and Wah Quong Sun at 714 Market Street.[65] The following year, Lung Quong On at 25 South Eighth Street and Jeu Hon Yee at 924 Locust Street (the latter owned by a Chinese woman) were added to the listing.[66] By the 1900s the number had increased to six.[67] The years 1912 to 1914 witnessed a sudden increase in Chinese grocers, to twelve.[68] In the 1920s the number of Chinese grocers decreased to six, at which point it remained steady.[69]

As the Chinese grocery businesses expanded, they attracted media attention. On 29 July 1900 the Sunday magazine section of the *St. Louis Republic* published an article, "The Chinese Colony of St. Louis" by Dick Wood, which portrayed a few respectable merchants running Chinese grocery stores, including Quong Hang Choung and Company at 722 Market Street, Quong On Lung at 17 South Eighth Street, and Quong Sun Wah and Company at 23 South Eighth Street. These three stores must have been well established, since they were listed in *Gould's St. Louis Directory* consistently from 1906 to 1910.[70] According to the article, most of these affluent merchants had acquired a thorough knowledge of English in America, as children at Sunday school. Lee Mow Lin, the owner of Quong On Lung, offered in fluent English a quite sophisticated view on the Boxer Rebellion in China.[71]

Unlike Chinese hand laundries, which served mainly non-Chinese and were dispersed across the city, grocery stores catered to the Chinese community and thus were clustered around the Chinese business district, resembling the pattern in other urban Chinese communities.[72] According to Wood, these stores sold merchandise imported from China, including tea, cigars, cooking ingredients, and cloth with intricately embroidered patterns. They also sold locally produced fresh fruits, vegetables, and meats. Crawfish, watermelons, and fresh vegetables in bunches were delivered to the stores daily by Chinese farmers on the other side of the river in Illinois. Some Chinese stores also handled the ordering and shipping of supplies to Chinese laborers in the southern and southwestern states.[73]

The Oriental Tea and Mercantile Company at 22 South Eighth Street was a typical Chinese grocery store of the 1910s to 1930s. The owners and operators were two brothers, Hom Yuen Sit and Gan Sit, who came to St. Louis in the 1910s from a village near Xinhui, Guangdong province. In their store they sold tea, spices, dry foods, preserved duck, salted fish, and Chinese porcelain, along with laundry and restaurant supplies. Gan Sit, the treasurer and sales clerk, drove a panel truck that scoured the city to deliver supplies to Chinese businesses and took orders for next deliveries.[74]

Annie Leong's family history offers another example of how Chinese grocery stores operated. Leong's father came to St. Louis in 1920 and established a Chinese restaurant. Four years later he brought his bride to St. Louis from his hometown, Xinhui in Guangdong province. Leong and her two older brothers were all born in Hop Alley and grew up there. During the 1920s and 1930s the Leong family owned a Chinese restaurant downtown and a grocery store in Hop Alley. The Leongs ordered merchandise for their grocery store from wholesalers in San Francisco, New York, and Chicago. All the children spent their time after school working in the family grocery store. Annie Leong recalled that time: "We got them [the retail goods] on credit and we have thirty days to pay. If you don't have a good credit, you have to pay right away. They gave us wholesale price, and we retail them. The whole family helps do the business. After the operation whatever is left is our profit."[75]

Grocery stores operated in much the same way in the southern states. Miller Chow's parents moved to Earle, Arkansas, in 1937 after six years working in a hand laundry in St. Louis. Like most Chinese in the South who were making their living by running groceries, Chow's parents owned two groceries in Earl. Chow, now a retired public-school librarian, recalled her childhood experience:

They [Chow's parents] went to South to run grocery stores. They had two stores, one in the city, one in the country. They were mom-pop stores with help from children. Mom ran one, Dad ran the other. Dad also bought a farm of 160 acres growing cotton and soybeans. When Dad went to farm, we children ran the store. We sold dry goods and all kinds of grocery, like a general store. Every day after school we worked in the grocery store and did our homework when the business was slow.

Earle is a small town with 2,000 people. There were two Chinese families in the town. There was a black part of the town, and a white part of the town. Our grocery stores were in the black area of the town. There are many small towns in Mississippi, and there is always a Chinese family in each town. Most Chinese ran grocery stores because they were not accepted too much in other things. We were called names by both whites and blacks.[76]

Grocery stores in St. Louis also resembled those on the West Coast and in Hawaii. Many Chinese grocery stores in California were family businesses; family members operated the store without pay. Wives and children worked alongside their husbands and fathers, packing, stocking, and selling goods. Connie Young Yu, in recounting her family history, remembers that Chin Shee, her great-grandmother, arrived in San Francisco in 1876 to join her husband, the owner of a successful Chinese dry-foods store. She lived in the rear of the store, where she bore six children. She not only took care of her children but also helped her husband operate his business. All the hard work and responsibilities made her face seem "careworn" by middle age.[77] Most Chinese grocers knew very little English—barely enough to tell customers the prices of their goods. Lily Chan, a Hawaiian-Chinese girl, noted in the 1920s: "They [her parents] did not know the English language, but they know enough as to keep a store."[78] Through diligence, frugality, and shrewdness, the Chinese grocers survived the harsh environment.

Some Chinese merchants in St. Louis operated general stores. In the 1920s one such store was Oriental Tea, which supplied Chinese laundries and restaurants. Bigger than most grocery stores, it had several partners, one of whom was Richard Ho's father. He brought his son, then ten years old, to St. Louis in 1928 from Guangdong. Richard Ho later worked for the store, driving a small panel truck, delivering ordered goods to customers and accepting new orders for the next round.[79] The Chinese general merchandise stores in St. Louis operated much like those on the West Coast, as scholarly writings have documented.[80]

Chinese restaurants and chop suey shops were also part of Hop Alley's economy. The first Chinese restaurants were started mainly to satisfy the needs of Chinese bachelors, who would come to eat on Sundays when they were not working. These restaurants usually served authentic Chinese dishes or delicacies that appealed only to Chinese. In January 1894, while researching a story on the St. Louis Chinese for the *St. Louis Republic*, Theodore Dreiser visited a Chinese restaurant at 19 South Eighth Street. It was midday, and the restaurant was not busy at all; the owner, cook, and waiter were sitting in the front room chatting, smoking, and drinking tea. When Dreiser showed the proprietor a letter of introduction from a Chinese friend written in Chinese, he was told, "Come a Sunday. Got glood dinner Sunday. Come a flive clock; bling flend." On Sunday at five, Dreiser and his friend entered the restaurant as instructed. Now the restaurant was packed with Chinese diners. Dreiser and his friend ordered "chicken, duck, rice and China dish" and apparently enjoyed the experience:

> The first dish set on the bare table was no larger than a silver dollar and contained a tiny dab of mustard in a spoonful of oil. Three dishes of like size followed, one containing pepper jam, the other meat sauces. Tea was served in bowls, and was delicious. The duck, likewise the chicken, was halved, then sliced crosswise after the manner of bologna sausage, and served on round decorated plates. One bowl of chicken soup comprised the same order for two, which was served with dainty little spoons of chinaware, decorated in unmistakable heathen design. Rice, steaming hot, was brought in bowls, while the mysterious China dish completed the spread. This dish was wonderful, awe-inspiring, and yet toothsome. It was served in a dish, half bowl, half platter. Around the platter-like edge were carefully placed bits of something which looked like wet piecrust and tasted like smoked fish. The way they stuck out around the edges suggested decoration of lettuce, parsley and watercress. The arrangement of the whole affair inspired visions of hot salad. Celery, giblets, onions, seaweed that looked like dulse, and some peculiar and totally foreign grains resembling barley, went to make up this steaming-hot mass.[81]

It is worth noting that Dreiser's description of his experience is laced with biases. His detailed account could only have reinforced Westerners' perceptions of the Chinese as "peculiar" and "exotic" creatures. The cartoon "In the Chinese Restaurant" attached to the story was even more prejudicial (see Photo 2.2). The three Chinese men portrayed in the cartoon are all eating Chinese food from huge bowls with chopsticks. Instead of holding their chopsticks in one hand as Chinese normally do, all three are holding them with both hands, the way Westerners hold a fork and knife. The man in front is holding a big bowl between his knees, and the head and tail of a rat are dangling over the bowl's lip. The menu posted on the walls

PHOTOGRAPH 2.2 "In the Chinese Restaurant," a cartoon attached to Theodore Dreiser's article on the Chinese in St. Louis (*St. Louis Republic*, 14 January 1894), portrayed the Chinese as rat-eating people. Courtesy of Missouri Historical Society, St. Louis.

reads BREWED RATS WITH FRIED ONIONS 15 CENTS. Portrayals such as this one (i.e., the Chinese as rat-eating barbarians) cast Chinese people in a negative light and discouraged the American public from accepting their food—and everything else about them as well.

Similar cartoons and descriptions of the Chinese as rat eaters were standard in the American press of the time. John Kuo Wei Tchen's excellent study *New York before Chinatown* provides ample evidence that American popular culture linked the Chinese with rat eating. According to Tchen, this linkage originated in American children's textbooks in the 1840s. By the 1870s and 1880s it had become *the* dominant image of Chinese across the country,[82] and as such did a great deal to justify Chinese exclusion and their confinement in enclaves.[83] The cartoon depicting the Chinese in St. Louis as rat eaters must be seen in this context.

Despite the distortions in the popular press, over time more and more Americans tried Chinese food, and the demand for it increased. For instance, in New York City in 1880 "at least five hundred Americans take their meals regularly in Chinese restaurants in orthodox Chinese fashion, with chopsticks . . . . Many of these Americans have acquired Chinese gastronomical tastes, and order dishes like Chinese."[84] As a consequence, shrewd Chinese entrepreneurs expanded services to the American public, and opened more chop suey shops across the country, including in St. Louis. According to the court records of the Eastern District of Missouri, Thomas Kee, who came to St. Louis in 1903, was running a chop suey house at 2032 Market street by 1906.[85] The *St. Louis Republic* reported that in 1910, St. Louis police raided a chop suey restaurant at 2301 Washington Avenue.[86] Both these restaurants were outside Hop Alley.

The first Chinese restaurants served mainly Chinese bachelor communities in isolated cow towns, logging camps, and mining districts. Once these restaurants began drawing non-Chinese eaters, some Chinese quickly realized that cooking was a stable economic niche. By the 1890s, Chinese restaurants were sprouting up in many parts of the United States.[87]

Chinese restaurants in St. Louis developed much as they did in the rest of the country. The first ones served Chinese laundrymen on their Sunday afternoons off, who had a craving for good Chinese food. Most of these restaurants were located in Hop Alley, since this is where the Chinese laundrymen usually came to relax. The Chinese restaurant Dreiser visited on a Sunday in 1894 was one of these restaurants. By the turn of the century, some restaurants were not only serving dishes for casual diners but also providing banquets for weddings and holiday celebrations. Dishes for these special occasions cost between $2 to $20 a plate—much more than the regular price of a dish, which was 40 to 80 cents.[88] A restaurant big enough to hold banquets could be quite lucrative; the owner could make a handsome income and begin to "Americanize" his appearance. One downtown Chinese restaurateur was described in the media as "a dapper little Chinaman" dressed stylishly in a "mohair suit, lavender silk hose, and tan shoes, diamond stud and Panama hat."[89]

As Chinese food became more popular in the first decades of the twentieth century, more chop suey shops opened in St. Louis. Chop suey shops and larger Chinese restaurants served European and African Americans as well as the Chinese. Annie Leong's parents opened a Chinese restaurant at 714 Market Street in St. Louis in 1924. It served Cantonese cuisine—shark fins, bird's nests, steamed fish, and barbecued pork, duck, and rooster—to Chinese guests. It was also frequented by American customers—the theater crowd.[90]

In the early 1930s, Richard Ho's father started a small Chinese restaurant on Jefferson Avenue that catered to the African American community; the racial segregation of the time barred blacks from dining places owned and operated by whites. The restaurant devised a simple menu of fried rice and duck noodles, and the patrons used forks instead of chopsticks. Business was brisk, and the restaurant continued to thrive after World War II, when returning black soldiers and their Japanese war brides came there to satisfy their yearning for rice and simple Chinese food. The restaurant also hired African Americans as servers—one of the early instances of racial collaboration and harmony in pre-desegregated America.[91]

Chinese restaurants depended heavily on unpaid family labor. Annie Leong recalled how her family restaurant was run in the 1930s and 1940s:

> The whole family worked. If you didn't get paid, it was okay. My mother worked in the dining room and kitchen. My dad worked as a chef. During the depression era, they survived and they made a living out of it. . . . We worked seven days a week, from eleven o'clock in the morning to mid-night. . . . We [she and her brothers] did everything. We wrapped wontons, took care of the dining room area, and set up restaurant. Then if they needed us, we could cook too. So we did whatever was needed. It was just natural, and we just did it. We were going to school and had to do our homework. After school, we would study, and it would get busy during dinner hours, and we took care of all the customers. In between, we would study a little, and then took care of customers. After the dinner rush was over, about eight o'clock, we could really have more time to study. I guess that was something we never thought about and that was something we did.[92]

Similarly, Richard Ho helped with his family restaurant after school every day throughout his teen years.[93]

The Chinese also opened tea shops. The first of these was Alla Lee's in 1859, at 106 North Tenth Street.[94] Lee would move his tea shop several times over the years, mostly outside Hop Alley. It was listed every year in the *St. Louis Directory* until 1880.[95] Jeu Han Yee landed in San Francisco in the 1860s as a child, stayed there for ten years learning to be a tea merchant, and then came to St. Louis. By the 1890s he had established himself as a well-known tea merchant.[96]

Hop Alley was also home to opium shops. The *St. Louis Post-Dispatch* noted thirty to forty opium dens in Hop Alley by 1899.[97] This figure was probably exaggerated by the media, as that year only four Chinese groceries were listed in the *St. Louis Directory* and no Chinese laundries or restaurants.[98] The number of opium dens in Hop Alley declined as a result of police raids. Court records from the Eastern Division of the Eastern Judicial District of Missouri indicate that most Chinese arrested in the 1910s were charged with unlawfully manufacturing or selling opium. The following cases give the flavor of the time.

On 8 July 1914, Hop Hing was found manufacturing five pounds of opium for smoking and was arrested. He was indicted on 4 March 1915 by the district court and was fined $2,000. Unable to pay, he was sentenced to thirty days in jail.[99] On 31 October 1914, Leong Choey was arrested after the police searched his residence at 700 North Jefferson Avenue and found two pounds of gum opium that did not have the proper U.S. revenue stamps. He was charged with unlawfully manufacturing opium without providing the bond required by commissioner of Internal Revenue, and was ordered to find sufficient bail in the sum of $1,500. He was arrested again on 19 April 1915, when he sold about one-eighth of an ounce of opium at the price of $1. He was indicted again for violating the provisions of an Act of 17 December 1914 titled "An Act to provide for the registration of, with collectors of Internal revenue, and to impose a special tax upon all persons who produce, import, manufacture, compound, deal in, dispense, sell, distribute, or give away opium or coca leaves, their salts, derivatives, or preparations, and for other purposes."[100]

On 10 May 1915, Sing Lung was charged with illegal possession of one pound of crude opium, which he had not registered with the Collector of Internal Revenue. The district court indicted him for violating the Act of 17 December 1914. His attorney, T. Morris, defended him as "a mere consumer of opium," but to no avail; the district court delivered him to the St. Louis City Jail on 24 February 1916.[101] On 13 August 1915, Wong Lung was arrested in his residence at 802 Market Street for possessing 30 grains of smoking opium without registering with the Internal Revenue. The district court judge, David P. Dyer, sentenced him to prison on 27 January 1916.[102]

By the 1910s, police raids had forced most opium shops to close. Only four or five were still in business, and generally, they charged more for the drug than their counterparts in New York and San Francisco. These opium dens appeared more like Indian camps than stores. The customers usually came at night. After paying, the opium fiend would crawl into a bunk, rest his head on a pillow, which was actually a wooden bench covered with cloth and matting, and enjoy the health-destroying smoke.[103]

The police searches also resulted in interracial business collaborations between Chinese and African Americans. Since the Chinese risked arrest and even deportation by running opium dens in Chinatown, some den owners began operating out of "Chestnut Valley," an African American neighborhood just north of Hop Alley. The 1896 Annual Police Report indicates that the Chinese owned fourteen opium dens in Chestnut Valley.[104] The Chinese also did banking with African Americans. It is estimated that in the late nineteenth and early twentieth centuries, half the African American businesses in Chestnut Valley were being bankrolled by Chinese moneylenders. White-owned banks generally refused to lend money to African Americans.[105]

There were also a few Chinese barbershops in Chinatown.[106] The earliest recorded Chinese barbershop was located at 21 South Eight Street. Dreiser described it as "dirty" and "bare of furniture." He suspected it was actually an opium den until he spotted a Chinese getting a haircut there.[107]

3. THE CHINESE AT THE ST. LOUIS WORLD'S FAIR

In 1904, St. Louis held the Louisiana Purchase Exposition, also known as the St. Louis World's Fair. Nations from around the world sent their products and cultural treasures there to display to the world. The Chinese Qing government dispatched two envoys to St. Louis to supervise the preparation of the Chinese exhibition. In May 1903, Sir Chentung Liang Cheng, envoy extraordinary and minister plenipotentiary, arrived for Dedication Week. That July, Wong Kai Kah, imperial vice-commissioner, arrived to oversee the construction of the Chinese Pavilion.[108] Wong conveyed his government's enthusiasm for the fair. "Embroideries, silks, porcelains, teas and other products of Chinese industry, and a great many other things illustrative of Chinese resources and progress will be exhibited," he told the fair's directors. "China has set aside 750,000 taels [about $500,000] for this purpose."[109]

Wong hired an English-run firm in Shanghai to design the main building, which was to be a replica of the country home of the

Manchu prince Pu Lun, who had been appointed the official head of the Chinese delegation. By the pavilion entrance, Chinese artisans raised a pagoda consisting of six thousand hand-carved pieces of wood inlaid with ebony and ivory. The eaves were decorated with figures from Chinese mythology in bright Chinese enamel. A replica of the palace bedroom with a square curtained court bed and carved tables and chairs offered visitors a glimpse of Chinese court life.[110]

Unfortunately, most of the two thousand tons of commercial exhibits from China did not receive the attention they deserved, as they were placed in other buildings, mainly in the Palace of Liberal Arts and the Education Building. These Chinese exhibits, from different regions of China, included scrolls, ivory, jade, porcelain, maps, stamps, and coins, as well as models of temples, houses, shops, and an examination hall.[111]

The enthusiasm of the Chinese to participate in the fair was dampened by suspicious American immigration authorities. The Chinese Exclusion Act had been passed in 1882 to prohibit the entry of Chinese laborers into the United States. To prevent any Chinese laborers from being smuggled into the country, the U.S. Immigration Service became more vigilant during the fair. Chinese merchants attempting to visit St. Louis for the fair were detained in a shed in San Francisco for days and weeks while awaiting clearance. Many of them returned early to China, unable to bear the humiliation of detention, interrogation, and the posting of a $500 bond in gold.

For those who did make it to St. Louis, American immigration officers set up strict rules of movement. There were 194 Chinese employed in the construction and operation of the exhibits. These people were registered, photographed, and required to report daily. A laborer who failed to report for forty-eight hours would be considered a fugitive.[112] During the fair the rumor spread that 250 Chinese had agreed to pay $850 for transportation to the fair with the intention of escaping.[113] The mistreatment these laborers suffered during the fair deeply upset Chinese St. Louisans.

During the construction of the Chinese Pavilion, the Chinese exhibits and topics relating to Chinese culture captured the attention of the local newspapers.[114] Wong Kai Kah gave a series of lectures on Chinese art and philosophy.[115] The Chinese delegation also threw many splendid parties for the city's elite; at these, the four hundred silk dresses brought by Mrs. Wong enormously impressed St. Louisans.[116] These events and activities helped create a more positive image for the Chinese in St. Louis.

CONCLUSION

St. Louis Chinatown history from the 1860s to the 1930s demonstrates a lively, dynamic, and productive ethnic community. This
contradicts the popular stereotype of Chinatown as a mysterious
quarter of sin, vice, and crime. Although a small group, the
Chinese in St. Louis contributed disproportionately to the city's
industrial and urban development.

Post–Civil War industrialization and urbanization attracted
laborers from other shores. But at the same time, economic reces-
sion and nativist sentiment resulted in the passage of the Chinese
Exclusion Act. Successive police raids on Chinatown between
the 1880s and the 1920s reflected a nationwide anti-Chinese sentiment. Systematic police roundups in Hop Alley reinforced the
negative popular image of Chinatown created by the press and
worked against the building of a Chinese community.

Despite institutionalized discrimination, Hop Alley showed
remarkable resilience and energy. St. Louis Chinatown was not simply a ghetto plagued by urban problems such as overcrowding, poor
sanitation, and crime. In fact, it was a lively commercial, residential,
and recreational center for the Chinese (as discussed in the following chapter). The hand laundries, grocery stores, restaurants, and tea
shops were essential businesses in St. Louis, and they enabled the
early Chinese to survive and sometimes even prosper. In particular,
the Chinese hand laundries were indispensable to St. Louisans, who
eagerly made use of them. The elbow grease of the Chinese laundrymen certainly made the industrial machine of St. Louis run more
smoothly. A handful of Chinese St. Louisans were contributing disproportionately to the city's economy; less than 0.1 percent of the
total population was providing 60 percent of its laundry services.

Clan dominance and geographical dispersion were two main
characteristics of the hand laundry business in St. Louis. Both
were closely related to patterns of urban development. Clan dominance was the result of chain immigration and urban ethnic
networking; the geographical dispersion of Chinese laundries
coincided with urban sprawl. As the city grew, the most affluent
left the downtown core for neighborhoods on the periphery.
Laundries, being service business, had no choice but to follow.
This was the pattern in all American cities.

Chinese laundries served the larger community; Chinese grocery stores, restaurants, and tea shops primarily served the

Chinese themselves. These businesses were important not only because they provided essential goods and services to the Chinese, but also because they absorbed Chinese immigrant laborers who would otherwise have been excluded from the labor market. Moreover, these businesses contributed to the cosmopolitan atmosphere that the city's boosters were trying hard to develop.

The unfair treatment the Chinese received during the 1904 World's Fair was further evidence of American antipathy at the time. However, China's participation at the fair and the Chinese cultural activities held before and during it did much to improve the image of Chinese St. Louisans.

The story of Hop Alley demonstrates the persistence, resilience, and ingenuity of a small minority group in the face of legal discrimination and social prejudice. Chinese St. Louisans' efforts to make a strong community out of Hop Alley enrich our understanding of the Chinese American experience in general, and expand our knowledge of Chinese immigrants to the United States.

3   Living in "Hop Alley," 1860s–1930s

St. Louis boasts a colony of Chinese women. Although the total population of the aforesaid "colony" is but four wee bits of femininity from the Flowery Kingdom—still it is a colony, and a large one, considering the obstacles which Uncle Sam places in the way of Chinese women who came to this country.
  —*St. Louis Republican*, 1908

HOP ALLEY was not just a commercial district; it was also a residential and recreational sanctuary for the Chinese of St. Louis. This chapter will examine how gender, class, race, sexuality, and religion defined the lives of Hop Alley's residents. A few Chinese women arrived in the Mound City almost as early as their male counterparts did; in addition to their domestic duties, they ran boarding houses and helped with family businesses. The affluent Chinese merchant wives enjoyed some of the leisure and comforts of American middle-class life; working-class Chinese women had to cope with the difficulties of daily survival. Because of the uneven sex ratio, the Chinese engaged in interracial marriages and sexual relations, yet few of them were accepted by the larger society. Christian institutions encouraged social interactions between the Chinese and European Americans, and this sometimes promoted the upward social mobility of Chinese youth. Recreational activities in Hop Alley helped ease the daily drudgery of laundry work, and Chinese social organizations attempted to improve the social conditions of the Chinese. The stories of the Chinese in Hop Alley are also told by the burial sites in Wesleyan and Valhalla cemeteries, where the Chinese men finally rested.

PIONEER WOMEN AND FAMILY LIVES

Most early Chinese immigrants were single men or married men who left their wives behind. For this reason, Chinese immigrant society prior to the 1960s has often been characterized as a "bachelor society."[1] Scholars believe that three main factors contributed to the shortage of Chinese women immigrants: (1) lack of financial resources among Chinese immigrant men, (2) restrictions in Chinese society, and (3) restrictive American immigration policies.[2]

Most early Chinese male immigrants came to America as indentured, contract laborers and coolies. They relied on the credit-ticket system, under which they obtained their passage from Chinese merchants, who were then reimbursed by relatives of the travelers or by future employers. The newcomers worked for the person who extended the credit, until the debt was paid off. This explains why Chinese male immigrants had to leave their women behind. Even after they paid the debt, their meager earnings did not permit them to support families in the United States.

Restrictions in Chinese society also prevented Chinese women from coming to America. The ideological, socioeconomic, and physical constraints imposed on women in feudal China crippled women and restricted all aspects of their lives. As a wife and daughter-in-law, a woman was supposed to bear children and serve her husband and parents-in-law. Confucian ideals placed filial piety above all other virtues; this meant that a daughter-in-law had to consider staying in China to serve her parents-in-law a greater moral responsibility than joining her husband in America. Also, for many parents of immigrant sons, it made economic sense to keep their daughters-in-law with them; doing so ensured that they would receive the remittances from their sons.[3] Immigration records reveal that some Chinese women who came to America to join their husbands did so only after their parents-in-law passed away.[4] Physical restrictions such as footbinding also prevented Chinese women from leaving their homes. The exact origins of footbinding are obscure. It may have begun with dancers at the imperial court during the Tang dynasty (618–907). By the Song dynasty (960–1279) it had been introduced among upper-class women. During the Qing dynasty (1644–1911) the custom became common in Chinese society at large. At a young age, girls had their feet tightly wrapped and gradually bent until the arch was broken and the toes were turned under. The "lily foot" produced by this practice crippled women to the extent that they could barely walk without support. This physical disability discouraged women from traveling overseas.

Recent scholarship argues that restrictive immigration laws and their enforcement were the main reasons for the imbalanced sex ratio in Chinese immigrant communities. Vincent Tang contends that the immigration acts of 1882, 1888, 1892, 1902, 1907, and 1924 succeeded in restricting the immigration of Chinese women.[5] George Anthony Peffer asserts that even before the Chinese Exclusion Act, the Page Law of 1875, which forbade the entry of Chinese, Japanese, and "Mongolian" contract laborers, and also women for the purpose of prostitution, effectively kept Chinese women out.[6] Sucheng Chan notes that in the decade before the passage of the Page Law, California passed several pieces of legislation to restrict Chinese women. "An Act for the Suppression of Chinese Houses of Ill Fame," passed on 21 March 1866, denounced Chinese prostitution and penalized landlords who allowed their properties to be used for immoral purposes. "An Act to Prevent the Kidnapping and Importation of Mongolian, Chinese, and Japanese Females, for Criminal or Demoralizing Purposes," passed on 8 March 1870, made it illegal "to bring, or land from any ship, boat, or vessel, into this state."[7]

As in other early Chinese immigrant communities, there were few Chinese women in St. Louis Chinatown. Censuses recorded six in 1890, two in 1900, and several in 1910 (see Table 2.1). However, private records indicate that Chinese women began arriving in St. Louis almost as early as their male counterparts. According to William Hyde and Howard L. Conard, who in 1899 edited the first history of St. Louis, *Encyclopedia of the History of St. Louis*, the first group of Chinese immigrants came to St. Louis from San Francisco in 1869. A Sunday school was immediately established at Eleventh and Locust Streets to teach the Chinese children English.[8] In January 1870 another group of Chinese, this one smaller, arrived from New York. The *Missouri Republican* reported that "among the number [there are] some women to take charge of the boarding house for the men at the works."[9]

Prior to the Civil War, the area south of Market Street was known as Frenchtown. The houses there were mostly single-family residences. As in most American urban communities, soon after the Civil War industrialization and urbanization swept away the single houses, and multifamily apartment buildings and boarding houses were constructed to meet the needs of the swelling population. Hop Alley was one of the streets in the area with many tenements and boarding houses. The typical rent in the late nineteenth century was a quarter a day or six quarters a week; room and board could be found for less than $15 a month.[10] Cheap housing attracted new immigrants, including the Chinese, who congregated around Hop Alley.[11] The first Chinese women to arrive managed boarding houses, which usually lodged a dozen single Chinese men each. These women earned their living by cooking, cleaning, and mending for the Chinese men—a working pattern very much resembling that of German and Irish immigrant women in the St. Louis, although most of the women in these latter groups worked for European Americans who were not immigrants[12]

Affluent Chinese merchant wives began arriving in the city around the turn of the century, and this was duly noted in the local newspapers. The *St. Louis Republic* recorded Mrs. Jeu Hon Yee, the owner of a Chinese grocery store at 924 Locus Street, as the only Chinese woman in the city since 1890.[13] She was joined after 1900 by Mrs. Fannie Toy, a San Francisco-born woman of twenty.[14] By 1908 there were a handful of Chinese women of merchant families. On 4 October 1908 the *St. Louis Republican* devoted an entire page to a story on four Chinese women. "St. Louis boasts a colony of Chinese women," the article started:

> Although the total population of the aforesaid "colony" is but four wee bits of femininity from the Flowery Kingdom—still it is a colony, and a large one, considering the obstacles which Uncle Sam places in the way of Chinese women who came to this country.
>
> The St. Louis contingent of Chinese women is proportionately larger, considering population, than any city in the country excepting San Francisco. Chicago boasts but half a dozen women from the land of Confucius, while New York, with its much-boasted Mott Street, and its half block of cramped Chinese quarters, has but five who are duly registered with the immigration authorities.[15]

This article was admitting that discriminatory laws against Chinese made Chinese women a rarity in America, and was placing the four women in the context of Chinese communities in major urban centers in North America. There were only six Chinese women in Chicago and five in New York, and both cities had much larger Chinese populations than St. Louis. The article's author seemed to be taking pride in introducing these Chinese women to St. Louisans.

According to the article, all four women were of the Chinese merchant class and were Americanized. Three of them—Juy Toy, Huy Tin, and Jo Hon Ye (whose name was spelled "Jeu Hon Yee" and "Jee Hon Yee" in other articles on the Chinese in St. Louis)— were the wives of well-to-do Chinese businessmen in St. Louis.

Miss Mei Chun, the fourth, was the daughter of a wealthy Chinese tea merchant.

Born in China in 1889, Juy Toy came to San Francisco as a little girl. Her father, a prosperous merchant in San Francisco, enrolled her in public school. She made rapid progress and graduated from San Francisco High School at seventeen—only the second Chinese girl to do so. After graduation, she was married to a St. Louis Chinese merchant, the proprietor of a chop suey restaurant on Sixth Street, a laundry on Marcus Avenue, and a mercantile store in San Francisco. She lived with her husband at 2629 Marcus Avenue in the city's affluent west end. Toy was proud of her acculturation. "I am no longer Chinese—I am an American," she told the reporter, "I was married like American women are and live just like people of this country do. Chinese dress and Chinese customs are no longer a part of my life and I am a member of an American church, and try to do just like the American women do."

Jo Hon Ye was born into a rich merchant family in Hong Kong and enjoyed all the pleasures that a wealthy family could afford. She married a Chinese merchant in San Francisco; however, in 1906 the San Francisco earthquake and resulting fire destroyed everything they owned. They came to St. Louis to start over. Within two years her husband owned a grocery store on Eleventh Street and was prospering again. Like Toy, Ye saw herself as a thoroughly Americanized woman.

Huy Tin was also a graduate of San Francisco High School. Her husband owned a dry goods store on Market Street, where she worked as a bookkeeper. The story noted that these three women were all cousins; this reflects the fact that the first Chinese women in St. Louis arrived as links in an immigration chain.

Mei Chun was the only unmarried woman among the four. A seventeen-year-old student at Forest Park University, she was "pretty," "clever," and "possessed of an education which few American girls can boast."[16]

These merchant wives made a deliberate effort to adjust to the American way of life, and they succeeded to a large degree. They wore Western dress and spoke fluent English. Like middle-class American women of the time, they enjoyed a life of leisure. They went to circuses and shows and attended various social functions. Toy went to entertainments frequently and was fascinated by romantic drama. "That is why I like to see the American plays so much," she commented. "The girl loves the man or she does not marry him." Mei Chun was reportedly "so popular that few social functions of the West End are complete without her presence." These women were adventurous, and they enjoyed the freedom that American life provided them. Ye was also fond of circuses and shows, but nothing delighted her more than the streetcars, which offered her kaleidoscopic views of city life: "I think the streetcars are so funny. They start and stop whenever the man who runs them wants them to, and one can see so many different kinds of people riding on them." She also enjoyed a thrill when she rode an elevator up and down in a department store.[17]

The Americanization of these women was also evident in their connections with various churches in the city. Toy went to the Union Methodist Church regularly and was a practicing Methodist in the same manner as her American counterparts. Tin belonged to the same church and took an active part in many church activities. Ye also belonged to a church and attended Sunday school and religious services every week.[18]

Another article, "House Keeping in St. Louis Chinatown," in the *St. Louis Republic* of 14 August 1910, confirmed that these Chinese merchant wives had been Americanized. It described Jo Hon Ye (spelled as Jee Hon Yee in this article) and Fannie Toy as "modest little women, quiet and refined, with beautiful manners." They wore "American dress" and had "adopted American ways." They spoke English "more or less perfectly"; Fannie Toy had been educated in San Francisco public schools and Ye had learned English in Christian missions. They kept house much the same as most Americans did, "with gaudy furniture and brass bedsteads and family photographs on the walls."[19]

The author of the article also noticed a sharp contrast between the well-off Chinese women and working-class Chinese men. The merchant wives spoke fluent English; few men could speak the language. The merchant wives appeared Americanized and well-adapted; the men were "less adaptable." The merchant wives kept flashy furniture in their apartments; the men lived in one-room flats with little furniture except "wooden bunks covered with matting" and "a table and a few chairs."[20]

The well-off Chinese merchant wives in St. Louis seemed different from their counterparts in larger Chinese communities; in the latter, women were more likely to be bound to traditions.[21] In other Chinese enclaves—such as those in the Rockies, in Hawaii, and on the West Coast (including San Francisco)—most affluent merchant wives lived in seclusion, upstairs from their families' businesses, and were cut off from European Americans and working-class Chinese. Their rooms were generally furnished with Chinese tables and chairs and decorated with Chinese ornaments.[22] They were rarely seen outside the home until they gave birth to a child.[23] After they had children, their primary responsibility was raising them. They preserved Chinese traditions in the foods they ate, the clothes they wore, and the ways they kept house and raised children. As a Chinese high school girl in Honolulu described in the 1920s: "The food [we eat] . . . are rice, meat, and fresh vegetables. In my family, my mother and I was dressed in Chinese costume . . . . I have often made fun of the customs of my racial groups. Some of the customs which I did not like were the serving of tea to visitors, forbidding to call the visitors by their first names, and the marriage customs."[24]

Perhaps the absence of a larger ethnic community released the Chinese women of St. Louis from traditional expectations. Without an ethnic community, these women had no choice but to interact with the larger society, and consequently they became more highly Americanized. Their fluent English helped them assimilate, and their financial security allowed them to enjoy a lifestyle similar to that of American middle-class women. Their socioeconomic status made it easier for the American public to accept and assimilate them.

While well-to-do Chinese women attempted to Americanize themselves, the wives of the small-time Chinese merchants and common laborers struggled simply to raise their large families in Hop Alley. In the first decades of the twentieth century, at least twenty Chinese families resided in Hop Alley; most of these were headed by poor laundrymen and family restaurant owners.[25] Lillie Hong's family history well illustrates their daily struggle. Lillie Hong and her mother Gene Shee came to the United States in 1924 to join Hong's father, owner of the Mandarin House restaurant at 4500 Delmar. They went to Seattle by the steamboat *President Coolidge*, then to St. Louis by train. They settled into a two-room apartment in a tenement building in Hop Alley, where Lillie's mother gave birth to four more daughters and two sons. The monthly rent for the apartment was $12, nearly half a laundryman's monthly income. One room was the bedroom, the other a living room-cum-kitchen. Since they had no refrigerator, they had to buy twenty-four pounds of ice every day to fill an ice box on the porch to keep food from spoiling. Gene Shee never learned to speak

English, so it was Lillie who had to buy ice every day from a nearby American grocery store. With the family growing constantly, ways had to be found to fit the family of nine into one bedroom. A large board served as the bed for all the children. Living conditions like this were typical among Chinese families in Hop Alley. After school, Lillie Hong had to take care of younger siblings and help her mother with the cooking, cleaning, and laundry—all of these classic second-generation responsibilities.

Like most Chinese children in Hop Alley, Lillie attended the nearest American public school, Madison School, which was eleven blocks away. There was a streetcar to the school, but Chinese parents could not afford the five-cent fare. The Chinese children would walk to school and back every day. In the city's hot, humid summers and wet, cold winters, the walk seemed endless. Also like many Chinese girls her age across the country, Lillie left school in the eighth grade; her parents felt she had received enough education.[26]

Lillie Hong's experiences growing up were not unique among immigrant families in St. Louis. In many ways her experiences mirrored those of other minorities and new immigrants. The bulk of the immigrant and minority population of St. Louis was crammed into the northern and southern sections of the city, along the river and on the edge of the business district. Immigrants from Germany, Greece, Ireland, Italy, Poland, and Russia, as well as black migrants from the South, lived in crowded row houses and tenements. Since the mid-nineteenth century the rapid growth of industry, commerce, and population had exceeded the absorption capacity of the area, thus creating the dilapidated neighborhoods or slums. This was not unusual for any American industrial city; even so, the area's shabby appearance shocked visitors. In 1842, Charles Dickens was depressed at the sight of the "crazy old tenements" of the old Frenchtown south of Market Street. In the north, the Irish immigrant community known as the "Kerry Patch" was a place of stark poverty and high crime. Visitors described the black neighborhoods in St. Louis as "stinking slums."[27]

The stories of four affluent Chinese women and Lillie's Hong's family history show a striking contrast between Chinese immigrant women of different social classes. Upper and middle-class Chinese women were highly Americanized and well assimilated and to a large extent enjoyed the same social leisure, material comforts,

PHOTOGRAPH 3.1 Lillie Hong with mother, brother Paul (in her arms), and sister Rose in the back of the family apartment in Hop Alley, 1927. Courtesy of Lillie Hong.

and individual freedom and independence as American middle-class women. This was possible because of their social privileges and economic advantages. Simply to survive, the working-class women had to struggle day after day with enormous family responsibilities. To summarize, class had a greater impact on Chinese immigrant women than either race or gender.

INTERRACIAL MARRIAGE, SEXUALITY, AND RACIAL RELATIONS

Because of the shortage of Chinese women, interracial marriages and sexual relationships involving Chinese men inevitably happened, in spite of the antimiscegenation laws. The American antimiscegenation laws were one of white society's reactions to the perceived threat of racially mixed marriages, in particular between whites and blacks. In 1661, Maryland passed the first antimiscegenation law to prohibit marriages involving white females and black males. Eventually, thirty-eight states followed suit.[28] In 1850, California lawmakers adopted a miscegenation statute to prohibit black–white marriages; in 1872 this law was included in Section 60 of the new Civil Code. Then in 1880 that law was drastically expanded to outlaw Chinese–Caucasian marriages; specifically, Section 69 was introduced to restrict marriages between a white and a "Negro, Mulatto, or Mongolian."[29] The old (and out-of-use) anthropological term "Mongolian" referred to Chinese, Japanese, Koreans, and other ethnic groups in Asia; that said, the law was designed to target the Chinese specifically, and was the state's response to anti-Chinese sentiment among the populace. In 1905, to make Sections 60 and 69 consistent and to deal with the fear of Japanese—another "Mongolian" people—the legislature amended Section 60 to make marriages between whites and Mongolians "illegal and void."[30] Similar antimiscegenation laws were in effect in many states until 1967, when they were finally declared unconstitutional.

Despite the antimiscegenation laws, there were a handful of interracial marriages involving Chinese men. Such intermarriages usually involved small entrepreneurs or laborers; the racial and ethnic background of their wives varied from region to region. In the South, most Chinese men were laborers from California or Cuba recruited by railroad companies or sugar plantations. They found wives among black women and Irish or French immigrant women. The 1880 census for Louisiana indicated that of the 489 Chinese in the state, 35 were married, widowed, or divorced. Of the married Chinese men, only four had Chinese wives; the rest had married non-Chinese women. Of these women, four were mulatto, twelve were black, and eight were white (six of whom were of Irish or French descent).[31]

As for the Midwest, in Minneapolis–St. Paul in the early twentieth century there were at least six interracially married Chinese men. They were laundry and restaurant owners and cooks, and their wives were mostly Irish or Polish women, who worked as vegetable washers in restaurants.[32]

In late-nineteenth-century New York City, censuses as well as newspapers revealed an developing pattern whereby Chinese men married Irish women. *Harper's Weekly* and other magazines and newspapers often featured stories about "Chinamen" and "Hibernian" women, in which the women strongly praised their Chinese husbands.[33]

Interracial marriages and sexual relationships were just as inescapable for the Chinese in St. Louis, mainly because of the sex imbalance among Chinese immigrants, but partly as well because of the nature of Chinese interactions with other races and ethnic groups. The earliest recorded interracial marriage was the union of Alla Lee and his Irish wife Sarah Graham. Their marriage seems to have been approved by both the Irish community and the larger society. Lee's friends were mostly Irish immigrants. In 1869, when the appearance of 250 Chinese laborers fanned St. Louisans' curiosity, a number of local reporters interviewed Lee and wrote articles about Chinese culture and customs. According to these articles, Alla Lee was a tall, handsome, intelligent, frugal, and hard-working "Chinaman," while Sarah Graham was a healthy, slightly plump, "Celtic beauty." Clearly, prior to the passage of the Chinese Exclusion Law in 1882 and the consequent anti-Chinese crusade across the country, the public attitude toward the Chinese was more curious than hostile. In this more tolerant climate, Alla Lee's interracial marriage was more or less accepted by the larger society. Alla Lee's marriage also affected his political life; he was recruited by the local politicians, most of whom were Scots-Irish Democrats. In the election year 1868, a local Democratic Party activist escorted him to the courthouse to take the oath of citizenship so that he could exercise his voting rights in favor of the Democrats.[34]

A similar interracial marriage took place a couple of decades later. In 1869 Amon Donn came to St. Louis from Canton, China, at the age of fourteen. He worked hard and was able to open a hand laundry downtown. He married an Irishwoman named Celia, and their marriage produced a son and three daughters.[35] In the absence of further information, we cannot say whether the marriage was socially accepted or resisted. The following sources reveal that later on, once anti-Chinese sentiment became more prevalent, Chinese-Caucasian sexual relations met with widespread social disapproval.

On 1 May 1910, a Sunday, census enumerators Henry A. Baker and Frederick Haid went to Hop Alley to count the Chinese residents, as most Chinese would gather there on Sundays. Besides about three hundred Chinese men and several Chinese women, the two encountered a number of Caucasian wives of Chinese men in the area.[36] The *St. Louis Republic* reported this with an undertone of disapproval.[37]

The same year, two white women involved in interracial romances incited a police raid. Sadie Walden, a twenty-six-year-old divorced European American woman, had met a Chinese man, Leon Ling, four years earlier at a Chinese Sunday school, where she was teaching the Chinese after her divorce. When she fell ill and ran out of money, Ling came to her assistance. Later she rented rooms above the Chinese chop suey restaurant at 2301 Washington Avenue where Ling worked. Still later, her seventeen-year-old stepsister Marguerite Helm came to live with her. Walden loved Ling and intended to marry him. She thought highly of the Chinese man and publicly displayed her passion for him. "Sure, I like Leon," she declared when she was incarcerated. "I will say that I have only praise for Leon Ling. He has never given me occasion to dislike him."

Meanwhile, her sister Marguerite fell in love with a Chinese merchant who owned a silk shop downtown. Marguerite consulted her mother about her marriage and was advised to wait until she was eighteen. On 22 August 1910 the St. Louis police raided the chop suey restaurant, supposedly to search for a Chinese man who was alleged to have murdered a white woman in New York with whom he had had a love affair. (This case was known as the "Chinatown Trunk Mystery." The Chinese man involved was also named Leon Ling. The case is discussed later in the section.) The two sisters as well as four Chinese men, including Leon Ling, were arrested but later released. Not intimidated by the arrest, Walden claimed that she was going to go with Leon for a marriage license very soon. Marguerite was tamed by apprehension. "I don't know whether I shall marry a Chinaman or not," she said, "but I will say that I have no cause to complain of the treatment I have received from the men of that race."[38]

This incident well exhibits the general antagonism toward sexual relations between European Americans and Chinese, who were perceived as culturally peculiar and physically inferior, and who were deemed unassimilable. Public disapproval was prompted by cultural bias and racial prejudice and reinforced by antimiscegenation laws.[39] The bias against racial mixing also reveals another facet of the Chinese exclusion crusade across the country: the notion that the presence of Chinese needed to be checked from every possible direction. Economic competition and cultural differences were common sources of racial anxiety. Sexuality was a different kind of source from these—it introduced social, cultural, and biological elements that could easily animate "sinophobic" racial riots. Although interracial marriage continued in some places in America (as discussed earlier), many interracial sexual relationships met social resistance and at times violence. Examples of the latter include the anti-Chinese riot in Milwaukee in 1889, the police raid of Boston Chinatown in 1903, and the policing of New York Chinatown from 1880 to 1915 for the purpose of stopping interracial sexual relations.

In March 1889 about 3,000 European American males in Milwaukee, Wisconsin, took part in a four-day anti-Chinese riot. It started with an anti-Chinese rally around City Hall, where the crowd screamed "Lynch 'em! . . . Hang 'em! . . . Scald 'em!" The rioters then marched in protest against the Chinese presence. Soon they began smashing the windows of Chinese hand laundries and chasing and threatening Chinese on sight. These rioters were angry about the city's growing Chinese population and the consequent increase in racial interactions—in particular, sexual relations between the Chinese laundrymen and European American girls. The local legal system and media deliberately denied that these relationships were consensual, and together cooked up appalling stories of white girls being sexually assaulted by Chinese laundrymen. These stories ignited the riot. Yet it seems from the white girls' somewhat fuzzy stories that they perhaps voluntarily sought out the Chinese men.[40]

On the evening of 11 October 1903, the Boston police and the Immigration Bureau jointly raided Chinatown and arrested more than fifty Chinese. The direct cause of this raid was the murders of members of Hip Sing Tong by members of the rival On Leung Tong. Indirectly, the authorities were also driven by fears of interracial contact, both commercial and sexual, between Chinese men and European American women. They were worried that white women were visiting opium dens and co-inhabiting with Chinese men.[41]

But the most boisterous police raid of all took place in New York at the time of the "Chinatown Trunk Mystery," also known as the Elsie Sigel Murder. On the afternoon of 18 June 1909, Sun Leung, the proprietor of a chop suey restaurant, reported to the police that his cousin, Leon Ling, had disappeared. A New York policeman went to search Ling's room and found a large trunk bound with rope. The policeman opened the trunk and found the body of a young white woman, later identified as nineteen-year-old Elsie Sigel, who had been missing for a week. Further investigation revealed that Sigel, a missionary worker from a prominent family, had been intimate with Ling. The murder of Elsie Sigel immediately grabbed the front pages of newspapers, which portrayed Chinese men as dangerous to "innocent" and "virtuous" young white women. This murder led to a surge in the harassment of Chinese in communities across the United States. Despite the combined efforts of police forces across the country, Leon Ling was never apprehended, and thus the murder was never solved.[42]

The anti-Chinese riots and the police raids of Chinese communities indicate that racial conflict was growing during this era and was being heightened by the Chinese exclusion mentality. Interracial marriages and sexual relations were the inevitable result of migration and assimilation. Social disapproval, race riots, and legal penalties for interracial sexual relations were indicators of an aberrant and destructive social trend. Racial tensions further isolated the Chinese and rendered them even more vulnerable to physical and verbal attacks by both police and the public at large.

SUNDAY SCHOOLS AND EARLY AMERICANIZATION

Interracial sexual relations were frowned upon by the general public; yet at the same time, interracial contacts within Christian institutions were cultivated by missionaries and encouraged by the larger society. Efforts to convert the "heathen" Chinese began in St. Louis in 1869, as soon as the first group of Chinese laborers arrived. A Sunday school was immediately established at Eleventh and Locust streets; it taught the Chinese children English with the goal of instilling Christian values in them.[43] In 1878, D. D. Jones, who could speak Chinese, was dispatched to St. Louis by the Chicago YMCA to establish a Sunday school. In 1897 the twenty-

eighth anniversary of the first Chinese Sunday school was cele-
brated to encourage further missionary work. By 1898 there were
Chinese Sunday schools at the Second Presbyterian Church,
Dr. Niccolls' Chapel on Taylor and Westminster Place, the
Presbyterian Church on Grand Avenue, and the Congregational
Church at 29th Street and Washington Avenue.[44]

The evangelical fervor directed toward the Chinese in St. Louis
was nothing new. Christianity had always been a driving force
in Western society; so was the desire to trade with the Orient.
The latter especially had been behind American overseas adven-
tures since the 1840s, when the "Celestial Kingdom" was
defeated by the cannons and gunboats of the industrialized Western nations. Protected by the right of extraterritoriality and Western military power, Christian missionaries had begun prosely-
tizing in China's coastal cities and treaty ports. After the Chinese
laborers began arriving in America in the 1840s, missionaries
immediately turned their sights on the heathen newcomers with
vigor and zeal. Some of the missionaries were China veterans.

Miss Chiles was one of these missionaries. In 1924 she founded
the St. Louis Chinese Gospel Mission, the first Chinese church
in St. Louis. Having worked in China for more than ten years, she
returned to her hometown St. Louis in 1924 due to deteriorating
health. Despite her poor health, she went from laundry to laundry to ask the Chinese to attend the church.[45] Having successfully
gathered a group of Chinese children, she began a weekly Chinese
Sunday school. It initially had to borrow space from St. Louis
Gospel Church on Washington Street; the American congregation
held services in the morning, and the Chinese service and Sunday
school were held in the afternoon. Chiles was strongly committed to teaching her Chinese followers English. However, she was
more successful with Chinese children than with women. Lillie
Hong recalled that "whenever Miss Chiles came to Chinatown,
these Chinese ladies would run away. They said it was too hard
to learn English."[46]

Some members of the St. Louis Gospel Church, who were small
business owners and working-class, assisted Chiles.[47] The Rad-
fords, a devout Christian couple, would drive children and adults
from Hop Alley to church for the afternoon service. Others, such
as the Bachmans and Ms. Comfort, taught Sunday school and visited Chinese newborns and their families.[48] Chinese parents, especially the fathers, often regarded church as a good place for their
children to go but not themselves. Hence, at least initially, most

of the congregation was women and children.[49] Lillie Hong started
going to church with her aunt on her arrival in 1924.[50]

Sunday schools became vehicles of upward mobility for ambitious St. Louis Chinese youth. At Sunday school they had an opportunity to learn English and the American way of life. Jeu Han Yee
arrived in San Francisco in 1870 as a child and lived there for ten
years. He came to St. Louis in 1880 and attended Sunday school
regularly. Through his Sunday school training, he became a skill-
ful writer and reader of English, and this helped him succeed as a
tea merchant.[51] Another Sunday school student, Jeu Hawk, came
to St. Louis as a boy in 1880. Eighteen years later he graduated
from a college in Des Moines, Iowa; later he became an eloquent
pastor for a Chinese congregation in Portland, Oregon.[52] Jo Hon Ye,
the merchant wife I introduced earlier, learned English as a child
at Christian missions. With her "more or less perfect" English
skills, she became the city's first female Chinese grocery owner and
was able to enjoy an Americanized lifestyle.[53]

The churches eased Chinese immigrant women's transition
from rural China to urban America. For these women, church-
sponsored activities provided a window onto American life and
culture. Domestic skills differed greatly between the villages of
Guangdong and the cities of America. The culture shock was
profound for these women; by learning American ways, they could
reduce their anxiety. Through the churches, they took classes in
domestic skills such as cooking, sewing, and housekeeping, and
as a result, America became less alien and intimidating to them.
Those women who attended church seemed more Americanized
than those who did not.[54]

For many Chinese, church was also a place to exchange information, find kinship connections, and maintain friendships with
other Chinese families. For instance, Tak Jung's family and the
Hong family often had Sunday dinner together after the Sunday
service.[55] Through the churches, Chinese families came into
closer contact with both American families and other Chinese.
Even with such a secular attitude, many Chinese families still
found church to be of spiritual significance.

RECREATION AND SOCIAL AWAKENING

In Dreiser's description of Chinese social life in St. Louis, gam-
bling seemed to be the main recreational activity. After a week
of toiling in laundries, the Chinese laborers longed to relax a lit-

tle. Many gathered to gamble till they lost all money they had on them. Others visited Chinese restaurants to eat authentic Chinese dishes and to chat with their clansmen about their families and relatives in China.

Dreiser perhaps suffered from the popular bias that most Chinese were opium fiends and gamblers; for whatever reason, he was unable to get past this limitation to truly understand Chinatown life. Unnoticed by Dreiser, many other Chinese social activities were taking place on Sundays. In the last decades of the nineteenth century, the Chinese in St. Louis were most likely to be bound by their clan associations, such as the Jue, Lee, and Leong associations.[56] Just as on the West Coast, most Chinese in St. Louis came from Canton and its adjacent counties: the so-called *Sam Yap* (San Yi, meaning "three counties," which included Namhoi [Nanhai], Punyi [Panyu], and Shuntak [Shunde] counties), and *Sze Yap* (Si Yi, meaning "four counties," which included Sunwui [Xinhui], Toishan [Taishan], Hoiping [Kaiping], and Yanping [Enping] counties). Among the Chinese in St. Louis, those with the surnames Jeu and Leong (from villages in Sunwui) and Lee (from Toishan) predominated, and they established surname associations for mutual aid and protection in a foreign land. Most of these surname associations rented flats in apartment buildings in

PHOTOGRAPH 3.2 Chinese women (mostly wives of laundrymen) outside the first Chinese church in St. Louis, which used space in St. Louis Gospel Center, 1924. Courtesy of Lillie Hong.

Photograph 3.3 Sunday-school children outside the St. Louis Gospel Center, 1924. Courtesy of Lillie Hong.

Hop Alley for clan business meetings and social gatherings. On Sundays, clansmen would bring Chinese ingredients to the flat and use its kitchen to cook special Chinese dishes that they did not have the time or means to make during the busy working week.[57]

Kinship networks were valued by the Chinese; even outsiders noticed them. Dick Wood, a reporter with the *St. Louis Republic*, observed that in restaurants, grocery stores, barbershops, and other local Chinese businesses, Chinese customers often purchased goods and services on credit. The name of the debtor was written on a large board in the store, along with the amount of debt. The debt was thus visible to all customers until the end of the year, when all debts were cleared. Sometimes a cousin of the same clan would pay a debt and the debtor's name would be wiped out; in this way the honor of the clan name was preserved.[58]

To the Chinese, Hop Alley was not a place of sin and vice, but a place of joy, comfort, good food, and relaxation. According to the *St. Louis Republic*, the Chinese "scattered" throughout the city, living behind their laundries, a "puzzling way peculiarly Chinese." On Sunday afternoons they would close their laundries and hurry to Hop Alley for recreation.[59] If the weather was nice, many Chinese men would sit on benches outside the shops in Hop Alley to bask in the sun's warm rays. They had been confined in dim and damp laundries for a week; now, for a moment, they were released from the drudgery. They could enjoy the warm breeze, catch up on news, share some laughter with clansmen, and watch Chinese children playing in the alley.[60]

Hop Alley served as a substitute for families back in China. Isolated for the rest of the week by cultural prejudice, the language barrier, and long, hard hours of work, the Chinese laborers found ethnic solidarity in Hop Alley. They came every Sunday, feeling that they were going home. In Hop Alley, the Chinese children called them uncle.[61] The Chinese were drawn so strongly to Hop Alley that census enumerators could count them simply by visiting the Chinese quarter on a Sunday afternoon.[62]

Hop Alley was more than a haven for Chinese bachelors. It was also a place where Chinese families living outside Hop Alley could shop, have fun, and visit friends. Lum Hey, the proprietor of a Chinese laundry on the edge of Chinatown, recalled that his wife came down to Hop Alley to shop for Chinese groceries once a week and that he and his friends would "go to see silent movies . . . near Chinatown for five cents a cowboy show."[63]

The Chinese found comfort and ethic cohesion in various social and cultural activities in Hop Alley. Since their first arrival, they had been celebrating the Chinese New Year. On 10 February 1880, the daily *St. Louis Republic* reported such a celebration in a Chinese laundry:

> The Chinese population in St. Louis yesterday arrayed in their best raiment and prepared to celebrate their New Year's day which always comes on the 9th day of February . . . at a Chestnut street laundry. There everything presented a holiday appearance. Bundles of washing were packed away under tables and corners, while the ironing-boards were covered with Chinese bon-bons, consisting of a species of eatables which no Christian would dare sample. The only delicacy which greeted the eye was a lot of oranges which were hanging to an artificial tree before which a celestial with head bent low, muttered some Asiatic prayer. He stopped short when the reporter entered, and looking up said:
>
> "Watchee wantee?"
>
> "Do you do any washing to-day?" asked the reporter.
>
> "No washee, no workee to-day. Dis Chinaman's lew year."
>
> " . . . Are you going to have a big time?"
>
> "No, no. Only little time. Out in Californy Chinamen have big time. Only little time here . . . . No joss-house here, no get dlunk, no good time, no big time, only little time . . . . Chilamen here today take it a rest. Put on best clothes. Go see udder Chilamen. Smoke pipe, get little dlunk. Just have a little time."[64]

Hop Alley was also a hub for the various Chinese social organizations that promoted social awakening in America and China. To augment the clan associations, other social organizations arose in the late nineteenth and early twentieth centuries. The Chinese Grand Lodge of Free Masons of the State of Missouri (also known as the Chinese Masonic Hall) was perhaps the city's oldest Chinese social organization, the forerunner of St. Louis On Leong. The Free Masons developed out of a Chinese secret society, Chih Kung Tong (Zhigongtang), which was established in 1674 in China with the aim of overthrowing the Manchu Qing Dynasty (1644–1911). Chih Kung Tong spread overseas, following the Chinese immigrants, and reached the United States in the 1850s. In the last decades of the nineteenth century, most large Chinese communities in America had branches of it. It was also known as the Chinese Free Mason Society.

The St. Louis Free Masons registered with the city on 21 October 1899. The corporation deed stated that "the objects and purposes of this corporation shall be . . . to promote fraternity among and provide for the relief and aid of its members, and the members of Subordinate Lodge of the State of Missouri, their widows, orphans and dependent relatives, to bury the dead, and to engage in such other charitable work as may not be in conflict with its laws."[65] This document indicates the organization's philanthropic goals; it also reveals that the group was a hybrid of Chinese and American social organizations. Its officers included a Grand Master (the presiding officer), a Deputy Grand Master (the assistant presiding officer), a Senior Grand Warden, a Junior Grand Warden, a Grand Treasurer, a Grand Secretary, and a Grand Lecturer.[66] The society combined elements of a secret society with those of a democratic organization. It was a Chinese society transformed by the American environment, and in that sense an impressive example of cultural adaptation among the early Chinese in St. Louis.

In 1903 the Chinese Empire Reform Society of Missouri was formed and registered with City Hall. This was a branch of a national organization that had been established at the beginning of the century to support the political reforms in China begun by the Qing court between 1901 and 1905.[67] Its officers included Jeu Shung, Lew Goon, Leong Yee, Leong Bow, and Leo Wu.[68] Its headquarters was at 25A South Eighth Street, the center of the Chinese quarter, and it was listed in the city directories until 1927.[69] It was more of a replica of its Western counterparts than the Free Masons were. Its officers included a president, a vice-president, a secretary, and a treasurer, all elected by the members. The society's business was managed by a Board of Trustees chosen by the members.[70] The society's objectives, quoted below, indicate its nature and its relationship to social and ideological trends in America and China:

> The objects for which this Association is formed are for social intercourse, mental and moral improvement, mental recreation, physical and mental development, benevolent, scientific, fraternal, beneficial and educational purposes and more in detail for the promotion of literature, science and fine arts, and for promoting the cause of temperance and moral reform, and to establish a Club or Clubs for said purposes and for establishing and maintaining a hospital or hospitals for the treatment of diseases among the Chinese people. It is the purpose of this Association in accomplishing the above objects among other ways to promote and encourage general education of the Chinese people in the principles of the Constitution and laws of the United States of America in the arts and sciences generally with a view of securing the adoption by the Chinese people of the leading improvements industrial and otherwise which have been and are being advantageously adopted by the English speaking people of the Earth and in every lawful way to bring about the amelioration of the Chinese people and to secure for them a freer diffusion of useful knowledge and generally to promote reforms in the customs and habits of the Chinese people and to do and perform anything and everything whatsoever to carry into effect the objects and purposes aforesaid.[71]

It is clear from this document that the organization was heavily influenced by the American middle-class reform movements of the late nineteenth and early twentieth centuries—movements that launched pragmatic crusades against alcoholism, prostitution, social poverty, and other urban vices. Like the American reformers, members of the organization were setting out to "ameliorate" the vices of Chinese society and to promote the education, health, and morality of the Chinese people.

This organization also reflected the reform movements then springing up in imperial China. After the catastrophe of the Boxer Rebellion in 1900, even the conservative Qing court felt compelled to reform itself. On 29 January 1901 the Empress Dowager solicited advice on reform from government bureaucrats at all levels as well as from foreign envoys.[72] Having heard from them, between 1901 and 1905 the Qing government undertook a series of reforms: old offices were abolished and new ones were created; military academies were founded and modern military training was instituted; political economy was added as a subject in civil service examinations; Chinese students were recruited from abroad for service at home; Manchus and Chinese were extended permission to marry each other; women were liberated from footbinding; and opium was banned.[73] Encouraged by all of this, Chinese intellectuals and social activists across the country and abroad founded many organizations advocating reforms. The agenda of the Chinese Empire Reform Society of Missouri was closely tied to the social reforms of the Qing court. Its main concern, however, was the "moral" uplifting of the Chinese.

In 1905 the Chinese American Educational Association was formed in St. Louis. Like the other two organizations, this one was restricted to Chinese males. Unlike the other two, it was dedicated to adoption of American culture and to the Americanization of its members—in particular, to establishing a night school for the Chinese in St. Louis. According to its corporation deed, it would hire American male teachers to teach its members and would maintain a reading room with books and newspapers. The organization was to be run by a board of governors consisting of a president, a secretary, a treasurer, and three other members. These were to be elected by the members for one-year terms. Jeu Shung, who was also the president of the Chinese Empire Reform Society in 1903, was elected as the organization's founding president, Gon Sun as its secretary, and Leo Wu (also a board member of the Chinese Empire Reform Society) as its treasurer. On 22 February 1905 the organization held its first meeting at its headquarters at 22 South Eighth Street.[74]

The above social organizations reflected the social awakening movements in America and in China. In contrast, the Chinese Nationalist League of America, formed in 1916 in St. Louis, was more closely linked to the Nationalist political movement in China:

> The purposes for which said corporation is formed are, to promote friendly and social relations among persons of Chinese birth or descent; to provide for the education of young boys and girls of Chinese birth or descent, and to employ teachers and maintain classes for that purpose.
>
> To improve social, civic, and economic conditions in the Republic of China; To use every effort to develop the resources of China and to establish trade and commerce relations between it and the United States and other countries; To make every effort to establish, maintain, and insure a sound republican, constitutional form of government, in fact as well as in name, in the Republic of China; To disseminate among persons of Chinese birth and descent true ideas of personal and public morality, as well as the principles of personal and political liberty and representative government; To foster and promote and in every way advance the spirit of Democracy and Equality in America and in China.[75]

This document indicates the organization's national agenda as well as its local program. Regarding the former, this group would strive to improve social and economic conditions in China by promoting Sino-U.S. relations and the values of liberty, democracy, and constitutional government. Regarding the latter, it would focus on improving general education among the Chinese in St. Louis. It is worth noting that the Chinese Nationalist League of America included Chinese girls among those whose lives it wanted to improve.

In 1928 the Chinese Nationalist Party or *Kuo Ming Tang* was formed in St. Louis. Its structure and programs closely resembled those of the Chinese Nationalist League of America.[76] The Chinese Nationalist Party in St. Louis was one of the overseas branches of the Nationalist Party in China, which in 1928 gained control of the country and established a government in Nanjing. The formation of the Chinese Nationalist Party indicates that the Chinese in St. Louis had sharp political instincts.

The above initiatives by the Chinese in St. Louis show that the early Chinese community was not insulated from social and political movements in America and China. On the contrary, the Chinese actively and enthusiastically involved themselves in social and political movements both in their adopted home and in their ancestral land.

FINAL RESTING PLACES: WESLEYAN AND VALHALLA CEMETERIES

Many Chinese came to St. Louis with the dream of making a fortune and then returning home to China. Few would realize this dream, and many ended up in Wesleyan and Valhalla cemeteries, their final resting places in America. The deaths and burials of the Chinese in St. Louis are thus significant windows onto their lives. The study of mortuary records helps us find missing pieces to the story of Hop Alley.

Wesleyan and Valhalla are the two main cemeteries for the Chinese of St. Louis. Prior to 1924, they were buried temporarily at Wesleyan until they could be transported back to China. After 1924, when Wesleyan was closed, Valhalla became their final resting place.

Wesleyan Cemetery was on Oliver Street Road near Hanley Road, outside the city limits and seven miles west of the courthouse. It was a ten-acre field and was populated with the remains of ordinary St. Louisans.[77] According to the records, Wong You, a Chinese laundry owner, was the first Chinese to be buried at Wesleyan, in 1879. After that year all deceased Chinese were buried there.[78] By 1894 around twenty Chinese were buried at Wesleyan, including Hong Sing, Wah Chi Lee, May Lin Foo, Sam Wo, Foo Gee Chin, and Wah Lung.[79] In 1894, William Schmieder, the sexton at Wesleyan, described to Theodore Dreiser how the Chinese buried their dead:

> They came out here in carriages, sometimes as many as 19 or 20 of them. They have the corpse in a coffin and rough box stowed away in a hearse, just like Americans. That's about all they do have like Americans. One of them will sit on the hearse with the driver, or in the first carriage, and drop little bits of white paper with holes in them all along the road. I always receive notice beforehand that they are coming, and so I have the grave ready. They'll drive in and take out the coffin. Then they always have a bottle with them that holds some kind of liquor and a little bit of china cup that holds about two thimblefuls. One of them will take the cup and pour it full of liquor. Then he'll go and kneel down about six feet away from the foot of the grave and begin mumbling something. At the same time he'll have the china cup between his thumbs before him and he'll keep swaying it up and down and crosswise until all at once he pours it around on the ground. Then he'll take the empty cup and go through the same motions. Everybody takes a turn doing this until all of them have blessed the grave. Then they throw the cup and bottle down alongside.
>
> Then I put the coffin down and when I begin to throw on the dirt they passes crackers around to one another and begin to eat. Some of them throw a bit of rice in the grave, another scatters the pieces of paper around, and another cuts the head off one or two chickens that they bring, and throw them in the grave. When the grave is filled they go away.[80]

Schmieder's description is a vivid and authentic account of Chinese burial ceremonies in St. Louis. From it we can draw some useful information. First, the burial ceremonies closely resembled those of traditional China, especially southern China.[81] Throwing paper money—"little bits of white paper with holes in them"—and blessing the grave with liquor, food, and chickens were all means for ensuring that the deceased would have money to spend and enough food to eat in the other world. Clearly, the early Chinese in St. Louis were consciously preserving Chinese traditions in a foreign land. Second, burial ceremonies were a means for binding members of the community together. The rituals enabled the living to mourn the dead, but they also bound

the living together. The gathering of Chinese at the burial ceremonies perhaps offered them a sense of kinship and solidarity.

The ceremonies Schmieder described were for ordinary members
of the community. When a well-to-do Chinese man died, the burial
service was more "imposing," as Dreiser put it. In 1889, Wah Chi
Len, a rich Chinese man, was buried at Wesleyan. This ceremony
was much more elaborate than those for ordinary Chinese. "Two
bands discoursed music at his graveside and a half dozen of his
country's flags drooped their silken folds upon the sod and decayed
upon his casket's breast with the lapse of time. Bowls of fine china
filled with choice food offerings were left upon his grave, and at regular periods thereafter friends came to decorate his resting-place."[82]

In 1927, Wesleyan Cemetery was leveled to make different use
of the land. Thus the On Leong Merchants and Laborers Association—the de facto Chinese government in St. Louis—had no
choice but to remove the remains of one hundred deceased Chinese for shipment to their home villages in China. On a mid-
November day in 1928, according to the *St. Louis Post-Dispatch*,
Lee Mow Lin, a prominent Chinese merchant in St. Louis and the
leader of On Leong, along with two other members of On Leong,
performed the pious task in a shelter of boards and canvas under a
tree in a corner of Wesleyan Cemetery. Surrounded by the remains
of one hundred of their fellows, Lee Mow Lin and his companions
washed and dried the bones before placing them in the metal boxes.
Some bones bore the marks of bullet wounds, and one had a gash
across the forehead, indicating the sudden and violent death of
their owners. The prepared bones would be shipped to San Francisco and loaded onto a steamer bound for Hong Kong with a cargo
of hundreds of wooden crates, each about three feet square and
containing four tin boxes. These boxes would contain thousands
of Chinese who had been interred in the United States. From Hong
Kong the parcels would be distributed throughout the interior of
China. Once the bones of those who died in foreign lands were
returned home, they would be placed in jars and buried near those
of their ancestors.[83]

This account indicates, first, that the social climate for Chinese
St. Louisans was harsh and often violent. The total Chinese
population in the last decades of the nineteenth century and the
first decades of twentieth remained steady at about three hundred.
Yet a hundred Chinese—one-third of the population—vanished
in the first fifty years of the community's existence. This high

mortality rate reminds us of the hard work the Chinese performed and the stresses, strains, discrimination, and violence they faced in an alien land.

Second, most of the early Chinese of St. Louis, like the Chinese in other parts of the United States, were sojourners who intended to return to their native villages in China. The sojourning nature of the Chinese immigrants was generally a result of two factors, one internal and the other external. The internal factor can be explained as the Chinese agrarian tradition, which encouraged social stability and discouraged migration and immigration. Those who migrated were regarded by other Chinese as "vagabonds" or "idling elements," and those who immigrated were despised by the governments as *hua wai zhi min*—"traitors" or "renegades" of Chinese civilization. Bound by this tradition, the Chinese overseas regarded themselves as sojourners and dreamed of someday returning to their ancestral home. The peculiarities of Chinese culture and the sojourning nature of Chinese immigrants were used as excuses for legal Chinese exclusion and for social discrimination. However, the sojourning lives of the Chinese in America, as indicated by how they lived in St. Louis, were at least as much a result of the host country's alien and frightening environment. The hardships of the work the Chinese accepted and the discrimination and the violence they faced discouraged them from making America their adopted home. It is consistent with this argument that C. Fred Blake in his study found no markers on Chinese graves at Wesleyan. The absence of grave markers tells us that the Chinese community of St. Louis was transitory in nature. The Chinese did not intend to stay permanently, so there was little point in spending scant funds to make grave markers.

Third, the temporary burials of deceased Chinese at Wesleyan demonstrates that the Chinese preserved their heritage. According to the Chinese tradition, *luo ye gui gen*, literally, "Leaves fall on the roots of trees," that is, "One should die or be buried in his ancestral land." This was the ideal for Chinese living outside their ancestral land. One who failed to return home while alive would expect his remains to be sent back. In faithfully performing this duty to the deceased, On Leong was preserving this tradition.

After Wesleyan Cemetery closed in 1924, On Leong purchased a section in Valhalla Cemetery on a hilltop in the northeast corner.[84] Since then Valhalla, a county cemetery, has been the final resting place for deceased Chinese. It holds several hundred graves of former residents of the Chinese community.[85] Unlike in Wesleyan Cemetery, all the Chinese graves in Valhalla have markers, which vary in size and ornamentation. My examination of the gravestones reveals that the Chinese community underwent changes and transitions. Since 1924 the Chinese burial plots have expanded far beyond that first section. A map of Valhalla shows that Chinese burials have spread into sections 6, 7, 8, 18a, 19, 20, FH#1, and FH#2.

The section purchased by On Leong in 1924 has thirty-seven flat gravestones, all of them square or rectangular and placed between 1924 and 1954.[86] These plain, flat stones contrast sharply with the more elaborate, upright gravestones of the European Americans surrounding them, revealing the social gap between

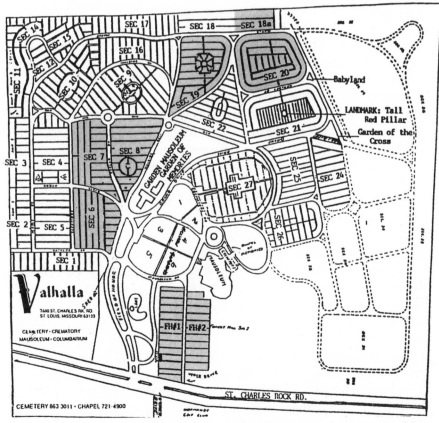

MAP 3.1 Chinese graves (shaded) in Valhalla Cemetery (reconstructed by Winston Vanderhoof, Truman State University Publications, with permission from Valhalla Cemetery).

the generally poverty-stricken Chinatown immigrants and the more affluent white St. Louisans. Most gravestones in this section were inscribed in the traditional style, with Chinese characters and no Romanized ones, indicating that Chinese families preferred to keep the Chinese tradition.

Section 18a of the Chinese section was added later. There are 142 flat, rectangular gravestones laid in twelve rows. Counting from west to east, the three stones in the first row, the nine in the second, the twelve in the third, and the eighteen in the fourth all date from the 1960s. The fourteen stones in the fifth row and the twelve in the sixth date mostly from the 1940s; the sixteen in the seventh from the 1980s; the fifteen in the eighth from the 1930s to the 1980s; the thirteen in the ninth and twelve in the tenth from the 1970s; the nine in the eleventh from the 1960s to the 1980s; and, finally, the eight in the twelfth row from the 1960s.[87] These dates on the stones indicate that this section was started from the center of the section (fifth to eighth rows) and gradually expanded piece by piece. This arrangement, Blake explains, shows that "when the plots in one were filled, each member of the On Leong Tong was asked to contribute a sum of money for the purchase of the next lot. In this way burial was under the control of the Tong and every member was guaranteed a place in the cemetery on the occasion of his or her death."[88] Yet, the arrangement could also be understood as a sign of On Leong's declining power since the 1960s, both in terms of financial capacity (On Leong could not afford to purchase the entire section), and in terms of social control over its members, who no longer felt compelled to be buried in this section.

The upright gravestones along both sides of the road in section 18a dating from the 1960s, and many other upright gravestones in sections 6, 7, 8, FH#1, and FH#2 dating from the 1970s, reflect dramatic economic, social, and cultural transitions in the Chinese community. First, the upright gravestones indicate an improvement in social and economic conditions for the Chinese; upright gravestones cost more than flat ones. Second, most of the gravestones in these sections have been inscribed with both names of the couple, indicating the community's gradual change from a "bachelor society" to a more family-oriented one since the 1960s. Third, the inscriptions of Chinese surnames or full names have been Romanized, reflecting efforts by the Chinese to integrate with the larger society. According to Blake, the side-by-side use of Chinese characters and Romanized letters on grave markers indicates Chinese efforts to accommodate American culture while preserving Chinese traditions.[89]

CONCLUSION

For most Chinese, especially Chinese bachelors, Hop Alley was a haven. In Hop Alley they could find joy, comfort, and solidarity—emotional commodities difficult to obtain anywhere else. The workplace, be it a laundry, a restaurant, a grocery store, or a tea shop, defined the daily life of the Chinese laborer; the institutions of family and community were meaningful to him on weekends and holidays. The lack of family life among the first Chinese immigrants was early on seen as evidence of Chinese cultural peculiarity, a sojourning mentality, and an inevitable failure to Americanize. Later it was used to help justify Chinese exclusion policies. Hop Alley offers a different picture; Chinese families lived there, and many Chinese immigrants tried hard to settle and even assimilate into the host society. For those with family and children, Hop Alley was both a home and a community. For those who could not have family with them due to financial constraints, Chinese cultural restraints, and the exclusion laws, Hop Alley was a necessary substitute for family life as well as an emotional outlet. Interactions with community members on Sundays restored the energy drained by a week of toil. To a certain degree, Hop Alley normalized their "abnormal" immigrant lives in America.

In the multicultural setting of St. Louis, interracial contacts inevitably affected the lives of the Chinese. Interracial marriage and sexual relations were direct products of the interracial interactions. The sharing of urban spaces and experiences resulted in intimate relations and even marriages between Chinese and European Americans. These relationships at different times encountered different social reactions. Before the era of Chinese exclusion, society was more tolerant of mixed marriages involving Chinese. After the passage of the Chinese Exclusion Act and the consequent nationwide anti-Chinese crusade, interracial sexuality made many Americans anxious.

Sexual relations between races were frowned on by the American public and by the legal system; yet at the same time, the churches encouraged the races to interact, both during services and at church-sponsored social activities. Sunday schools were effective means of evangelizing the "heathen" Chinese.

Many young Chinese took advantage of the Sunday schools to acquire an education they could not otherwise have achieved. Having done so, they were able to climb in the world and assimilate with European Americans. Meanwhile, for many Chinese women, the religious and social services offered by the churches eased the culture shock of immigration.

The recreational activities of the Chinese point to early efforts at community building. The various clan associations tried to meet their members' social and emotional needs by offering recreational facilities and by organizing cultural and social activities. The rise of more Westernized social organizations indicates that Chinese St. Louisans not only were trying to make their lives in America easier, but also were concerned about broader social and political movements in both America and China.

The mortuary records further reveal how immigrant life evolved for the Chinese. Wesleyan Cemetery served as a temporary graveyard for deceased Chinese before their remains were shipped back to the ancestral land; in contrast, Valhalla Cemetery has become the permanent final resting place for Chinese St. Louisans, much earlier than one might have expected.

4 Governing "Hop Alley"

On Leong Chinese Merchants and Laborers Association, 1906–1966

"On Leong" means peaceful. If they have problems and don't know what to do or if there is a dispute about payment of debt, they go to one of the two co-presidents instead of going to a lawyer. The men at the meetings hear the story—like a jury. They consult and the co-presidents hand down a decision. You know, we Chinese like to keep our problems within our community and solve them ourselves.

—Annie Leong, *St. Louis Globe-Democrat*, 1962

LIKE OTHER URBAN CHINESE immigrant communities, Hop Alley developed a self-protective and self-governing organization, the On Leong Merchants and Laborers Association, commonly known as On Leong Tong. After it was founded in the early years of the twentieth century, it became the dominant community organization in St. Louis Chinatown. The public referred to its presidents as "the mayors of Chinatown," reflecting the fact that the Chinese preferred to solve their problems within their own community.[1] As this group's name included the word *tong*, it was widely and mistakenly perceived to be a criminal secret society.[2] This chapter examines the origins, nature, and functions of On Leong and its impact on the St. Louis Chinese community.

FORMATION AND FUNCTIONS OF ON LEONG

The efforts by the Chinese to build a community in St. Louis were exemplified by the On Leong Merchants and Laborers Association. Other social organizations existed before On Leong, but none possessed its power and influence.

The national On Leong Association was in existence by the 1890s, with branch associations in the eastern states and later the Midwest.[3] With support and guidance from the national association, the

Chinese in St. Louis formed the On Leong Tong Chinese Merchants Association in 1906.[4] They registered it with City Hall in 1912.[5]

The term *On Leong* is the Cantonese variant of *An Liang*, which is derived from the Chinese aphorism *chu bao an liang*, meaning "eliminating despots [*chu bao*] and bringing peace to people [*an liang*]." Generations of Chinese peasant rebels and secret societies had adopted this slogan while challenging the established order and advancing their own political agendas. In an alien land, merchants—the elite of Chinese immigrants—felt the need and obligation to establish a social organization that would protect their interests and also assist newcomers from China. As a vulnerable minority, Chinese immigrants were unable to *chu bao* (eliminate those who excluded them legally or discriminated against them socially). The best they could do was *an liang* (bring peace and social order) within their own communities through mutual aid and self-governance. Thus the On Leong Merchants and Laborers Association was founded as a self-reliant and quasi-legal social organization of Chinese immigrants.

On Leong Merchant and Laborers Association was popularly known as On Leong Tong. The word *tong* in Chinese means "hall"; in none of its senses does it suggest crime or secrecy. In China the term *tong* often indicates a school, a church, a district association, or a herb dispensary.[6] In America, Chinese organizations with *tong* in their names include both benevolent societies and criminal ones. Because *tong* is such a loaded word in English, these organizations all tend to be misconstrued as criminal secret societies—especially during clashes between Chinese criminal gangs.

An article in the *St. Louis Republic* on 14 August 1910 addressed this confusion about the Chinese tongs:

> A good deal of mystification and misunderstanding about the Chinese tong exists in the American mind. We confuse all tongs with the one called Highbinders, a gang of the criminal class of the Chinese, most of them hired cutthroats and thieves, and nothing could be a greater injustice. The Chinese tong—or secret society—is an organization branching from the ancient Free Masons. The secret society of Free Masons has flourished in China for thousands of years and the tongs are merely branches of the original society. They are based on exactly the same principle as are our secret societies and should not be confused with the criminal Highbinders. The Gee Kong Tong holds its meetings in elaborately appointed lodgerooms in which only tong members are allowed to enter. The better clans of tong members will not tolerate the Highbinders and there have not been any in St. Louis for several years. An occasional Highbinder soon leaves town after an interview with police or the more law-binding Chinese.[7]

Scholars have also tried to end the public's confusion. Sociologist C. N. Reynolds in 1935 stated that the Chinese organizations (or tongs) in America had their roots in secret societies in China. He differentiated Chinese community organizations such as the Six Companies (discussed later) and trade and craft organizations from the fighting tongs. He noted that many tongs in America had modified their criminal activities and taken on benevolent and protective functions.[8]

Several decades later, Yung-Deh Richard Chu explored the origins, structures, and functions of the various Chinese secret societies in America. According to Chu, three types of Chinese social organizations developed in America. The district associations emerged to assist new immigrants by providing free lodging, food, and employment services. Soon after, clan associations were formed to provide services to those who lacked support from the district associations. As the district associations grew, various clan associations within the same district began to compete with one another for hegemony. As a consequence, the smaller clans began to coordinate their efforts secretly in order to avoid being controlled by the bigger clans, and began using violence to force the larger clans to act reasonably. When the environment in America turned hostile after the passage of the Chinese Exclusion Act in 1882, a third type of organization, the secret society, became very active and widespread. Chu concluded: "The tongs have both their vices and positive aspects, especially for the peculiar situation of the Chinese immigrants. They can not be simply regarded as Chinese version of Mafia existing merely for pursuing organized crimes."[9]

A more recent study by sociologist Kuo-lin Chen places Chinese criminal organizations (i.e., criminal according to American law enforcement agencies) in the following categories: triads, tongs, gangs, heroin smugglers, and smugglers of illegal immigrants. Based on "sworn brotherhood"—whereby secret societies bind their members by an oath of brotherhood—the tongs in America today include Chih Kung (Gee Kung, Zhigong), On Leong (Anliang), Hip Sing (Xiesheng), Tung On (Tongan), Fukien (Fujian) American, Hop Sing (Hesheng), Bing Kung (Binggong), Suey Sing (Cuisheng), and Ying On (Yingduan).[10]

Chih Kung, On Leong, and Hip Sing are the most influential tongs. Chih Kung, the oldest of all, was formed in 1850 in Hawaii and expanded to British Columbia in the late 1850s, finally establishing itself in San Francisco in 1863.[11] Some members of Chih Kung established On Leong in 1894. Its headquarters were moved to New York a few years later and have remained there ever since.[12]

The works discussed above categorize On Leong as one of the secret societies and note that it is involved in both benevolent and criminal activities. Historically, the national On Leong had been involved with tong wars; that said, its St. Louis branch does not seem to resemble a secret society in either structure or functions. Its officers are elected, including the president, vice-president, secretary, treasurer, and seven directors, who together constitute the governing board. It more closely resembles a local Chamber of Commerce, and the media have referred to it as a Chinese version of the Business Men's League.[13]

On Leong in St. Louis bears a closer resemblance to the Chinese Six Companies. Up until the civil rights movement of the 1960s, most Chinese immigrant communities in America were controlled by fraternal organizations known as the Six Companies. Their memberships were based on lineage and geographical origins. Specifically, they were the Kong Chow Company (Gangzhou Huiguan), the Sam Yup Company (Sanyi Huiguan), the Yeoung Wo Company (Yanghe Huiguan), the Yan Wo Company (Renhe Huiguan), the Ning Yung Company (Ningyang Huiguan), and the Hop Wo Company (Hehe Huiguan). All six were founded between 1851 and 1862 on the West Coast. In 1882, in response to the harsh treatment of Chinese immigrants from the public and from lawmakers, they formed a national umbrella organization, the Chinese Consolidated Benevolent Association (CCBA or *Zhonghua Huiguan*), commonly known as the Chinese Six Companies.[14]

The Chinese in St. Louis were different from those on the West Coast and did not join the CCBA network; instead, they were controlled by On Leong.[15] Unlike the CCBA, On Leong was a trade and professional organization that promoted and protected all Chinese businesses in the United States regardless of lineage and geographical origins. On Leong's 1912 corporation deed gave its mission as follows: "to bring about cooperation of its members in buying and importing goods, wares and merchandise, and obtaining better facilities of transportation for the same, to provide relief for its sick members, to bring about a better social and friendly relation among its members, and to elevate them morally and educationally."[16] Clearly, the main objective was to protect and promote commerce—the buying, importing, and transporting of goods. The corporation deed also indicates that On Leong had $2,000 in capital stock divided into two hundred shares equally held by the four members of the board of directors: Lee Look, Hang Jue, Heuy M. Fot, and Gin

Suey.[17] Judging from this, in 1912 the board members were more like business partners.

In 1919, On Leong underwent major changes. First, it expanded its membership to include not only merchants but also common laborers. This suggests that On Leong was attempting to transform itself from an elite trade organization into a community service organization. To reflect this structural change, On Leong changed its official name: "tong" was dropped and "laborers" was added. This reveals that On Leong was aware of the negative connotations of "tong" and that the American public equated tongs with criminal organizations. In 1919 the reorganized On Leong again registered with City Hall, this time as On Leong Chinese Merchants and Laborers Association. The corporation deed of that year indicates that the organization was more democratic in both name and structure. By this time On Leong had purchased a headquarters for meetings and other activities. The officers of On Leong consisted of a president, a vice-president, a secretary, a treasurer, and seven directors, all elected annually by the members.[18]

Despite the differences in organizational structure, On Leong's societal functions were very similar to those of the Six Companies. For Chinese immigrants in America, On Leong was an unofficial local government—it was the legislative, judiciary, and administrative authority within Chinese community. To control competition among Chinese entrepreneurs in St. Louis, On Leong declared a "one mile one laundry" rule, whereby Chinese laundries had to be at least a mile apart. (Later on, a "one mile one restaurant" rule was also declared.) A similar rule had been established by the Chinese laundry associations in San Francisco and Virginia City in the 1860s. Those who violated the regulation were often punished. First they were warned by On Leong, and a warning was often enough that the offender would close his shop voluntarily. A laundryman who refused to heed this first warning was often forced to close the business later, after a mysterious tragedy—a fire on the premises or the murder of a family member.[19] Enforcement measures like these were effective; however, they were the same methods as criminal societies used, and thus they only strengthened the popular image that On Leong was a criminal organization.

More often, On Leong served as a Chinese court on American soil. Here it applied Chinese legal codes and customary laws to try criminals and wrongdoers in cases presented to the board.[20] This reflected the tradition among Chinese secret societies to take the law into their own hands; however, it was even more a reaction to the Chinese experience as immigrants in America. When Chinese were murdered in the United States and American law enforcement agencies were seen to be delaying or ignoring the cases, On Leong would step in and prosecute the crimes within the Chinese community, utilizing Chinese laws.[21] The president of an On Leong organization, elected every year by its members, was generally regarded inside and outside the community as the mayor of Chinatown, especially because of this judicial authority. In a similar way, the Chinese Six Companies arbitrated disputes among members and represented Chinese immigrants in their dealings with American authorities.[22]

Besides this, On Leong was the most powerful economic force in the Chinese community. The association owned properties that earned considerable income. Most presidents of On Leong were prominent local entrepreneurs who had donated large sums to the association; most members at large were petty merchants and common laborers. However, On Leong did not have absolute economic control over its members. In contrast, the Six Companies wielded almost complete control over the economic lives of Chinese immigrants. The companies required Chinese immigrants to register with them on landing and to pay fees and debts before departing for China.[23]

On Leong provided useful services to its members and their families. An especially valued service was translation aid. Most new Chinese immigrants were unable to speak English and so faced tremendous difficulties during their first steps on American ground. On Leong hired a group of young, bilingual Chinese to act as interpreters. They would go to the train station to meet the new immigrants, bring them to their apartments, and help them settle down and find work.[24] On Leong also helped many new immigrants get licenses to start laundries.

On Leong was also a social center for Chinese immigrants. Its headquarters were often used by members at no charge for weddings, funerals, celebrations of new-born babies, and other social gatherings.[25] The Six Companies provided similar services: language schools, temporary lodging for newcomers, charity to the destitute, and so on.[26]

On Leong helped Chinese immigrants meet their spiritual needs. It approached burial ceremonies for its members as a sacred task. Many Chinese immigrants came to America with the intention of working hard, saving as much money as possible, and eventually returning home to their families. Some returned to their villages in

China with savings after years of toil on the "Gold Mountain." But many others who came to America died by violence or of diseases. They were buried temporarily in local cemeteries, and there awaited transportation back to their homeland. On Leong made it its duty to return the bones of deceased members to China (see Chapter 3).

Like most traditional Chinese organizations, On Leong maintained a number of traditional rituals. Members of On Leong depended on Chinese gods for protection and good fortune. The meeting hall at On Leong's headquarters had an altar with a shrine to Guan Gong, the protector of merchants. When On Leong's eleven board members gathered for their monthly business meeting, they would light incense and bow to Guan Gong before starting the meeting. During the Chinese New Year celebrations, the most important ceremony was a homage to Guan Gong. The members would donate between two and five dollars to cover the costs of this ceremony. The proceeds supplemented On Leong's annual membership fees, which were twenty-five dollars.[27]

Like the Six Companies, On Leong was a fraternal organization that excluded Chinese immigrant women. The 1919 On Leong corporation deed stipulated that "the active membership of the organization shall consist male only, and they of the Chinese race."[28] Although members' wives were sometimes allowed to attend meetings, women seldom participated in decision making. However, On Leong provided services to Chinese families and in that way indirectly helped Chinese women. Also, beginning in the 1950s many women helped On Leong provide services to the community. Annie Leong well illustrates the St. Louis On Leong's openness to women. Annie, who was raised in an apartment right above On Leong's headquarters in Chinatown, became a significant force in On Leong. Although never a member, she served as its unofficial spokeswoman after 1950 and contributed tremendously to the organization. She was the mistress of ceremonies at various celebrations sponsored by On Leong. She served as interpreter for the senior On Leong officers, and she entertained local newspaper reporters during the 1950s and 1960s.[29]

The protective functions of the traditional Chinese community organizations have long been recognized. Julia I. Hsuan Chen has noted On Leong's "generous" contributions to "all good causes."[30] William Hoy has praised the Six Companies' campaigns against Chinese exclusion legislation, which involved protest and appeals directed at all levels of government.[31] Him Mark Lai has recognized the CCBA's role in ensuring the smooth functioning of communities.[32] Peter Kwong has categorized the functions of the district or clan associations in New York Chinatown as "defensive" (in dealings with the larger society) and "offensive" (in efforts to develop businesses within Chinatown), and believes that both functions have had positive effects on the community.[33] Sue Fawn Chung's recent study of Zhigongtang (Chih Kung Tong) praises the protective features of this organization: it shielded communities, created surrogate families, established basic rules of conduct among members, helped immigrants find work, extended economic assistance through systems of mutual aid, arranged entertainments and traditional festivals, provided facilities for travelers, and made funeral arrangements.[34]

Scholars also believe that these protective functions have also served to control communities. Lai has meticulously analyzed the CCBA's control over Chinese immigrants. On landing, a Chinese immigrant would be placed under the protection or control of the association with regard to food, lodging, and employment. An immigrant could not purchase a steamship ticket for China until he had cleared his debts and obtained a departure permit from the association.[35] Similarly, Kwong claims that the unofficial political structure in Chinatown helped the elite exploit the working class.[36] The traditional Chinese organizations' control over Chinese immigrant communities was comparable to Tammany Hall's hold over New York City's Irish immigrants, except that Tammany Hall had transformed itself into a political machine in mainstream urban politics.[37]

On Leong did not achieve total control over its members the way the CCBA did. Also, it never was On Leong's intention to blend its members into the larger society. This self-confinement mentality was partly a result of the socioeconomic position of the Chinese immigrants—and, for that matter, of American society. Prior to World War II, most Chinese immigrants were from impoverished rural areas of China and spoke little or no English. As a result, they had little understanding of American ways. This naturally nourished the self-confinement mentality; Chinese immigrants relied heavily on one another for comfort and security. At the same time, they had been legally excluded by immigration authorities, persecuted by law enforcement agencies, economically segregated from the mainstream labor market, and socially isolated from the majority of Americans. The hostility they faced in America gave them no choice but to develop systems of mutual aid and protection.

Meanwhile, as business leaders, the "mayors of Chinatown" had a vested interest in keeping the community isolated and dependent on its own internal structures. Many writers have noted this.[38] An isolated community guaranteed a steady pool of laborers and a profitable market. Yet economic factors alone cannot explain On Leong's leanings toward self-confinement. Consider that until the 1960s the main occupation of Chinese St. Louisans was laundry, and that the major clientele of these laundries was white Americans.

In St. Louis the more important reasons for this self-confinement were cultural and psychological. The dominant position of the Chinese business class over Chinese immigrants was a distinctive feature of overseas Chinese societies in America, just as it was in other parts of the world. This pattern of social control was a departure from the system in traditional China, where a social elite of gentry-scholars dominated every level of the governing machine, and where merchants were despised as social parasites who would corrupt both government and society. Secure in their wealth and power, the Chinese gentry-scholars had little incentive to immigrate. The absence of the gentry-scholars among Chinese immigrants thus gave Chinese merchants—who were better educated and more sophisticated than common laborers—the opportunity to emerge as leaders of their communities. Thus the more confined a Chinese immigrant community was, the more indispensable the Chinese business leaders were. These men had elite status, and to keep it they tried to maintain the community's established order.

On Leong inherited elements of Chinese tradition, but it also adopted cultural practices of the New World. Its organizers quickly learned the rules and customs of the American business world. In the 1910s, Chinese businesses were expanding rapidly and the Chinese population was growing steadily. As one result, On Leong required a bigger space to hold meetings. In 1914 it purchased a three-story building at 20 South Eighth Street as its new headquarters; on 10 October of that year it moved in. The *St. Louis Republic* reported this event in "Hop Alley Feast Like B. M. L.":

> The Chinese Merchants' association celebrated the removal into their new headquarters at 20 South Eighth Street yesterday. . . .
> This association is to the Chinese about what the Business Men's League is to the rest of St. Louis.
> The Chinese are apt pupils. They have been reading of the functions of the B. M. L., and their celebration possessed all features of that organization, and then some.
> First, they had a banquet. It has come to be recognized in St. Louis that no function of the B. M. L. is complete without a banquet. The Chinese brethren has a series of them.

Music, too, features the functions of the B. M. L., and the Chinese
were not daunted. While they had no celebrated vocalists like George
W. Simmons or William Flewellyn Saunders, they got along fairly well.
Harmony has no particular place in a Chinese musical production. But
they sang, anyhow.

Each Celestial chose his own song, and delivered in his own pet key.
While the words were not overly intelligible to the American ear, that
made no particular difference, and as rapidly one banquet table was
emptied, other banqueters took their places, and the revelry lasted all
day and until late in the night.[39]

Clearly, this report is patronizing as well as laced with stereotypes. Nevertheless, it tells us something about how On Leong
developed. This elaborate celebration reflected On Leong's growing
economic strength and the adaptability of Chinese businessmen,
who were not only scions of traditional Chinese merchants, but
also modern businessmen eager to absorb new ideas and grab new
opportunities to survive and prosper in a more competitive world.

In performing its legal, economic, social, and spiritual functions,
On Leong eased many newcomers' initial cultural shocks and
difficulties, and successfully maintained community peace and
order. In these ways it was instrumental to the building of
St. Louis's Chinese community.

"The Mayors of Chinatown"

The presidents of On Leong Merchants and Laborers Association
were referred to by the American public as the "Mayors of
Chinatown." Most of them were affluent merchants and powerful
men in the Chinese community. The unofficial title of "Mayors
of Chinatown" suggests some form of despotic rule. In fact,
although a few leaders of On Leong were involved in criminal
activities that tainted the reputation of the organization, most
presidents of On Leong provided valuable services to the community and were highly respected. To understand On Leong and
its contributions to the community, it is worth examining the
personalities of its leaders during its peak years.

Jeu Sick (presidency: ?–1917)

Jeu Sick was one of the early presidents of St. Louis On Leong.
From the little that the sources tell us about him, he was probably
one of the worst. According to the *St. Louis Globe-Democrat*, Jeu
Sick was a wealthy merchant and the leader of On Leong in the
1910s. On 15 December 1917 he shot and killed Leong Fou, his

business competitor, behind a house at 714 Market Street in Hop Alley. He then turned the gun around and shot himself in the stomach, and died before medical aid could be summoned.[40] His dramatic and violent death contributed to the misconception that On Leong was associated with tong wars.

Lee Mow Lin (presidency: 1917–1929)

Lee Mow Lin came to America as a child and spent some years in San Francisco, where he learned the grocery business, before moving to St. Louis. His business, Quong On Lung, at 17 South Eighth Street, was one of the city's first Chinese grocery stores and was listed in the 1897 *Gould's St. Louis Directory*. In the decades around the turn of the last century, Chinese groceries were struggling to survive and the failure rate was quite high; few such businesses lasted longer than five years. Quong On Lung, however, managed to stay in business on the same premises until 1914.[41]

Lee Mow Lin's business success and his influence in Hop Alley attracted the attention of the local media. Dick Wood of the *St. Louis Republic* visited Quong On Lung and other Chinese businesses and wrote an article for his paper's Sunday magazine, which ran on 29 July 1900. The article took up an entire page, including photographs of Chinese grocery businesses and of social life in Hop Alley. According to Wood, Quong On Lung stocked a wide range of Chinese goods, including dry foods, tea, cloth, and medicines.[42] Wood portrayed Lee Mow Lin as a well-educated and highly respected Chinese merchant. A convert to Christianity, he had acquired a thorough English education at a church school in America when he was a young boy.[43] Because of his education, intelligence, and business success he came to be regarded as the spokesman for St. Louis Chinatown.

Wood's visit to Hop Alley took place at a critical time for the Chinese: the Boxer Rebellion was raging in their ancestral home. By the turn of the century, in the wake of the Opium Wars, the Chinese had grown angry at the increasing presence and influence of foreign aggressors. Members of *Yi He Quan* ("righteous and harmonious fists"), known in the West as the Boxers because they practiced martial arts, rose up to challenge the foreign powers. On 13 June 1900 the Boxers besieged the legation quarter in Beijing, where only 450 foreign guards were available to protect 475 foreign civilians, including twelve foreign ministers, as well as 2,300 Chinese Christians who had fled there for protection. The Western powers immediately dispatched an international relief expedition. The war in China aroused anxiety among the Chinese in St. Louis. Lee Mow Lin gave Wood his opinions on the Boxer Rebellion, which largely reflected those of his community. First he dispelled the rumor that massacres were taking place in China; then he expressed his confidence that the Chinese government and Chinese philosophy would prevail over the forces of evil:

> We can't believe all the things the papers have told. It surely could not be that our Government has been unable to protect the lives of foreign Ministers and their households. If such were the case, we, the Chinese merchants of St. Louis, would certainly have been informed through Chinese sources.
>
> If such were the case, it would mean untold suffering to many millions of our home people. Should the lawless element in China triumph over her centuries of economic adjustment, it would mean more of a reign of terror to the law-abiding representatives of our own race than the Western world is capable of grasping.
>
> In China, we have had dissensions and rebellions, as has been the case with many other nations not nearly so old, and there may be some who would gladly welcome a change in the Government, a shifting around of rulers—much the same as new blood is welcomed in the leader of a herd. The lawless element may gain, or may already have gained, the upper hand, but if so the bad effect will be nullified by the great unity and philosophy of the Chinese as a race.[44]

This statement reveals Lee Mow Lin's political skill and sophistication: he was defending the integrity of the Chinese government and Chinese culture while condemning the turmoil and violence generated by the Boxers. This is the best evidence available of Lee Mow Lin's character.

As a successful businessman and a strong leader, Lee Mow Lin dominated On Leong from its founding in 1906 until 1929. Many non-Chinese St. Louisans viewed him as a "venerable sage of the Chinese quarter."[45] Under his leadership, On Leong provided legal, social, and spiritual services for the community.

Joe Lin (presidency: 1929–1940)

Born in China in 1881, Joe Lin became a prominent restaurateur in St. Louis. His Orient Restaurant, at 414 North Seventh Street, was in operation from 1937 to 1952.[46] He was elected president of On Leong in 1929 and held that post until 1940. Between 1937 and 1947 he also served as president of the National Association of On Leong—a position usually held by leading merchants from New York City or Boston. He was referred to as the Mayor of Chinatown by the local media from 1929 until his death in 1947.

Like most of the early Chinese immigrants, Joe Lin had left his wife and children behind in China. Also like most of his fellow Chinese, he was keenly interested in politics in China. In 1927 the Nationalist Party, or Kuo Min Tang (KMT), split with the Chinese Communist Party (CCP) after a four-year coalition; the following year the KMT consolidated its grip on China. The KMT–CCP split affected the Nationalists in St. Louis. As a Nationalist, Joe Lin was enthusiastic about a republic in China; however, he did not favor the Nationalist government. He abhorred the corruption and backroom dealings within the party and the government it led.[47]

Joe Lin's leadership ability was most visible during the Sino-Japanese War, when he organized various activities to raise funds for the Chinese resistance. Immediately after the Japanese launched a total war against China on 7 July 1937, On Leong called on the Chinese of St. Louis to contribute to the Chinese war effort and named Joe Lin as treasurer of the fund. Although most Chinese in St. Louis were impoverished laborers in laundries and restaurants, they made weekly contributions as often as they could. Thus the community was able to donate a thousand dollars every week to buy weapons and ammunition for fighting the Japanese.[48] On 17 June 1938, Joe Lin gave a speech at a fundraising event organized by the St. Louis Committee of the United Council for Civilian Relief in China. This event was a great success, with 250 attending.[49] Joe Lin had friendly relations with his American customers, and sometimes they too donated to China's war effort.[50]

Joe Lin died at sixty-six on 13 December 1947, in the city's Jewish Hospital, where he had undergone an operation for a brain tumor. His funeral indicates just how influential he was in the Chinese community and among Americans. It was held on 23 December and was so elaborate and well attended that the *St. Louis Globe-Democrat* featured it in a story headlined: "All Limousines in City Hired for Mourners." The article began: "A lavish and colorful funeral service, followed by a procession including a 30-piece brass band and 46 limousines which tied up the heavy downtown Christmas traffic, marked the last rites yesterday of Joe Lin, unofficial mayor of St. Louis Chinatown."[51] The funeral cost $5,000—a considerable amount even by present standards. It was attended by five hundred people, including local Chinese, leaders of On Leong associations from twenty-eight cities, and many of Joe Lin's American friends. This speaks eloquently to the power that On Leong held over the Chinese immigrant community.

Interestingly, the service combined Eastern and Western rites, which reminds us that Joe Lin, like so many Chinese immigrants, had been able to adapt to America. Christian services were held in Cantonese dialect. A brass band played traditional Western funeral music, including "Onward Christian Soldiers" and "Adeste Fidelis." Joe Lin was buried at Valhalla Cemetery.[52]

Charles Quinn Chu (presidency: 1940–1950)

Charles Quinn Chu (or Charles Quin Chu), also known as Charles Quinn, was another powerful and charismatic leader. Born in Hong Kong in 1900, he came to St. Louis in 1912 with his parents. His father owned an importing business at the corner of Eighth and Market streets, in the heart of Hop Alley. Growing up in Chinatown, Quinn spoke fluent Cantonese and English. His restaurant, the Shanghai Café, was at 6314 Delmar Boulevard; there, as a sideline, he also sold Chinese *objets d'art*.[53]

A prominent businessman, Quinn enjoyed social respect and a comfortable lifestyle. His family lived at 434 Melville Avenue, a colonial brick house furnished handsomely in Western style with just a touch of the Orient. A new Pontiac parked outside his house further indicated his economic well-being. Quinn and his wife, Lum Shee, had one son, Chu Wah Chu, and two daughters, Rose Chu and Peggy Chu, all of whom went to college. In 1949 his older daughter Rose, a graduate of Washington University School of Dress Design, married Man Hing Au, a graduate of the Washington University School of Medicine.[54]

Quinn was tall in stature and congenial in nature, and he gradually emerged as a leader in Chinatown. Though he had been On Leong's president since 1940, he was referred to as the Mayor of Chinatown only after Joe Lin's death in 1947. Like Joe Lin, Quinn expanded the influence of the Chinese in St. Louis during his tenure as president of the St. Louis On Leong and as president of the National Association of On Leong from 1938 to 1948. He accomplished this in a number of ways—in particular, by holding the National Convention of On Leong in St. Louis in April 1949.[55]

Although his tenure as president of On Leong ended in 1950, Quinn remained influential and continued to be known as the Mayor of Chinatown until his death in 1976. News reports from time to time portrayed him as a powerful leader. Dickson Terry of the *St. Louis Post-Dispatch* interviewed him in December 1950. During the interview, Quinn explained On Leong's functions to Terry. When asked about the Communist takeover in China, he said that all the

PHOTOGRAPH 4.1 The gravestone of Charles Quin Chu (1899–1976), the last "Mayor of Chinatown," in Valhalla Cemetery, 1999. Note the inscription in both English and Chinese. Huping Ling Collection.

Chinese in St. Louis were anti-Communist and that they were going to hold an anti-Communist parade.[56] This indicates Quinn's efforts to protect members of On Leong from investigation by the FBI at a time when the United States was consumed with McCarthyism.[57]

Quinn retired from the restaurant business in 1961 and died of a heart ailment at the Clayton House Health Care Home in 1976 at seventy-six.[58] With his death, and more importantly, with the emergence of a new social organization, the St. Louis Chinese Society, most of whose members were Chinese professionals, On Leong began losing its grip on the Chinese community in St. Louis. The age of Mayors of Chinatown had ended.

Joe Lin and Charles Quinn were the most powerful of all the "mayors" of Chinatown, with influence both inside and outside the Chinese community. However, they and their families never acquired same clout among Chinese St. Louisans as the Moy, Wong, and Lin families did in Chicago Chinatown. The clan rivalries in Chicago, first between the Moys and the Wongs and later between the Moys and the Lins, resulted in tong wars, murders, and political disarray within the community.[59] In St. Louis there were no feuding clans, and this helped On Leong maintain a united community front.

HEADQUARTERS OF ON LEONG

The headquarters of On Leong had been moved several times during its history. In the early years of On Leong, the voluntary relocation of its headquarters was a result of the growing need of the Chinese community for more space to facilitate the various functions. After 1966, when Hop Alley was demolished under the urban renewal programs, the forced removal of On Leong headquarters reflected the discriminatory nature of urban renewal as it demanded the clearance of the districts where ethnic minorities resided, and were deemed unsafe and unsanitary and therefore doomed. Meanwhile, the forced removal of On Leong headquarters also indicates the powerlessness and lack of resources and means of On Leong in fighting discrimination and social injustice.

The First Headquarters: 20A South Eighth Street

On Leong's first headquarters, from 1914 to 1948, was at 20A South Eighth Street. This building had a Chinese grocery store downstairs and meeting rooms upstairs. The store was operated by Wing Chong Tai Company from 1914 to 1917 and then by Yen Lung & Company from 1918 to 1944.[60] In the first decades of the twentieth century, South Eighth Street was the busiest commercial street in Chinatown. Besides Yen Lung & Company, there were seven other Chinese grocery stores along it.[61] Around this time the Chinese community was maintaining a steady population of more than three hundred.

This headquarters was in the heart of Hop Alley and thus a convenient gathering place. On Leong held its board meetings there, and clansmen gathered there to celebrate the Chinese New Year. In 1936 more than three hundred Chinese crowded the meeting hall on New Year's Day. The festive spirit was visible everywhere in Chinatown. The owners of Chinese stores set out bowls of candied fruits, lily roots, and tangerines so that passers-by could help themselves. Adults handed out lucky money wrapped in red paper to Chinese children. Firecrackers were set off, and a dragon dance was performed. About fifteen men paraded in the dragon costume, with the man in the head leading the rest in a line down the street.[62]

The Second Headquarters: 720–724 Market Street

In September 1948, to better serve the community and to prepare for the national convention to be held in St. Louis the following year, On Leong began looking for a larger headquarters. At the time, a property at 720–724 Market Street was for sale. The Chinese already owned several other properties on the east side of Eighth Street and south of Market Street. By purchasing this building, they would be consolidating the Chinese holdings north to the main traffic artery. The On Leong board, which included Charles Quin (president), Yee Hing (vice president), and Joe Jones (secretary-treasurer), inspected the two-story brick building and decided to purchase it. On Leong agreed to pay $100,000 for the 12,000 square feet of floor space, which included five stores on the first floor and a number of meeting rooms above. The rooms would be able to accommodate the eight hundred people expected to attend the convention.[63]

On 2 April 1949 the annual National Convention of On Leong Merchants and Laborers Association opened as planned. The freshly renovated building was furnished with handsome teak chairs and desks and costly Oriental rugs. A fourteen-course dinner of Chinese delicacies, including shark's-fin soup and abalone with oyster sauce, was held for the 125 delegates and their wives and children from twenty eastern and midwestern cities.[64] The three-week convention impressed the delegates and promoted St. Louis Chinese businesses. It is worth noting that the wealth displayed by On Leong at the convention was in sharp contrast to most Chinese St. Louisans, who were earning about $30 a month. The concentration of economic power enhanced On Leong's social and political control over the community.

After the convention the headquarters continued to be used for community activities. For instance, the Chinese Youth Association used the meeting rooms for its monthly dances. In 1949, Annie Leong's family restaurant, the Asian Café, relocated from 714 Market Street to the downstairs of On Leong headquarters. On weekends, Annie and her friends would go upstairs to attend the dances held by the youth association.[65]

The most elaborate and important activities held at the headquarters were the annual Chinese New Year celebrations. On 27 January 1952 about fifty guests attended the celebration of the 4,650th Chinese New Year (according to the Chinese lunar calendar). The association served Chinese oyster soup (made of seaweed, with a steamed oyster on top), as oysters were a symbol of long life for the Chinese. Charles Quin delivered a speech expressing his hope that China would soon be freed from Communist rule.[66]

On 7 February 1959 about a hundred members of On Leong celebrated the 4,657th Chinese New Year. In keeping with Chinese tradition, no women were invited to the ceremony at the headquarters, although they could attend a more elaborate celebration a few weeks later. The ceremony started before midnight. The men, nearly all of them Chinese-born, solemnly approached a shrine at the end of the meeting room. The statue of Guan Gong, the protector of merchants, was placed in the center of the shrine. Before the idol were three delicate cups filled with wine. In front of the cups two red candles were burning. A jar of sand had been placed between the candles. The men bowed to their protector and then lit joss sticks, which they planted in the sand. Hai Leong, the president of On Leong, struck a brass gong to begin the Chinese New Year. Following the ritual, the men were served a dinner of oyster-and-seaweed soup and variety of vegetarian dishes.[67]

In 1962 the fifty-ninth annual National Convention of On Leong was held in St. Louis. Between 19 and 23 April, 104 delegates from thirteen eastern and midwestern states gathered at the headquarters. The main business of the convention was to hear advice on problems facing Chinese in individual communities and to pass

PHOTOGRAPH 4.2 The co-presidents of On Leong, Robert Chu and Hai Leong, ringing the gong to start the Chinese New Year, 5 February 1959. From the collections of the St. Louis Mercantile Library at the University of Missouri-St. Louis.

judgment on specific issues. Al Delugach of the *St. Louis Globe-Democrat* visited the convention and wrote about the event:

> They take their food seriously. Serious enough to import five Chinese cooks from Chicago to fix their vittles. Some of the delicacies they whip up are shark fin soup, chicken stuffed with bird's nest, abalone sauté with oyster sauce, steamed imported Chinese black mushrooms and other goodies . . . .
>
> It's a men-only affair. All the men we talked to were genially uncommunicative about the sort of problems that actually are dealt with. They would smile and reply something like: "Any problem."
>
> Miss Leong, 27, who manages the Asia Restaurant downstairs, gave us some additional help: "'On Leong' means peaceful," she pointed out, "If they have problems and don't know what to do or if there is a dispute about payment of debts, they go to one of the two co-presidents instead of going to a lawyer. The men at the meetings hear the story— like a jury. They consult and the co-presidents hand down a decision. You know, we Chinese like to keep our problems within our community and solve them ourselves." . . . .
>
> Upstairs are curved teakwood furniture, incense burners, red drapes, a Gwan Gung (protector of merchants) idol and hosts of flowers.
>
> Before a gong signaled the start of the daily business session and our departure, we observed that the delegates' places bore white pads of paper, fresh-sharpened pencils and ashtrays—just like the more usual businessmen's conventions. The only difference: the name tags were in Chinese characters.[68]

This convention was one of the last major events organized by the St. Louis On Leong. In the 1960s the St. Louis city government leveled Hop Alley to make way for a parking garage for Busch Stadium. In 1963, there had been discussions about the relocation of Chinatown, and the sad news affected the annual celebration of the Chinese New Year. Annie Leong, who was born in 1935 behind the On Leong headquarters, lamented the loss of the community: "I hate to see this place go. I'm the last of the Chinatown babies."[69]

The Chinese residents were at loss what to do, and the leaders of On Leong were not sure where to move the headquarters. The co-presidents, Ing Hong and Wai Lee, and the secretary, Joe Jone, had no immediate plans for its future.[70]

The uncertainty continued until the end of 1965, when On Leong bought a building at 1509 Delmar, the old R. E. Funsten Company nut-packing plant. The vacating of the old headquarters was emotionally difficult, and for that reason the New Year celebrations of 1966 were canceled.[71] On Leong chose 4 August 1966 as moving day. Beulah Schacht of the *St. Louis Globe-Democrat* recorded the sad moment:

I've been following the Chinese around our old little Chinatown, an area which once stretched from Seventh to Ninth streets and bounded by Market and Walnut streets, for so long they opened the door and let me see the moving-day mess.

But, they moved so quietly to their new quarters that a policeman came in right on my heels and said: "You should tell somebody. We didn't know you were here."

All through the years, on very special occasions, the association has received gifts from China and from other associations in the United States—gifts which would be impossible to replace. They were housed for so long in the headquarters at 720 Market St., there are tears in the eyes of the old-timers when they are reminded of the move.

The precious carved teakwood chairs are covered with the usual "moving dust," the intricately embroidered silk banner have been carefully placed on the very long ceremonial table and the shrine which houses Gwan Gung, protector of merchants, has been given special care.

Framed embroidered silks have been carefully stacked against walls but there was no sign of the big gong which is sounded shortly before midnight to celebrate the arrival of the Chinese New Year.

Annie Leong, who has called the new headquarters "the Chinese nut house," said it's going to be very difficult to make it take on the appearance of the old one.[72]

Two weeks after the move, along with all the other buildings in the area, the old headquarters was torn down to make way for the stadium project.[73] The physical disappearance of Chinatown did much to hasten the decline of On Leong's influence in the Chinese community.

WAR EFFORTS AND ON LEONG

In 1931 the Japanese invaded Manchuria in northeastern China. The Nationalist government under Chiang Kai-shek declared a policy of "unification before resistance"; it insisted that only after completely eliminating the Communist Party and its influence in China could the Nationalist government organize an effective resistance against the Japanese invasion. Meanwhile, the League of Nations condemned the Japanese aggression, albeit without taking any effective action to stop it. Encouraged by the weakness and ineptitude of the Nationalist government and the international community, Japan launched a full-scale war against all of China on 7 July 1937.

When news of the Japanese invasion reached the United States, Chinese communities throughout the country began organizing fundraisers to assist China's war effort. Six Companies called an emergency meeting on 21 September 1931, immediately after the Japanese invasion of Manchuria. This meeting gathered representatives of ninety-one Chinese organizations throughout North America. It resulted in the founding of the China War Relief Association of America, which ultimately had forty-seven chapters in the western hemisphere. The most urgent business of the association was to raise money for the war effort in China. One effective means of fundraising was the "Bowl of Rice Movement"— a collective effort made by Chinese in America to raise funds and gather supplies to send to China.[74]

Under the leadership of On Leong, Chinese St. Louisans joined this effort at once. On Leong formed a fundraising committee with Joe Lin, the president of On Leong, as its treasurer. To the sacred cause, 350 Chinese in St. Louis contributed enthusiastically and generously. Even though suffering from poverty and the Depression, they gave as much as they could every week. Joe Lin described the fundraising activities in the *St. Louis Globe-Democrat* of 14 October 1938: "We are accepting subscriptions from anyone. A lot of Americans who patronized my restaurant voluntarily have given me small sums from time to time. Most of the money being raised is from Chinese, however. As treasurer of the fund I transmit money from it at intervals to a New York bank, which in turn sends it to a bank in China."[75]

On Leong also organized many fundraisers. On 17 June 1938 a Bowl of Rice fundraiser was held at the Hotel Chase by the St. Louis Committee of the United Council for Civilian Relief in China. Joe Lin and the Reverend Phillip Y. Lee of Chicago Chinese Christian Church spoke at this event, and were heard by 250 St. Louisans, most of them Chinese. Chinese musicians performed, and Chinese boys and girls served tea to the guests. The fundraiser was a great success.[76]

According to the 11 August 1939 edition of the *St. Louis Globe-Democrat*, Chinese St. Louisans contributed about $1,000 every week to the war effort. Charles Quinn, secretary of the Chinese Emergency Relief Society, said that the contributions had been made weekly since the Japanese invasion in July 1937; the Chinese gave a certain percentage of their income. The same system was employed throughout the United States and other countries. From July 1937 to July 1939, Chinese in the United States contributed $15,000,000, and those in Canada gave $13,000,000. Approximately $500,000 was used to purchase weapons to fight the Japanese.[77]

According to On Leong's records, in 1944 it raised between $35,000 and $50,000 to aid China's war effort. Many individuals contributed from $500 to $1,000. Given the fact that most Chinese were earning $30 a month, their contributions were enormous.[78]

ASSESSMENT OF ON LEONG

In St. Louis, On Leong Merchants and Laborers Association was a complex phenomenon. Chinese immigrant society in America was controlled by businessmen who possessed better education and economic means and who thus were able to emerge as community leaders. Although publicly known as "On Leong Tong," On Leong was by no means associated with tong wars. The development of On Leong was not a result of the cultural peculiarity of the Chinese, who were wrongly accused of a tendency to form criminal secret societies. On the contrary, On Leong, and other prominent Chinese community organizations, were products of the social and economic environment in America. As members of a legally, socially, and economically oppressed group, Chinese immigrants enjoyed protection from neither the Chinese government nor American authorities. Lacking this protection, the Chinese had no choice but to rely on their own resources if they hoped to survive in an alien land. Thus On Leong developed to meet the social, economic, and legal needs of Chinese immigrants.

On Leong's reputation was tainted by the criminal activities of some of its members. Generally, however, it was a benevolent and protective trade and community organization as well as a powerful group of businessmen within Chinese community. In this sense it resembled Chinese community organizations such as the CCBA and other traditional Chinatown community organizations. Also, the power of business leaders over the community suggests that Chinese immigrant society in St. Louis—and perhaps elsewhere—was strongly hierarchical.

The various functions of On Leong were comparable to those of the CCBA. In its heyday, On Leong made strong efforts to protect its members on all fronts. It maintained peace and order in the Chinese community by acting as the strong albeit unofficial government of Chinatown. It negotiated for the Chinese community with the American authorities in legal and economic disputes. It provided translation services, lodging, and business assistance for new immigrants. It organized traditional celebrations and ceremonies. It arranged funeral ceremonies for its members and the shipping of remains to China for reburial. All of these were vital to the Chinese community at a time when its members were segregated from mainstream society and vulnerable to social ridicule and even physical attacks.

Yet at the same time, the protective and hierarchical nature of On Leong prevented it from bridging the gap between the Chinese community and the larger society. The protection provided by On Leong was necessary for the social and economic functioning of the community; it was also essential for the success of its business leaders. On Leong's self-confinement nature was shaped from outside by the social and economic environment of the United States and from inside by the social and economic hierarchy of the Chinese community itself.

The "Mayors of Chinatown," like most of their counterparts in other Chinese communities across the country, were mostly benevolent community leaders. Their better education, their English skills, and their financial ability enabled them to emerge as leaders of the immigrant community. Their colorful personalities and the events of their individual lives reflect the shifting economic and social climate in both the motherland and the host society.

The forced move of On Leong headquarters in the 1960s reveals that in terms of St. Louis as a whole, On Leong never enjoyed more than limited political power. For both good and ill, On Leong played a significant role in Hop Alley until 1966.

5   Dwindling "Hop Alley," 1920s–1966

Chinatown in St. Louis, a block of Oriental food shops and old tenement buildings filled with poignant memories of families that grew up and drifted away, soon will be gone.

—*St. Louis Post-Dispatch*, 1965

THE NUMBER OF second-generation Chinese children began to rise after the 1920s. As with other immigrant children, Chinese children's experiences were strongly connected to work: either they did chores at home or they worked in family businesses. Despite the heavy workload, the children of Hop Alley excelled academically; they also became Americanized in appearance and social values. Meanwhile, the Great Depression halted the steady growth of Chinese businesses and forced many to restructure. The economic base of the community changed as a result. Despite the Depression, Chinese St. Louisans participated enthusiastically in the country's war effort. World War II helped bring an end to the Chinese exclusion acts; this in turn led to a rising class of Chinese professionals after the war. Postwar prosperity brought about the urban renewal movement, the intent of which was to beautify the city and promote its economy. It was at this time that the central business district was torn down and rebuilt and that Hop Alley was leveled, thus bringing to an end St. Louis Chinatown's hundred-year story.

NEW GENERATION

The U.S. Census indicates that by the 1920s and 1930s, the number of native-born Chinese in Missouri was increasing steadily. In 1900 there were only 10 native-born Chinese in the state. This number had climbed to 84 by 1910, 105 by 1920, and 250 by 1930 (see Table 5.1). Since most of the Chinese in Missouri lived in St. Louis, these figures constitute a reasonable indicator of the demographic changes in St. Louis: more and more Chinese St. Louisans were young and American-born.

108

TABLE 5.1 Chinese population in Missouri by place of birth and by sex, 1870–1940

Census year	Total Chinese	Native	Foreign-born	Male Native	F-B	Female Native	F-B
1870	3	—	—	—	—	—	—
1880	91	—	—	—	—	—	—
1890	409	—	—	—	—	—	—
1900	449	10	439	10	437	—	2
1910	585	84	451	74	441	10	10
1920	412	105	307	87	296	18	11
1930	634	250	384	188	333	62	51
1940	334	179	155	104	129	75	26

Source: Tabulated according to *Sixteenth Census of the United States: 1940 Vol. II, Characteristics of the Population*, 312.
Note: Dash "—" in the table indicates data not available.

Most Chinese St. Louisans were in the laundry, restaurant, or grocery business; thus most young Chinese were the children of laundry operators, restaurant owners, or grocers. Many were born in the cramped apartments of the tenement buildings in Hop Alley or in the backrooms of their parents' business. Lillie Hong's family lived in a two-room apartment in Hop Alley. One room was the bedroom, the other the living room and kitchen. In this apartment, in the late 1920s and early 1930s, Lillie Hong's mother Gene Shee gave birth to Lillie's four sisters and two brothers.[1] James Leong, another Hop Alley youth, was born in St. Louis in 1924 at 4360 Lee Avenue, his father's laundry. Leong felt that he and his siblings were "born into" the laundry business: "We were all born there at that same address, and we didn't go to hospital. We had a midwife who took care of it all."[2]

The 1920s was a decade of prosperity for many Americans. For the residents of Chinatown, most of them poor immigrants, it was not; few shared the growing wealth, and most faced a continuing struggle for survival. Most young Chinese lived difficult lives, just like their elders; they had to juggle school with the heavy burden of helping operate the family business. Most rose early to help their parents open the shop, restaurant, or laundry. Then they would walk to school, and then back from school, and continue with their household chores or business responsibilities. James Leong's childhood routine was a typical one among second-generation Chinese children. As the son of a Chinese hand laundry worker, he rose at six every morning, fired up the boiler, and worked in the laundry for an hour before going to school. He began this routine in 1931 when he was seven and would continue it—for work to school, from school back to work—until he graduated from college.[3] Similarly, during her school years between 1927 and 1935, Lillie Hong helped her mother cook, do the laundry, and care for her younger siblings every day after school.[4] Annie Leong and her two brothers worked at the family restaurant, the Asian Café at 714 Market Street, every day after they returned from school. They waited on diners, bused the tables, and prepared food for the kitchen. They did their homework between customers.[5]

For second-generation Chinese, this pattern held across the country: they were brought up strictly and burdened with heavy responsibilities. In San Francisco, a Chinese college girl recalled in the 1920s: "We were brought up more strictly than most girls, even according to Chinese ideas, and my sister and I have kept those habits, never going to dances, or having company, always working."[6] In Hawaii, a high school student wrote about his childhood in 1926: "My father was a rice planter, and miller. I used to work with my father but oftentimes he sent me home to look after my baby sister while my mother did the cooking . . . . My brothers and I also helped in the mill and my mother sometimes helped sewing up the bags of rice. My chief duty there was to thread the needles."[7]

Other immigrant groups in St. Louis also relied on child labor. For example, Italian immigrants were keenly aware that "a family's wealth depends upon the number of hands it has."[8] "The earnings of all members of the family are pooled together in a family budget," observed a community social worker in the 1930s. "Girls and boys are expected to participate in this until they marry." An Italian dictum advised parents: "When hair begins to grow between the legs, one is fit to marry and work." Gary Ross Mormino's study of Italian Americans in St. Louis notes that Italian immigrant parents customarily withdrew their sons and daughters from school when they were fourteen. In the late nineteenth and early twentieth centuries, the jobs available to Italian immigrants were mainly unskilled and poorly paid—in clay mines and brickyards. Many Italian immigrant teenagers followed their fathers to the workplace. In 1910, 15.5 percent of the workers in St. Louis brickyards were young Italian immigrant men between fourteen and twenty. While boys worked in brick-yards, Italian immigrant girls sorted tobacco leaves in factories.[9]

Chinese children followed a pattern different from that of other immigrants' children. Children of European immigrants were hired by brickyards and tobacco and shoe factories; those of Chinese immigrants worked at home or in the family business as unpaid help. Some European immigrant children took pride in bringing their meager wages home to help the family;[10] children of Chinese immigrants perceived sharing family chores and working in the family business as a duty. These different mindsets regarding work reflected the racial segregation in the labor market. European immigrant children joined the mainstream labor market; Chinese children, like their parents, had been excluded from that market.

Despite the heavy family responsibilities, many Chinese children were excellent students. Unlike their counterparts on the West Coast, who could only attend Chinese (i.e., segregated) schools, the Chinese youth in St. Louis enrolled in public schools. Madison School, eleven blocks from Chinatown, was the public school for most of the children of Hop Alley. According to the *St. Louis Globe-Democrat Magazine* (4 September), in 1927 there were about thirty Chinese students between ten and sixteen at Madison. P. J. Hickey, the principal, extolled their academic ability:

> They are very good students . . . exceptionally able in mathematics, and generally in this subject they keep about two grades ahead of the rest of their work. The younger girls learn to read very quickly and seem to take particular delight in it. All of them are exceptional in handiwork. The girls, especially, are facile in drawing, painting and cutting out such things as dolls. They have an artistic sense and a fine ability of fine-line drawing noticeable in all Chinese work, which is difficult for Americans to get.[11]

Tak Jung had a similar experience at another public school. Jung came to St. Louis from south China in 1930 when he was nine to join his father, who had opened a laundry at Academy and Delmar avenues in what was then the west side of St. Louis. Jung recalled his first days at the public school:

> [I had] very loving teachers and patient teachers, 'cause at that time, only two Chinese in the whole school . . . . I 'm very ahead in math, just the English language is difficult and I had a very hard time to pro-nounce the "r." I couldn't roll the "r" for a long time, but the teacher said, "watch my mouth and see how my tongue goes." She was a very good teacher. I will never forget her.[12]

Some Chinese children even excelled at sports. By the beginning of the twentieth century, St. Louis had two major-league baseball teams: the Browns (AL) and the Cardinals (NL). As symbols of local pride, they inspired thousands of young St. Louisans of all ethnic groups to play baseball. Even so, most St. Louisans found it hard to imagine the local laundryman's son playing baseball. A few Chinese boys did take up the game and quickly captured the media's attention. In particular, Henry Lang, a fifteen-year-old at Madison School, caused a sensation. Lang was born in Canton, China, and came to America with his parents in 1923. He was enrolled at Madison School the day after his family arrived in Chinatown. Though he spoke no English before coming to St. Louis, and though he had only two years' education in his homeland, after four years at Madison he was ranked among the top students in the seventh grade.[13]

Lang liked sports as well as academics. He was good at a number of modern games. He was a relief pitcher on Madison's baseball team and helped it win a grade-school championship in 1926. He had begun learning the game in 1925, playing casual games of catch. The following year he began playing for the school team as an outfielder. Once he realized he was too slow on his feet, he began to learn pitching at the suggestion of Principal Hickey. He was determined to be a good pitcher. "He not only got every boy who could curve a ball to show him the tricks," the *St. Louis Globe-Democrat Magazine* commented, "but he bought a book by Bill Doak, the major league hurler, whose success indicates that he ought to know all about it and, by hard practice, learned several curves and a knuckle ball. He learned a change-of-pace delivery, too, and has a floater that is useful to mix with his fast one and curves. He occupied the mound in practice games at the school three or four times."[14]

Tak Jung also had athletic ability. He was captain of his school's baseball team and would later recall it with great pride: "Our team win after a semester, then the principal rewards us with a bar of candy like Baby Ruth or Butterfinger." Playing baseball well was important to him because it helped his American peers accept him. Whenever he played well, the white boys would say: "Hey, the Chinese are not too bad. They're not stupid, they're pretty good ball players." The desire "not to be looked down upon, not to be second class" motivated Jung to "keep ahead" in the sport throughout his youth.[15] The participation of Chinese students in sports helped break local stereotypes of Chinese.

Public education exposed Chinese children to Western traditions and American culture. One of James Leong's fondest childhood memories was of Christmas festivities at school: "We just draw Santa Claus on cardboard. Draw, maybe make him red and then you stick cotton on him . . . . I remember in kindergarten how Santa Claus came in."[16]

Even outside the schools, American ways affected Chinatown children. Tak Jung remembered how exciting it was to go on family picnics at a nearby park. The children would "jump for joy because [it's a] great time to bring sandwiches. Sometimes we ask our mother, can we buy soda out there. The park would have soda or hot dog."[17]

With the inescapable American influence, this new generation Americanized quickly. Most of them, whether native or foreign born, carried an English given name. Henry Lang was nicknamed "Hop Leong" by some mischievous schoolmates, presumably because of his connection with Hop Alley, but he preferred his American name. He wore the same clothes as American boys, and he was "American in many of his ways."[18]

The Chinese girls were just as Americanized in their appearance. Many wore a fashionable fur coat, like other American girls their age.[19] Annie Leong reminisced about her teen years: "We were following fashion and try to dress fashionably."[20] Interaction between the Chinese girls and their white peers also occurred in public schools. Although most Chinese girls walked to Madison School with their Chinese friends, they were very friendly with the other girls in their classes.[21]

Like other American teenagers, the Chinese socialized as much as they could. A Chinese Youth Association was formed in the 1940s, consisting mainly of Chinese middle and high school students living in the Chinatown area. It used the On Leong headquarters for dances and other gatherings. It also organized a variety of social activities for Chinese youth such as bowling and hayrides. Annie Leong was a member of the Chinese Youth Association and had many fond memories of its activities:

We [the Leong family restaurant] moved to 720 Market Street in 1949. On Leong owned that building, that's why we moved downstairs to the restaurant. We had the Chinese Youth Association. We used the facilities at On Leong, which is upstairs from the restaurant. We had activities like bowling, hayrides, and other things. There was a dance once every month. So the young kids would have a place to go. You could always borrow their facilities. In the 1950s, we got up to about fifty [people], in the same age range as mine or a little older. We did most things as a group. We went to the movies, bowling, not dating per se, just boys and girls going [out]. But some of them did dating. That was nice because these were all the Chinese families, so we knew that everybody knew everybody else because we were growing up together at that time. You know those Chinese families, they were all scattered out, and they weren't concentrated in Chinatown. We learned the new dances and whatever popular music at the time. You bought records, you listened to them on radio, watched them on TV.[22]

Many young Chinese were Americanized in their appearance and social values; others were still confined by Chinese traditions and strict parental authority. As the oldest daughter in a family with seven children, Lillie Hong never had the opportunity to socialize or date. After school she had to take care of her younger siblings and help her mother with laundry, cooking, and other household chores. Her formal education continued up to the eighth grade; at that point her parents decided she had had enough education and withdrew her from school. To gather enough money to return the family to China, Lillie's parent married her—in 1935 when she was seventeen—to Chooey Hong, a Chinese laundry owner twenty years her senior.[23] Similarly, Tak Jung's father advised him "to go back to China to marry a girl who could speak Chinese" or "somebody with Chinese heritage or upbringing." An obedient son, Jung went back to his family's home village in the 1940s to look for a wife even though he did not quite understand "why the parents like the son to go back to the old country to pick his wife."[24]

This process of Americanization mirrored that of second-generation Chinese throughout the United States. Many Chinese children on the West Coast wanted to be "hundred percent Americans," and to that end they dressed like flappers, went to parties, and participated in school sports and marching bands.[25] Like their white counterparts, some young Chinese college girls took singing and dancing lessons. Some were even recruited by Forbidden City—a Chinese nightclub in San Francisco that had its heyday in the 1930s and 1940s—as professional singers and dancers for the "Oriental" floor show. "We did this in the 1930s and 1940s," recalled France Chun, a singer at Forbidden City. "We were a shock to the Chinese community and a confusion to the Caucasian people."[26]

Like the younger generation of Chinese in St. Louis, Chinese students studying in the United States were Americanized and were determined to apply their knowledge to benefit China. An example was Hsi Fan Chao, a female Chinese graduate student at

Washington University. Born into a prominent family in Harbin, Manchuria, in 1912, she had been inspired by her uncle's experiences at Yale University, and she dreamed about seeing for herself "what was going on" in the world beyond China. A child of Chinese Christian parents, she began studying at the missionary school when she was six. Shortly after her eighteenth birthday she left her luxurious home and came to America to study at Iowa State University. In her first six months in America she was homesick and had difficulty with English. But she overcame these obstacles and obtained a master's degree from the Iowa State University. She then enrolled as a graduate student at Washington University, where she majored in social work. In May 1934, when interviewed by Adalyn Faris McKee of the *St. Louis Globe-Democrat*, she impressed McKee with her appearance and intellectual strength. She looked "typically modern and typically American, from the top of her curly black bobbed head to the tips of her high-heeled slippers."[27] She was also well versed in the social and economic issues of America and China. She planned to return to China to initiate courses in social service, home management, and subjects that would improve the living conditions of the Chinese working class.[28]

Other Chinese college students in St. Louis were equally associated with political and social developments in China. In 1938 a group of Chinese students at Washington University and St. Louis University cooperated with On Leong in arranging celebrations for the Day of Double Tens.[29] Two student leaders in particular were active in this: Sung Kong-Nying, son of the manager of the Bank of China and a first-year dental student at St. Louis University, and Andrew L. Wan, a senior at the St. Louis University Dental School. The scion of a wealthy Chinese family, Sung learned his English at St. John's University, an Episcopal school in Shanghai. Wan had been in the United States for nine years and had attended schools in Quincy, Illinois, before coming to St. Louis University. Like Hsi Fan Chao, he expected to return to China after his graduation.[30]

It is important to note that the young people of Chinatown and the college students from China came from starkly different social and economic backgrounds. Most of the former were children of working-class immigrants from impoverished rural areas of south China; the college students were from elite families in China's biggest cities. The children of Hop Alley combined their schooling with endless household chores and business responsibilities;

most of the college students had led comfortable lives in China. Yet the two groups also shared a great deal—their outlook and interests, and their experiences in America. The younger generation of Chinatown residents in many ways shared a common outlook and interests with the college students. The students from China involved themselves in the Chinese community's activities and cared about the well-being of the Chinese in general.

THE GREAT DEPRESSION AND ITS IMPACT ON CHINESE IN ST. LOUIS

The economic collapse of the 1930s devastated the United States. After the stock market crashed in the autumn of 1929, the U.S. economy went to a tailspin. By 1932 the median income of American families had plunged to half what it was in 1929, and at least one-quarter of American breadwinners were unemployed.

As one of the major industrial cities of the country, St. Louis suffered job losses above national levels. In 1930 the national unemployment rate rose from 3.2 to 8.7 percent; in St. Louis it rose to 9.8 percent. In 1931 the national figure jumped to 15.9 percent; in St. Louis it jumped to 24 percent. In the spring of 1933 the national unemployment rate reached its peak of 24.9 percent; in St. Louis it was 30 percent.[31]

The Chinese of St. Louis worked as operators or laborers in hand laundries and were not immune from the Depression. The Great Depression engendered a population dispersion and economic reshuffling for Chinese St. Louisans. Economic calamity drove two demographic changes: a movement of Chinese from St. Louis back to China or to other American states; and the gradual decline of Chinese hand laundries. In the century's first decades the Chinese population of Missouri had been increasing steadily: from 449 in 1900 to 535 in 1910, 412 in 1920, and 634 in 1929. By 1939 the figure had dropped to 334—an almost 50 percent decrease (see Table 5.1).

Many Chinese immigrants saw their economic prospects vanishing and decided to return to China. Lillie Hong's parents made that decision. In 1935 they married off their eldest daughter Lillie. As "payment" for her, they received $1,000 from Lillie's husband. With this they were able to return to China with their younger children. Lillie remembers the moment sadly: "I wanted to help them out . . . . I didn't have any choice because my parents were going back to China and they needed the money."[32]

Some Chinese St. Louisans went to California, New York, or other states to seek better economic opportunities. Lillie Hong's childhood friends all left St. Louis with their families; most of them went to California.[33] A few later established small colonies in northern California.[34] Miller Chow's parents came from Canton to St. Louis in 1931 and began working in a hand laundry with her uncle. When the Depression hit St. Louis, the laundry business threatened to collapse. In 1937 her uncle went to New York; her parents went to Earle, Arkansas, where they managed to start two grocery stores and a farm.[35] The rapid decline of the Chinese population of Missouri was the result of individual decisions like these.

The Depression and the drop in St. Louis's Chinese population led to a decline in the Chinese laundry business. This paved the way for a structural reorientation of the Chinese economy in the 1960s. Statistics indicate a steady increase in the number of Chinese laundries in the 1910s and 1920s, followed by a rapid decrease after 1931 (see Table 5.2).

Since 1927, Chinese hand laundries had been listed separately in the city directories, reflecting their growing significance in the laundry business. Although the Depression resulted in a slow-down for Chinese businesses, laundries continued to be the main occupation for the Chinese, and about half the Chinese in St. Louis were in the laundry business.

THE CHINESE AND WORLD WAR II

World War II affected the lives of millions of Americans. For the Chinese it was even more significant and far-reaching in its effects. Historians have noted several positive changes: Asians were permitted to serve in the American armed forces, and they were permitted to enter more occupations in the mainstream employment market. The participation of China and Chinese Americans in the war helped improve the image of both in America. Public attitudes toward the Chinese softened, and this soon led to the repeal of the exclusion laws that had restricted the entry of the Chinese into America and violated the civil rights of those already here.[36]

Like the Chinese throughout the country, the Chinese St. Louisans were affected by these changes. A few days after the Japanese raid on Pearl Harbor, Missouri Governor Forrest C. Donnell alerted Missourians that the army could guard only four strategic bridges in the state. That left 588 Missouri bridges unprotected.[37] Servicemen were desperately needed. Feelings of anger, fear, and excitement were

TABLE 5.2 Numbers of Chinese laundries, restaurants, and groceries in St. Louis, 1900–1966

Year	Number of Laundries	Number of Restaurants	Number of Grocers
1900	—	—	3
1901	—	—	3
1902	—	1	3
1903	1	—	—
1904	1	—	—
1905	—	—	—
1906	—	2	6
1907	—	1	6
1908	—	2	5
1909	—	4	6
1910	—	—	5
1911	31	6	4
1912	56	9	6
1913	53	6	10
1914	83	9	12
1915	97	3	1
1916	108	6	1
1917	102	8	3
1918	112	8	6
1919	102	12	8
1920	98	12	6
1921	100	10	6
1922	91	7	6
1923	96	12	4
1924	114	6	4
1925	140	6	3
1926	148	9	4
1927	149	10	1
1928	143	12	6
1929	165	15	6
1930	161	10	5
1931	155	12	4
1932	128	8	2
1933	123	8	—
1934	123	8	—

TABLE 5.2 (*Continued*)

Year	Number of Laundries	Number of Restaurants	Number of Grocers
1935	104	11	1
1936	123	7	—
1939	89	13	1
1941	78	18	—
1944	48	13	1
1946	61	14	1
1952	41	13	—
1956	42	14	—
1959	37	15	—
1963	24	21	—
1966	10	13	—

Source: Tabulated according to *Gould's St. Louis Directory for 1900–1952* and *Polk's St. Louis City Directory for 1956–1966*.
Note: Dash "—" indicates no data available.

soon transformed into patriotic fervor. On 8 December long lines of enlistees were waiting outside the Federal Building on Market Street, where armed forces recruiting officers were processing applications.[38] Many of the city's young Chinese, like 15,000 of their counterparts across the country, were among those enlistees.[39] Tak Jung was one of the Chinese who showed his loyalty to the United States by joining up. He would spend more than two-and-a-half years in the U.S. Army.[40] More young Chinese St. Louisans followed him. On 6 November 1943 the *St. Louis Globe-Democrat* featured a group of Chinese St. Louisans who had enrolled in the U.S. army: Private Y. T. Hom and Corporals Shew Key Lee, Suey Chung, and Lawrence D. Wong.[41] Corporal Shew Key Lee was stationed at the Jefferson Barracks during the war. He had been born in China and came to the United States before his twenty-second birthday in 1935 to claim his citizenship through his father.[42]

Richard Ho's experiences during the war provide some insight into Chinese participation in the war effort. Ho started out as a defense worker at Curtiss-Wright United in St. Louis. He then was drafted into the U.S. Air Force and stationed in Texas. When the war ended he was honorably discharged back to St. Louis. Because of his military service, he was able to become a naturalized citizen. He then traveled to Hawaii by steamer and was immediately recruited as a serviceman at Hickam Field, a U.S.

Air Force base. In September 1946 he was reassigned to the 5th Air Force and stationed in Nagoya, Japan. In 1948 he returned to Hickam Field.[43]

Some Chinese enlistees were able to utilize their college education and Chinese-language ability to serve America, as exemplified in the wartime experience of Hong Sit, a Hop Alley–born college graduate who joined the army in 1943:

> It [the military training] was strenuous . . . . Before being inducted, I was expecting terrible ordeals ahead. Both Sam [Sit's brother] and cousin Wayne had entered the service earlier, and both reported it was "hell on earth." . . .
>
> There were the usual obstacle course and endurance races, plus crawling on our belly under barbed wires with a pack and rifle while a machine gun fired just over our heads. Our barracks had to be immaculate, clothes hung pressed and pleated, shoes shined, and beds made with blankets so tight that the inspection officer could bounce a coin on it . . . .
>
> Before long I was back in Camp Crowder, Missouri, as a Second Lieutenant, training a new Signal Center Team. We soon received orders to ship out by train to the West Coast . . . . We finally boarded a troop ship at Long Beach. It took a month to reach our destination in Bombay, India . . . . After an arduous and mosquito-infested train ride on hard benches, we arrived in Calcutta, then flew over the hump, from Camp Kamchaparan to Kunming, China. Then it was another back-breaking, liver-shaking truck ride along the eastern terminus of the Burma Road to Kweiyang [Guiyang], our home for the next half year. We set up a communication center and soon were preparing for the big push to throw the Japanese invaders out of China . . . . When the war was over and our Signal unit was disbanded, I received orders to accompany Chinese troops to take over Taiwan from the Japanese . . . . After Taiwan, I found myself assigned to Beijing, as translation officer of the interpreters section.[44]

While the men of St. Louis were fighting at the front, the women were making ammunition. During the war, thousands of women across the country took jobs in heavy industry left behind by American men. By 1943 the government was urging women to do their patriotic duty and take places on the assembly lines. Millions of American women responded. By the end of the war the American labor force included 19.5 million women.[45] These "Rosie the Riveters" built airplanes, tanks, and ships. Like their counterparts anywhere in the country, St. Louis women worked on the assembly lines. According to a news item in the *St. Louis Globe-Democrat*, one-third of the workers at the St. Louis ordnance plant were women.[46] On 31 July 1942 the *St. Louis Globe-Democrat*'s Edna Warren and a number of other female reporters visited that plant to see St. Louis's women ammunition makers:

PHOTOGRAPH 5.1 The Chinese St. Louisans participated in World War II as enlisted men or factory workers. From left: Private Y. T. Hom (left front), Corporal Shew Key Lee, Mrs. William C. Ping, Rose Lee, Mae Young, Corporal Suey Chung, and Corporal Lawrence D. Wong (right front), 1943. From the collections of the St. Louis Mercantile Library at the University of Missouri-St. Louis.

> We saw thousands and thousands of women working in stifling heat of a July day, in the midst of thundering machinery and the barking of machinegun testing of the cartridges, working as calmly and as efficiently as if they were shelling peas on their own shady back porches. Women of all ages from 18 to more years than any of them would admit. Women of all strata of society and former occupations. College graduates, waitresses, stenographers, school teachers, laundry workers, saleswomen, clerks, shoe factory workers, cooks, students, housewives, bookkeepers, housemaids, credit managers, auto glass inspectors—all now small arms ammunition workers, transformed into units as disciplined and efficient as soldiers . . . .
>
> Straight as an automobile assembly line ran the production line through the building, from raw material to finished product. Long narrow strips of shining brass, rolled and stacked to the ceiling like giant cheeses filled the end which we entered, and at the opposite end of the building we saw the finished cartridges with which some United Nation airmen will salute the enemy.[47]

According to the article, the women at this plant greatly enjoyed their work. They were proud not only of their patriotic contributions but also of the wages they were earning. Most of

them were categorized as "gaugers" and could earn $30 a week—
better pay than for most jobs available to women at the time. The
factory also employed women as cartridge inspectors; those positions required at least two years of college.[48] Among the cartridge
inspectors were a few Chinese women. Rose Lee, for example, a
"small and pretty" young Chinese woman, was one of the inspectors at the St. Louis plant.[49]

The war created employment opportunities outside St. Louis
Chinatown, not only for Chinese women but also for a few
Chinese men. Joe Ho was born in Canton, China, in 1916 and
came to St. Louis with his father in 1927. An ambitious young
man, he did not want to work in a laundry or a restaurant like
most Chinese. So he studied aeronautics for six years. His dream
finally came true thanks to World War II. Yet because he was not
naturalized, it took him eight months to find work as a final
assembler at Curtiss-Wright.[50]

During the war the American government and the public became
more sympathetic to China and to the Chinese in the United States.
A Gallup poll taken in 1942 indicated that the public's image of the
Chinese had improved. The Chinese were now perceived as "hard-
working, honest, brave, religious, intelligent, and practical."[51] This
was evident in the case of Mrs. Lee Wing. She was born in China
and on 17 October 1930, in China, married Lee Wing, the proprietor
of a tavern at 2708 North Newstead Avenue in St. Louis. Their first
two children were born in China but were citizens of the United
States through their father's citizenship. In 1939 Mrs. Wing and her
children fled their war-torn country and entered the United States
on a visitor's visa for one year. She was given several extensions of
her visa but was ordered to return to China alone after the last one
expired in January 1942. On her behalf, in the summer of 1942 the
local Chinese and some sympathetic Americans petitioned the U.S.
Congress to grant her the right to stay with her family, and a bill
was duly introduced in Congress. After a six-month investigation
by the Attorney General's office, Congress adopted the bill. On 27
December 1942, President Franklin D. Roosevelt signed the bill
authorizing her permanent residence in the United States.[52]

This incident constituted a prelude to the final repeal of the Chinese exclusion laws in 1943. These laws, first proclaimed in 1882,
had been "an untouchable cornerstone of American immigration
and naturalization policy," as historian Roger Daniels has commented.[53] However, the change in the public mood was now strong
enough to reverse this policy. Fred Warren Riggs has described in

detail how pressure-group politics succeeded in this situation.[54] Facing pressure from the public and from specific interest groups, Congress repealed a number of exclusion laws. On 13 December 1943, President Roosevelt signed the "Act to Repeal the Chinese Exclusion Acts, to Establish Quotas, and for Other Purposes."

The act consisted of three parts: (1) it repealed all past acts relating to the exclusion and deportation of Chinese aliens; (2) it permitted Chinese aliens in the United States to apply for naturalization; and (3) it allowed for the admission of 105 Chinese per year, with up to 75 percent of the quota to be awarded to those born and raised in China. The first two parts were long overdue and corrected past injustices perpetrated against the Chinese. However, some restrictions adhering to the 105 quota made the third part of the statute racist and especially restrictive to Chinese. The law defined a Chinese person as one who had "as much as one half Chinese blood" and stipulated that a Chinese must be charged to the Chinese quota of 105 irrespective of his or her country of birth. The law also declared that Chinese wives and children of American citizens would be chargeable to the Chinese quota of 105, whereas European wives and children of American citizens would be admitted on a nonquota basis.[55]

Nevertheless, the repeal of the Chinese exclusion laws was absolutely supported and welcomed by the Chinese in the United States. While congressmen were debating the repeal of Chinese exclusion, the Chinese in St. Louis were joining the national debate and eagerly anticipating its passage. In October 1943, when President Roosevelt recommended that the Chinese Exclusion Act be repealed, the Chinese of St. Louis rejoiced. Around this time Margaret Maunder of the *St. Louis Globe-Democrat* visited different groups of Chinese in St. Louis, including factory workers, entrepreneurs, community leaders, and servicemen.[56] All of them felt that it was only fair to repeal the act. The younger generation saw the law as hampering their opportunities in the country. Joe Ho had come to St. Louis in 1927 when he was eleven with his merchant father. Although his wife and five-month-old son, Kenneth, were citizens, Ho could not automatically assume his wife's nationality. A final assembler at Curtiss-Wright, he regarded St. Louis as his home and was "looking forward to the day" when he could become an American citizen.[57] Wing Leong, a young Chinese born in St. Louis, responded to the criticism that Chinese did not assimilate with Americans and that they sent their money back to China: "As long as they're not allowed to become citizens, they won't anchor themselves here and intermingle. They don't feel that they really belong."[58]

The younger Chinese hoped that their generation would be granted citizenship. The older Chinese proprietors did not anticipate an influx of Chinese immigrants—the chief concern of opponents of repeal. Quon Fong was an eighty-three-year-old man who had been in the country for seventy years. He doubted that common Chinese would come to America—they would be too busy developing China once the war ended. Lin Ah Kui, owner of a small laundry at 1708 Market Street, where he had worked since 1921, agreed with Quon Fong: "Since 1924 the Chinese population in this country has greatly decreased. That number will decrease even more after the war. Chinese people will be too busy with reconstruction work, railroads, mining and housing to leave their country." Joe Lin, now sixty-three, the proprietor of the Orient Café at 414 North Seventh Street and the "Mayor of Chinatown" in the 1930s, expressed a similar view: "When the war is over, China will be the land of opportunity . . . . The country will be modernized. People will have opportunity in their own country and the Chinese Government will provide employment for many who might otherwise be looking for work abroad."

Some young Chinese St. Louisans were in fact planning to return to China to help in reconstruction once the war was over. Corporal Shew Key Lee was born in China but had obtained his American citizenship in 1935 through his father. Having lived in St. Louis for eight years, he still considered China his home and planned to go back there after the war to buy a farm or to join Chiang Kai-shek's army. Rose Lee, the young Chinese woman working at the St. Louis ordnance plant, also thought that many Chinese in the United States would return after the war: "I think everyone with an education will be glad to go back and help with reconstruction. There is much to do. China will need us."[59]

The war provided unprecedented opportunities for Chinese St. Louisans; however, it also produced dark moments for "enemy aliens." In the week following the Pearl Harbor attack, nineteen Germans and one Italian were labeled "dangerous" and were imprisoned. The Japanese in St. Louis were never interned like those on the West Coast (120,000 of them), but they were carefully investigated. Thirty-three Japanese residents were interrogated by the St. Louis police but were not found guilty. However, all property and assets owned by Japanese and Korean residents were seized and frozen. The Kobe Restaurant at 919 Market, the Oriental Kitchen at 3189 South Grand,

and Oriental Food Supply at 3950 Delmar were ordered to close and were guarded by the police day and night. Tetsu Uyeda, a Japanese resident who managed the Bridle Spur Hunt Club, was arrested by the FBI as a suspected spy.[60] Afraid of being mistaken as Japanese, many Chinese residents avoided public places.[61]

PIONEER PROFESSIONALS

After World War II the Chinese in St. Louis witnessed another transformation. The economic boom started by the war continued into the postwar years; Americans were enjoying the greatest economic expansion of the century. The American gross national product rose from $200 billion in 1945 to almost $300 billion in 1950 and over $500 billion by 1960. Riding this national trend, St. Louis also witnessed economic expansion. The major businesses—St. Louis Union Trust Company, Union Electric, Southwestern Bell, Ralston-Purina, Monsanto Chemical, and McDonnell Aircraft, and others—expanded rapidly. Economic expansion attracted newcomers from other parts of the country as well as from overseas; the area's population rose from 1,090,278 in 1940 to 1,262,145 in 1950 and 1,263,145 in 1960.[62] As thousands of Americans moved to St. Louis, professionals from China also came to the city for the economic opportunities it offered. The early Chinese professionals were engineers, physicians, and scientists. One of these was William Tao, whose case exemplifies the arrival of the pioneer Chinese professionals.

William Tao was born into a well-off family in Beijing, China, in 1917. In 1937 he was admitted to Zhejiang University, where he majored in mechanical engineering. He was hoping to contribute to China's automobile industry. After graduating in 1941 he was assigned to a position with the China Transportation Company, where he was placed charge of transporting supplies along the Burma Road for China's war effort. After the Japanese surrendered in 1945, the Chinese government sent him to manage a rubber factory in Qingdao, Shandong province. At this point he thought hard about his career choices and goals and decided to study overseas. In 1947 he was awarded a scholarship by the Mechanical Engineering Department at Washington University. He came to St. Louis alone, and was joined by his wife and their first son a year later.

Tao's first years in St. Louis were difficult. He worked hard to maintain a good academic record. He also served as a graduate assistant during the day and did part-time engineering design

PHOTOGRAPH 5.2 William Tao (front right) started the engineering design firm William Tao & Associates in 1957. After struggling for several years, his company began establishing a reputation for vision and creativity. The photograph shows a welcome sign for the executives of McDonnell and William Tao & Associates posted during a visit to the Trane Company in Wisconsin, 1979. Courtesy of William Tao.

work at night. After completing a master's degree he stayed on as an instructor. He taught during the day and designed building projects at night to prepare for his future engineering consulting business. In 1955 he and a partner began a private engineering practice; later, with the help and moral support of his wife, Anne Tao, he became the sole proprietor. In 1957 he named his practice William Tao & Associates Consulting Engineers (WTA). Over the next few years the company grew and its reputation rose. In 1963, WTA was commissioned to do all the electrical and mechanical engineering for the seventeen-story Pierre Laclede Building in Clayton. This marked the beginning of a distinguished career designing high-rise buildings throughout St. Louis, in many other states, and overseas.[63]

Tao was soon followed by three physicians: Dr. Andrew Lu, a graduate of Zhendan University in Shanghai and an orthopedic surgeon; Dr. Louis Yuan, also a graduate of Zhendan University and an anesthetist and surgeon; and Dr. Jerome T. Y. Shen, a graduate of St. John's University in Shanghai and a pediatrician. All three came to St. Louis for advanced training at the medical school of St.

Louis University and local hospitals.[64] Dr. Lu's story in particular provides some insight to the life of the early Chinese professionals.

Dr. Lu was born in Shanghai in 1920. His father was a building contractor who provided the family with a comfortable living. He went to Zhendan University, a Catholic university run by French Catholic churches. After he completed his M.D. at Zhendan, he and his wife, an obstetrician, were recruited by an American Catholic Church in Changsha, Hunan, to work in the parochial school. In 1948 the church sponsored him to come to America for his internship. He interned at a Catholic hospital in New York for a year at a monthly salary of $10, and then at another hospital in New Jersey the following year.

With the help of the church networks, Dr. Lu came to St. Louis in 1950. He enrolled at the medical school of St. Louis University, also a Catholic university. There he studied orthopedics. He graduated in 1956 and opened the St. Louis Orthopedic Group with another orthopedic surgeon, a European American. Specializing in polio, which was still a common disease in the 1950s, he was known as a sympathetic and generous doctor. He often treated Chinese patients, especially those who were students, without charge. Like Tao, Dr. Lu also left his wife and two young daughters in China; he lived alone in St. Louis until his wife and daughters joined him in 1955. His first years in St. Louis were lonely; two Chinese biochemistry students at St. Louis University, two Chinese doctoral students in physics from Hong Kong at Washington University, William Tao, and Dr. Lu himself were the entire Chinese student/professional community in St. Louis.[65] This tiny group was tightly knit.

The two Chinese physics students at Washington University would later emerge as prominent leaders of the overseas Chinese community. Shien-Biau Woo was born in Shanghai in 1937. His family later moved to Hong Kong. In 1955, when he was eighteen, he came to the United States; the following year he was awarded a bachelor's degree in physics and mechanics from Georgetown College in Kentucky. From there he came to St. Louis for graduate training in physics at Washington University.[66]

Woo's passion for public service took root during his years in St. Louis. He saw how hard the city's Chinatown residents had to work to make ends meet—in laundries, restaurants, grocery stores, and odd jobs. They wanted very much to pass their Chinese heritage to their children, but they lacked the energy, the time, and the education. So Woo decided to open a Chinese-language school.

With the help of On Leong and Chia Wei Woo, the other Chinese physics student at Washington University (who later became president of the Hong Kong University of Science and Technology), Woo set up such a school.[67] Although it was forced to close after only two years, Woo had gained valuable experience and a better understanding of Chinatown communities; both would help his later career in public service.

Woo attained his master's and doctoral degrees from Washington University in 1962 and 1964 respectively and was hired by the University of Delaware as a physics professor. As a junior faculty member, he became a founding president of the faculty bargaining unit; he was its chief spokesman and negotiator from 1971 to 1973. In 1976 he was appointed by the governor of Delaware as a trustee of the university—the first faculty member to be named to the post. Woo's involvement in public service gradually expanded to encompass the state and the nation. In 1984 he ran for his first public office and was elected Lieutenant Governor of Delaware on the Democrat ticket.[68] Although his political career developed mainly in Delaware, his involvement in the St. Louis Chinatown in the 1950s and 1960s undoubtedly prepared the ground for his career in public service.

The pioneer professionals included not only the technically trained newcomers but also children of Hop Alley. Wing Leong and Kuong Leong, Annie Leong's brothers, were unwilling to work all their lives in a restaurant or a laundry; they wanted to become professionals. They learned to read and write Chinese as children and worked in their family restaurant every day after school. Despite their family responsibilities, the Leong brothers got good grades at school and went to college. Wing obtained a master's degree at Washington University and was hired by Emerson Electric Company as an engineer after graduation. Kuong earned his degree from St. Louis University and later became a manager of data processing for Biederman Company.[69]

URBAN RENEWAL AND THE END OF "HOP ALLEY"

The urban renewal movement in St. Louis can be traced back to the beginning of the twentieth century. The success of the 1904 World's Fair encouraged the city's boosters to continue their ambitious plans to make St. Louis one of the most prosperous and livable cities in the country. Influenced by the Progressive spirit, they saw their main goals as stimulating new industry through "scientific" and honest government, and improving the urban environment.

Luther Ely Smith, a prominent lawyer, advocated a new riverfront complex, which would include a park—Jefferson National Expansion Memorial Park—with a symbolic monument. The Depression delayed Smith's plans; however, they were placed back on agenda around the time of Franklin Roosevelt's New Deal. A $7.5 million municipal bond and the $9 million federal fund for WPA projects enabled the city to acquire and clear forty blocks of riverfront for the project. More delays ensued: taxpayers opposed the bond issue in 1936, and then the war distracted the nation from civic projects. In 1948 a group of distinguished architects selected an arch as the design for the memorial. Finally, in 1954, Missouri senator Thomas Hennings persuaded Congress to allocate $5 million for the project. Congress provided another $12.25 million in 1958, $6 million in 1965, and $9.5 million in 1976 to help complete the Gateway Arch and the Museum of Westward Expansion.[70]

The completion of the 632-foot-high steel arch realized the dreams of the city's boosters; it also made St. Louis an international tourist destination. The income generated by the arch—an estimated $503 million—made downtown renewal possible. In 1951, St. Louis established a Land Clearance for Redevelopment Authority to "undertake the acquisition, relocation, demolition, and site improvements of the urban renewal areas." Charles L. Farris, a developer who was calling for a new downtown stadium, was appointed by the mayor as its director.[71]

In 1955 the Redevelopment Authority began clearing land. The 454-acre Mill Creek Valley site between Lindell-Olive and Scott avenues was cleared in 1955, and Twentieth Street and Grant Avenue in 1959. The downtown district was next on the list for demolition. A group of downtown businessmen established the Civic Center Redevelopment Corporation and contracted with the Redevelopment Authority to carry out the downtown renewal project. The century-old commercial district with its homes and industries was to be flattened to make way for thirty-four office buildings, twenty-six factories, and extensive parking and loading facilities.[72] The centerpiece of this project was to be Busch Stadium. Under this scheme, Hop Alley would make way for a parking lot.

The Chinese community reacted to this news with deep sorrow. Its people were reluctant to move but offered no organized resistance. By early February 1963, Chinatown residents were greeting one another with *Gung Hay Fot Choy* but wondering whether a "happy and prosperous New Year" was going to be possible.[73] Many who grew up in the alleys of Chinatown lamented the imminent disappearance of the district. The old men who lived above the Chinese businesses or in tenements worried where they would go. The community's leaders were no more prepared than anyone else; the presidents of On Leong wondered openly whether to find a new building for their association.

The sense of uncertainty dominated Chinese residents during the next few years. The Chinese of Hop Alley lived the next few years in a state of flux. The New Year celebrations of 1965 were subdued, and would be remembered as a time of mourning for the passing of Chinese traditions, since the old Chinatown and On Leong had long been associated with the preservation of those traditions. With their community about to vanish, many worried that their traditions would disappear as well. Nin Young, the president of On Leong, expressed his anguish: "This neighborhood is our home. We are going to stay as long as we can."[74]

In 1965, On Leong was still holding on both physically and psychologically. By then, 75 percent of the buildings bounded by Seventh, Eighth, Market, and Walnut streets had been purchased by the Civic Center Redevelopment Corporation. City officials began negotiating with On Leong to purchase the two buildings owned by the association on South Eighth Street. On Leong was hesitant, for it had just spent $75,000 on renovating its headquarters. Dozens of hand-carved teak chairs inlaid with marble had been imported from Hong Kong to beautify the meeting rooms. At one time the association had been planning to construct two new buildings on property it owned on the west side of South Eighth Street. There would have been Chinese stores at street level and apartments for Chinese above the stores. The leaders of On Leong were also concerned about the neighborhood's older residents. Around thirty elderly Chinese men were living above the shops on South Eighth Street and in two buildings bordering Hop Alley behind the Asian Cafe. According to Nin Young, it would be difficult to find a place where all the old generation could live near one another.[75] Annie Leong expressed the same concern: "I was born in this building. It's home and I don't want to leave. I think some of the older Chinese people will be lost when they're forced to move out of this block. I guess I feel like a landmark myself. This neighborhood with its closely-knit, old-fashioned Chinese families built character—juvenile delinquency didn't exist in Chinatown."[76]

By Chinese New Year in 1966, all that was left of Chinatown was the On Leong headquarters, the adjoining Asian Restaurant at 720 Market Street, and a couple of buildings on South Eighth Street housing the Lun Sing and Oriental Tea and Mercantile importing companies. Those buildings also provided rooms for some twenty elderly Chinese. On Leong finally bought a new headquarters building—1509 Delmar, which had once been the R. E. Funsten nut-packing plant and was jokingly called "the Chinese nut house" by some members of the community.

The first day of August in 1966 saw the closing of the Asian Restaurant, which had long been popular among St. Louisans. Thus the last remaining business in an old and respected St. Louis neighborhood was gone. Three days later, On Leong moved to 1509 Delmar. Two weeks after that, the last building in Chinatown was leveled, and Hop Alley had vanished.

CONCLUSION

The 1920s and 1930s saw the emergence of the second-generation Chinese. To help their families survive, the children of Chinese immigrants had to work before and after school, either at home or in family businesses alongside their parents. Dependence on children's labor was a significant aspect of immigrant life in America. But at the same time, these children were Americanizing themselves and assimilating into the larger community. While this was happening, the Depression scattered Chinese St. Louisans to other parts of the country or back to China. The Depression also shifted the Chinese economic center of gravity: many hand laundries closed as more Chinese moved into the restaurant business.

World War II dramatically improved the public image of China and the Chinese, and this led to the repeal of the Chinese exclusion laws, which had existed for more than half a century. This crack in the door to America brought the first Chinese professionals to St. Louis. By now, Hop Alley–born Chinese were beginning to go to college and then stepping into professional fields.

The postwar era brought a general improvement in the lives of millions of Americans, including Chinese Americans; it also sparked urban renewal projects in St. Louis and other American cities. The intentions of these projects were good, but they inevitably meant the end of St. Louis's historic Chinatown.

II. BUILDING A CULTURAL COMMUNITY, 1960s–2000s

6   Emerging Suburban Chinese American Communities, 1960s–1980s

Hop Alley is long gone . . . . Numbering about 2000, St. Louis Chinese community includes dispersed residents and descendents of old Chinatown, once home for more than 200 people. Some still run restaurants, laundries, groceries. But most children of the old families are college educated professionals and well-assimilated members of neighborhoods throughout the city. They have been joined during the last 30 years by technically educated, primarily Mandarin-speaking immigrants attracted by the universities and employment opportunities.

—Margie Wolf Freivogel, *St. Louis Post-Dispatch*, 1971

WHEN HOP ALLEY vanished under the debris of urban renewal in 1966, the Chinese community of St. Louis began to undergo a quiet yet profound transformation. The decades of the 1960s to 1980s saw two major shifts among Chinese St. Louisans. The first was demographic: The Chinese began remaking themselves as suburbanites, scattering throughout the West County (the municipalities west of the city). Meanwhile, continuing urban renewal thwarted the community's efforts to build a new Chinatown. By this time, Chinese professionals—both the new arrivals and those who were American-born—were depending less heavily on an ethnic district for their jobs and their leisure activities. The second shift was economic: The Chinese began moving away from laundry businesses toward food service and related retail industries. At the same time, the professional Chinese began finding employment in the mainstream economy. Throughout these two transitions, the Chinese continued to suffer from a lack of political clout. This was most vividly illustrated during the second "removal" of Chinatown and the campaign to save the Sam Wah Laundry.

THE LAST HEADQUARTERS OF ON LEONG
AND THE SECOND REMOVAL OF CHINATOWN

After moving to 1509 Delmar Boulevard in 1966, On Leong continued to serve the Chinese community. However, with the disappearance of Hop Alley and the coming of Chinese professionals, On Leong was gradually losing its influence in the community, especially after the 1970s.

The Third Headquarters at 1509 Delmar Boulevard (1966–79)

On 4 August 1966, On Leong moved headquarters to 1509 Delmar. Several Chinese businesses followed it to the new neighborhood. Also, some retired Chinese men formed a "colony" in a group of houses west of the association.[1]

Three weeks later, on 24 September, On Leong held a ceremony to celebrate the beginning of the new Chinatown. Two hundred guests attended, representing On Leong and other Chinese organizations from all over the country—New York, Boston, San Francisco, New Orleans, and many other cities. Present were the national co-presidents of On Leong: Bob Lee of Boston and Stanley Chin of New York. By midnight the statue of Guan Gong had been placed carefully in his renovated red and gold shrine. The following morning two huge roasted pigs, a boiled chicken, rice wine, and rice were placed before Guan Gong. In the afternoon the gongs were struck and the festivities began. Irene Au, a celebrated Chinese entertainer, was invited to the ceremony to sing Chinese songs.[2]

The gongs seemed to have revived the spirits of Chinese St. Louisans. They were hoping to build a new Chinatown around the 1500 block of Delmar, and they almost succeeded. The block later became quite close to what could be called a Chinatown. Chinese parties and wedding receptions were held in the On Leong hall, and Chinese films were sometimes shown there.[3]

Following the grand opening ceremony, the Chinese celebrated a relatively quiet Chinese New Year in 1967. The Cultural Revolution had begun in China the previous year; it was targeting intellectuals, the children of former capitalists and landlords, and individuals with overseas relatives. Many Chinese St. Louisans feared for their relatives back home. Out of sensitivity to the situation in China, the Chinese in St. Louis muted their celebrations.[4]

PHOTOGRAPH 6.1 After the ceremonies dedicating the new On Leong headquarters at 1509 Delmar Blvd., two huge roast pigs were served. Annie Leong stands between the national co-presidents of the association, Bob Lee (left) of Boston and Stanley Chin of New York, 25 February 1966. From the collections of the St. Louis Mercantile Library at the University of Missouri-St. Louis.

In 1971, the decline of On Leong's power and influence became more evident as the celebration of Chinese New Year, a symbolic indication of the power structure in the Chinese community, was no longer sponsored by On Leong. That year the festivities were organized by the St. Louis Chinese Society, which had been founded by a group of Chinese students and professionals in 1962 (see Chapter 7). This new organization had 400 members; On Leong by then represented 150 families. The St. Louis Chinese Society was offering "programs, fellowship and a chance to celebrate Chinese holidays, including the Chinese New Year."[5] On Leong was slowly losing its central place in the community.

Yet On Leong and the original Chinatown had not been forgotten. St. Louisans missed the old Chinese neighborhood, especially after On Leong was forced to move again in 1979. The impending

PHOTOGRAPH 6.2 Nin Young and Jim Leong, co-presidents of On Leong, and Annie Leong of the Asian Food Products Co., celebrate the Year of the Sheep with ceremonial wine, 5 February 1967. Courtesy of St. Louis Mercantile Library. From the collections of the St. Louis Mercantile Library at the University of Missouri-St. Louis.

move reminded St. Louisans of Hop Alley, and people grew nostalgic. An article in the *St. Louis Globe-Democrat* reminisced:

> St. Louis once had a Chinatown and it flourished near Eighth and Market Streets with laundries, restaurants, shops and the people who ran them. It was on the southern range of the city on a block bounded by Walnut, Market, Eighth and Seventh Streets . . . . One of the busiest places in Chinatown was the On Leong Merchant Association now located above the Asian Food Product store in the 1500 block of Delmar Boulevard. The canopy outside the association building was held by dragons at each corner. It was the hub of Chinatown business.[6]

The second removal of the Chinatown was forced by the development of Franklin Industrial Park, a twenty-two-acre parcel intended for small factories. An eight-block site bounded by Fourteenth, Eighteenth, and Cole streets and Delmar Boulevard, it was one of several projects planned by the city government to "make use of vacant land, decaying buildings and long-ignored railroad yards."[7] The project was intended to create jobs, but in doing so it forced the last vestiges of Chinatown to relocate again. Affected were the new On Leong headquarters, Asia Food Products at 1509 Delmar, and six Chinese families living in flats between Sixteenth and Seventeenth streets on Delmar.

There is no evidence that the site for the industrial park had been selected for reasons of race. Paul Nagel, a project specialist in the city's Planned Industrial Expansion Authority, stated that "it just happened" that the site was the "new Chinatown" area.[8] That being said, it was the second time in living memory that the St. Louis Chinatown had been forced to move. In other words, it was the second time that an urban renewal project had unintentionally victimized the Chinese. Lack of political influence made the Chinese an easy target for urban renewal projects. This had a deleterious effect on their efforts at community building.

On Leong was again forced to look for a new location for its offices and for displaced families. Ideally, the new headquarters would have at least five or six storefronts and easy access to bus transportation, and be in an area of heavy foot traffic.[9]

The Fourth Headquarters at 3608 South Grand Boulevard (1979–97)

For its new headquarters, On Leong found a building in an old German neighborhood in south St. Louis—3608 South Grand Boulevard. On Leong had its reasons to choose this neighborhood. This three-story brick structure, known as the Grand View Arcade Building, had once housed the Melba Theater.[10] It was spacious enough for five or six shops at street level and for plenty of meeting rooms and apartments upstairs. The area was well served by public transportation and had plenty of foot traffic, and Chinese businesses would be able to take root there. Already in the area were the South Grand Sears store, the South Side National Bank, and a number of restaurants including Arthur Treacher's Fish and Chips, White Castle, and Pizza-A-Go-Go. Some Chinese restaurant and grocery businesses would be a strong addition to the existing businesses there. Most importantly, the leaders of On Leong predicted that the south side would not be developed by the city for some time. Annie Leong, the unofficial spokeswoman of On Leong, told Edward L. Cook of the *St. Louis Globe-Democrat* that "we looked everywhere for a place. We wanted an area with vehicular and pedestrians. And we felt the city wouldn't be developing South St. Louis for a while."[11]

Along with this move, On Leong continued to lose importance. With all the postwar opportunities and a more diverse Chinese American community, mutual aid and recreational facilities—the mainstays of On Leong's services—were no longer as necessary. Furthermore, the older Chinese entrepreneurs were retiring, and the younger Chinese businessmen were less interested in joining On Leong, seeing it as too tied to traditions. On Leong's somewhat unflattering reputation among the newer generation resulted in a power vacuum in the St. Louis Chinese community. However, because it had lasted so long, and because it was now mainly a trade association for restaurateurs, On Leong held on to enough members to continue playing a role in the community.

NEW ARRIVALS

While Chinatown and On Leong were struggling for survival, the city began receiving new arrivals from China. By 1960 the there were 663 Chinese in the St. Louis area. Ten years later there were over twice as many—1,451. By 1980 there were 2,418—a fourfold increase within two decades (see Table 6.1).[12]

The rapid population increase in St. Louis reflected the national demographic trend for Chinese Americans over the same period (see Table 6.2). The Chinese exclusion acts had been repealed; however, the quota for Chinese immigrants was only 105 per year. Nevertheless, nonquota immigrants were being allowed to immigrate to the United States. More Chinese scholars were coming to teach at American colleges—an average of about 137 per year, compared to 10 per year in the previous decade. More importantly, under the War Bride Act of 28 December 1945 and the G.I. Fiancees Act of 29 June 1946, the alien wives and children of veterans and American citizens were being permitted to enter America as nonquota immigrants. During the three years that the War Bride Act was in force, around 6,000 Chinese war brides were admitted.[13] Thus in 1947, 3,191 Chinese immigrants entered the United States, most of them

TABLE 6.1 Chinese population in St. Louis, 1950–1980

| | St. Louis City | | St. Louis County | | |
Year	Male	Female	Male	Female	Total
1950	166	119	24	29	338
1960	242	206	109	106	663
1970	295	216	468	472	1451
1980	524		1894		2418

Source: Tabulated according to *Census of Population: 1950, Vol. 1 Characteristics of the Population*, Part 25, Missouri, 143; *Census of Population: 1960, Vol. 1 Characteristics of the Population*, Part 27, Missouri, 153; *1970 Census of Population, Vol. 1 Characteristics of the Population*, Part 27, Missouri, 155–56; and *1980 Census of Population, Vol. 1 Characteristics of the Population, Chapter B. General Population Characteristics*, Part 27, Missouri, 14.

on a nonquota basis.[14] Many came under other laws besides these. The Displaced Persons Act of 1948 and the Refugee Relief Act of 1953 enabled several thousand Chinese to immigrate to America. The former allowed "displaced" Chinese students, government officials, visitors, and others who had temporary status in the United States to become permanent residents; the latter allotted 3,000 visas to refugees from Asia and 2,000 visas to Chinese whose passports had been issued by the Chinese Nationalist government, which had been driven from power on mainland China in 1949.[15] On 22 September 1959 the U.S. Congress passed an act whereby more Chinese on the quota waiting list were able to obtain nonquota status.[16] Thus by 1960 the number of Chinese in the United States had reached 237,292, of whom 60 percent were American-born.[17]

The 1965 Immigration Act also contributed to the population increase of Chinese Americans. This act, officially styled "An Act

TABLE 6.2 Chinese American population in the United States, 1950–1980

Year	Total	Male	Female	Ratio of Sex
1950	117,629	77,008	40,621	1.8:1
1960	237,292	135,549	101,743	1.3:1
1970	431,583	226,733	204,850	1.1:1
1980	806,040	407,544	398,496	1.0:1

Source: *Census of Population, 1950–1980*.

to Amend the Immigration and Nationality Act of 1924," abolished the quota system that had been in effect since 1924 and established three immigration principles: family reunification, the need to recruit skilled workers, and the obligation to admit refugees. Accordingly, visas would now be allocated among quota immigrants from the Eastern Hemisphere in the following percentages: 20 percent of total annual visas to unmarried children of citizens of the United States; 20 percent to spouses and unmarried children of permanent residents; 10 percent to professionals, scientists, and artists with "exceptional ability"; 10 percent to married children of citizens of the United States; 24 percent to siblings of citizens of the United States; 10 percent to skilled and unskilled workers in occupations "for which a shortage of employable and willing persons exists in the United States"; and 6 percent to refugees.[18]

Most new immigrants came to America for economic reasons. Chinese refugees from Vietnam since 1975 and immigrants from Cuba, Jamaica, and other Caribbean islands were lured by the economic opportunities in America. Besides these people, many professionals—the wealthier and better educated from China, Taiwan, Hong Kong, and Southeast Asia—have also arrived since 1965. These new immigrants have benefited from the 1965 Immigrant Act, which gives priority to refugees, to those who have close family members in the United States, and to applicants who have skills, education, and capital.

Most postwar and post-1965 new immigrants settled in American cities. By 1980 nearly 60 percent of the new immigrants from China were living in the larger Chinese urban communities in California and New York.[19] Studies focusing on San Francisco and New York indicate that most residents of Chinatowns are working-class new immigrants with limited English and few marketable skills. Chalsa M. Loo found that the residents of San Francisco Chinatown were far from the "model minority" stereotype. They were overwhelmingly foreign-born (81 percent); they were less educated; in 1979 they were earning $4,000 to $4,900 a year and living in crowded apartments.[20]

Similarly, Peter Kwong's study of the New York Chinatown revealed a "class cleavage" in this large Chinese urban center: the "Uptown Chinese," professionals with better education, lived in the suburbs and enjoyed incomes higher than the national average; the "Downtown Chinese" in the Chinatowns were new immigrants who spoke little English and worked mainly as manual laborers or in service industries. The conflict between the two groups had resulted in a polarized community.[21] Min Zhou's study arrived at different conclusions, finding that new immigrants, regardless of their socioeconomic background, tended to "cluster" in Chinatowns. As a result, Chinatown economies had great potential.[22]

The new arrivals in St. Louis seem to have differed in a number of ways from those in the larger Chinese communities (such as New York City). To start with, the Chinese in St. Louis were much more likely to be professionals or technicians. By 1979, 66.2 percent of the Chinese in St. Louis County were managers, professionals, technicians, or administrators; 10 percent were in sales; and only 21 percent worked in service jobs or as laborers. Among the Chinese in the city of St. Louis itself, 54.4 percent were managers, professionals, technicians, or administrators, 7 percent were in sales, and 36 percent worked in service jobs or as laborers.[23] In New York City in 1980, 39.7 percent of Chinese men and 46 percent of Chinese women were managers, professionals, technicians, or administrators; 60.3 percent of men and 64 percent of women were in sales or service occupations or were laborers.[24]

Furthermore, the Chinese in St. Louis were more likely to be suburbanites. This trend toward the suburbs started in the 1970s. In 1959, 68 percent of Chinese St. Louisans were living in the city proper. Ten years later, 64 percent of them were living to the west and south of the city in the sprawling suburbs of St. Louis County. By 1979, nearly 80 percent were living in St. Louis County (see Table 6.1). In contrast, in the same decades about half the Chinese in the New York City area were living in the city itself and the rest outside the city.[25]

There was no glaring class divide among the Chinese of St. Louis, because the great majority were professionals or entrepreneurs. And because they tended to live in the suburbs, there were few vestiges in St. Louis of a Chinese enclave economy.

TRANSFORMATION OF THE ECONOMY

Beginning in the 1960s, the economy of Chinese St. Louisans went through a remarkable transformation. The Chinese hand laundries disappeared one by one, and Chinese restaurants popped up like mushrooms, especially in shopping malls and plazas. At the same time, the newly arrived Chinese American professionals were being heavily recruited by a number of major employers in the region: Washington University, Monsanto Chemical, McDonnell-

TABLE 6.3 Numbers of Chinese laundries, restaurants, and grocers in St. Louis (city and county), 1952–1980

Year	Number of Laundries		Number of Restaurants		Number of Grocers	
	City	County	City	County	City	County
1952	49	—	13	—	1	—
1956	44	—	14	—	1	—
1959	41	—	15	—	1	—
1963	25	—	21	—	1	—
1966	10	0	13	2	1	0
1969	5	0	16	5	1	0
1972	2	0	20	8	1	0
1975	1	—	17	—	1	—
1976	1	—	40	—	1	—
1980	1	—	41	—	1	—

Source: Tabulated according to *Gould's St. Louis Directory for 1952*, *Polk's St. Louis City Directory for 1956–80*, and *Polk's St. Louis County Directory for 1966–73*.
Note: Dash "—" indicates data not available.

Douglas (later Boeing, after it was purchased by that company in 1999), Ralston-Purina, Emerson Electric, and Anheuser-Busch.

From Laundry to Restaurant

As noted in Chapter 5, the Chinese hand laundry business peaked in the 1920s and began to decline in the 1930s. After the 1950s Chinese hand laundries began disappearing so quickly that the *St. Louis Directory* no longer listed them separately. That business was nearly extinct in the area by the early 1970s. By then, the Chinese restaurant business had replaced it as a key occupation for Chinese St. Louisans (see Table 6.3).

The shift in the Chinese business community from laundries to restaurants was not an accident. The decline of hand laundries was a direct result of competition from the newer steam laundries, which began in the 1930s, and from coin laundries, which became ubiquitous in the 1950s. In the late 1920s only a couple of steam laundries were listed in the St. Louis city directory. In 1931 the number of steam laundries suddenly jumped from 1 to 66.[26] Competition between hand laundries and steam laundries was heating up throughout the United States. Renqiu Yu investigated this struggle between the Chinese hand laundries and the steam laundries. The competition between the "two pillars" of the Chinese laundry business, Yu notes, was economic as well as political. The hand laundrymen saw themselves as part of the "laboring class"; the steam laundry owners considered themselves part of the "gentry." The latter, "exercising power over the community by virtue of their wealth and education, promoted their own interests in the name of 'ethnic solidarity.'"[27]

In St. Louis the competition between hand laundries and steam laundries was of a different nature than in New York; in the former it was intertwined with racial differences. Chinese operated hand laundries; non-Chinese (mainly European Americans) owned steam laundries.[28] The white steam laundry owners worked hard to convince the public that steam laundries were more hygienic. In the end, they succeeded, and as a result the number of Chinese hand laundries in St. Louis declined drastically in the 1930s and 1940s (see Table 6.4).Coin laundries, also owned by European Americans, began to appear in the 1950s. Much cheaper and more

TABLE 6.4 Comparison of Chinese hand laundries, steam laundries, and coin laundries in St. Louis (city), 1928–1963

Year	Chinese Laundry	Steam Laundry	Coin Laundry
1928	143	4	0
1929	165	1	0
1930	161	1	0
1931	155	66	0
1932	128	79	0
1935	104	61	0
1936	123	65	0
1939	89	62	0
1941	78	68	0
1944	48	60	0
1946	61	55	0
1952	49	86	37
1956	44	72	60
1959	41	54	107
1963	25	38	168

Source: Tabulated according to *Gould's St. Louis City Directory for 1928–1952*, and *Polk's St. Louis City Directory for 1955–1963*.

convenient than hand laundries, they had driven most Chinese hand laundries out of business by the 1960s. Clearly, the competition between the Chinese hand laundries and the steam and coin laundries reflected a conflict between labor and capital; furthermore, it reflected differences in economic status between an ethnic minority group and the majority. Most Chinese hand laundrymen, whether they were owners or workers, were manual laborers who lived from hand to mouth and had limited savings at best. To open a steam laundry or coin laundry demanded considerable capital for machinery, and the operating costs were higher. It follows that the competition between the laundry businesses in St. Louis reflected a conflict between the Chinese working class and European American capitalists. Most hand laundrymen were Chinese, and the steam and coin laundries were owned by European Americans, and as a result the class conflict was masked by racial differences. The Chinese hand laundries lost the economic battle. This was more than a victory of technology over labor; it also reflected, to a certain degree, the uneven distribution of social wealth between the advantaged majority and disadvantaged minorities.

While the Chinese hand laundries were closing down, Chinese restaurants were beginning to open. The growth of the Chinese restaurant business, especially after the 1970s, was a nationwide phenomenon and was driven by a number of factors. As a result of the more liberal 1965 Immigration Act, the number of Chinese immigrants to the United States more than tripled in 1966, and this population grew fourfold over the next decade.[29] Many Chinese restaurants in urban Chinese communities opened in order to meet the demands of the growing Chinese immigrant population. The Chinese restaurant business also grew as a result of the American public's yearning for ethnic food. The civil rights movement, which was dominated by African American and Mexican American activists, increased the public's acceptance of cultural and ethnic diversity. The Vietnam War, although unpopular in America, brought Americans closer to Asia and its cultures, including its cuisines. President Richard Nixon's visit to China in 1972 heightened the public's curiosity about things Chinese. As a result of these developments, Americans began eating more rice and Chinese food became one of the most popular ethnic foods in the 1970s. As the public learned more about Chinese food, savvy American diners began frequenting Chinese restaurants.

Reflecting these trends, the Chinese restaurant industry in St. Louis entered a new era. By the late 1970s there were more than forty Chinese restaurants in the city—a fourfold increase over the previous decade. These restaurants were not only more numerous; they were also more exquisite and offered more variety. By now they were serving more than chop suey and Cantonese cuisine. Other Chinese cuisines—Mandarin (or Peking, or Beijing), Shanghai, Szechuan (Sichuan), Hunan, and so on—were now competing with Cantonese. Many St. Louisans welcomed this new variety, although others were nervous about experimenting too much. In 1976, John Heidenry, the restaurant critic for the magazine *St. Louisan*, followed Theodore Dreiser's footsteps and explored most of the important Chinese restaurants in the area, in order to provide a practical guide for the Chinese food lovers.[30]

Heidenry listed eight Chinese restaurants in his guide. According to him, Chinese restaurants in St. Louis were now offering Cantonese, Peking, and Szechuan cuisine. The Rice Bowl at 3157 South Grant served Cantonese cuisine; the House of Cheng at 5612 South Grand served inexpensive homestyle cooking, including chow mein (fried noodles), chop suey (chopped meats and vegetables), egg foo yung (scrambled eggs mixed with pork, beef, or seafood), fried rice, and lo mein (noodles with sauce). The other six restaurants offered a mix of Mandarin and Szechuan styles. In 1973, Lantern House, a Mandarin restaurant at 6605 Delmar, was chosen by *Esquire* magazine as the best Chinese restaurant in the United States. Yen Ching, a newer Mandarin restaurant at 1012 South Brentwood, in the tony Brentwood neighborhood, served expensive but exquisitely prepared dishes. Both Lantern House and Yen Ching were rated highly by the reviewer. The Peking Restaurant at 7903a Forsyth also served Mandarin cuisine, but at reasonable prices. The Shanghai Inn, downtown at 606 Pine, served cheap Szechuan food. The Pagoda at 3679 North Lindbergh offered a mix of all cuisines. The Jade Teahouse at 10045 Manchester Road was a typical suburban mall restaurant that served Chinese food.[31]

From Heidenry's guide, it is apparent that Mandarin cuisine was the easiest to find in St. Louis. This reflected recent demographic changes in the Chinese community: the earlier Chinese immigrants had been mainly Cantonese-speaking; many of the new immigrants from China, Taiwan, and Hong Kong spoke Mandarin instead. Inevitably, Cantonese dominance of the restaurant business had been broken. Restaurateurs from other regions of China were now competing with their Cantonese counterparts.

The eight Chinese restaurants listed by Heidenry were obviously the more prominent ones. There were many smaller ones—chop suey shops—scattered throughout the city and suburbs. In 1976, twenty-three of the forty-plus Chinese restaurants listed in the city directory were chop suey shops. The large Chinese restaurants had adopted exotic names and offered luxurious surroundings; most chop suey shops were more basic. The chop suey shops simply used "chop suey" as the business name such as in Chop Suey Bowl, combined the owner's name with "chop suey" such as in Bing Lau Chop Suey, or placed a distinctive name before "chop suey" such as in Bangkok Chop Suey.[32]

The chop suey shops were much simpler to run and required less initial capital than fancy restaurants. A chop suey shop usually needed only a kitchen and a front area with a counter and a few chairs. They were cheap to furnish and their overhead was low. They could be run by two people, typically a husband and wife, with the husband cooking and the wife waiting on customers. The overwhelming predominance of chop suey shops among Chinese restaurants indicates that chop suey was a popular and inexpensive alternative food for many St. Louisans. Most chop suey shops served basic Cantonese-style food: chow mein, lo mein, and Americanized Chinese dishes such as chop suey and egg foo yung. Chinese restaurants had developed these dishes long ago to accommodate American tastes, so most non-Chinese diners already knew what they were. This, and the lower initial capital investment, made it inevitable that chop suey shops would be the most common model for Chinese restaurants in postwar St. Louis.

Most owners of Chinese restaurants and chop suey shops were old Chinatown residents and new immigrants with limited English and few marketable skills. Don Ko, who owned several Chinese restaurants between the 1960s and the 1980s, was one of the former. Ko immigrated to the United States in 1948 from Hong Kong at seventeen to join his father, a merchant in St. Louis. Ko worked in a Chinese hand laundry for five years. In 1953 he married Ann, who was born in an apartment near Hop Alley in 1932. The Kos owned a hand laundry called Don's Laundry at 4318 East Avenue from 1954 to 1964. When that business began to decline, they sold it. In 1968 they and a partner opened a Chinese restaurant, Ho Choy. Ho Choy had hundred seats, which made it a large one. Ann worked in the front serving customers while Don and the partner cooked. They ran Ho Choy for two years before selling out to the partner, that partnership having soured. The Kos then started a takeout shop in 1970 in an African American neighborhood. Business was brisk and they had orders all day long, but they were not making much money, since the takeout orders were usually small. Four years later they sold the takeout shop and opened a sit-down restaurant, the Dragon Inn at 5814 Natural Bridge Avenue. Ko's seven children all helped with the restaurant business, busing tables, washing dishes, and doing whatever was needed. The restaurant and other businesses the Kos owned enabled the Kos to send all their children to college.[33]

Yee M. Kwong's experience was typical of new Chinese immigrants with limited English skills. Kwong studied engineering in China. In 1965 he went to Hong Kong, where he worked as an engineer for four years. In 1969 he and his wife came to St. Louis to join his father-in-law, who owned a Chinese restaurant. Kwong had studied Russian in college, as Russian was the foreign language most often taught in China before 1966, but he had difficulty with English. He worked in Chinese restaurants throughout his years in St. Louis, first as a restaurant worker, later as an owner of his father-in-law's restaurant. He found it a difficult business to be in: "You put all your time in, and your family also put all time in." Besides the help from his family members, Kwong had to hire many part-time workers, mostly Chinese college or graduate students.[34]

The shift from laundries to restaurants was taking place in Chinese communities throughout North America. By 1970, restaurants had surpassed laundries as the biggest sector in Chinese American economy, and there were more than 9,300 Chinese restaurants across the country.[35]

The Chinese grocery business grew in tandem with the restaurant sector and the Chinese American population. Chinese groceries in St. Louis peaked in the 1910s, declined during the Depression, and nearly died out in the 1930s and 1940s. In those decades almost no Chinese groceries were listed in the St. Louis Directory.[36] In the 1950s, Annie Leong's family opened a grocery business in addition to their family restaurant, the Asian Café. After Hop Alley was torn down in 1966, Annie reopened the grocery store on Delmar Boulevard under the name Asian Food Products; this shop stayed in business from 1967 to 1978.[37] In 1978 a new Chinese grocery store, Asian Trading Company, was opened by a Chinese couple from Taiwan. The same year, Din-Ho Market also opened. The year after that, Edwin and Jean Chiu moved to St. Louis and opened a third Chinese grocery store, Central Trading Company.[38] The Chius, originally from Hong Kong, had run a restaurant in England for more than ten years before immigrating to the United States in 1978. They first stayed in Chicago, and a year later came to St. Louis to join a relative. The relative told them that a Chinese grocery store was for sale. The Chius decided to go into the grocery business instead of the restaurant business, since it would not involve working nights, which meant that Jean Chiu would be able to look after their young children after the store closed at six.[39]

Chinese groceries in St. Louis were mainly retail during the 1910s; by the 1970s and 1980s they were more diversified. The daily operations of the Central Trading Company exemplify how the grocery business worked in St. Louis. It ordered merchandise from warehouses in New York and California, paying wholesale prices, and sold the goods at retail. In the morning, some of its employees would deliver merchandise—usually Chinese cooking ingredients—to restaurants at a less than retail markup. Meanwhile, the store retailed goods throughout the morning and the early afternoon. After two in the afternoon most of the store's workers would begin preparing wholesale merchandise for the next morning's deliveries.[40]

As Chinese groceries expanded their operations, they also grew bigger. The earlier Chinese groceries in Hop Alley were mainly family stores operated by unpaid family members; the groceries now had to hire their help and pay them wages. Most of these workers were Chinese—typically they were new immigrants with limited English and few marketable skills. For instance, the Central Trading Company had between twenty and thirty full-time and part-time employees.[41] Some of the employees were Cantonese speakers; others were new arrivals from other backgrounds.

Chinese restaurants catered to both Chinese and non-Chinese; in contrast, Chinese groceries drew their customers almost exclusively from the Chinese community. This limited the number and size of the Chinese groceries. At the same time, the restaurants and the rapidly growing Chinese population of the city provided a stable and expanding market for Chinese groceries. By staying open seventy hours a week, these stores were able to thrive.

Most Chinese entrepreneurs focused on the restaurant business, but a few ventured into other businesses that had long been dominated by European Americans. Walter Ko was born in Canton, China, in 1949 and moved with his family to Hong Kong in 1960. He received elementary, secondary, and two years of preparatory school education in Hong Kong. In 1973 he and his family immigrated to the United States to join an uncle in Chicago. Ten months later they came to St. Louis. Like most new Chinese immigrants at the time, the Kos worked in restaurant. In 1977 they opened the first Cantonese dim sum restaurant in St. Louis. Business was brisk, but Walter Ko had never wanted to be a restaurateur. So he enrolled in a two-year engineering program at Forest Park Community College and followed this with a degree in engineering management from the University of Missouri at Rolla. He studied the market and saw opportunities in the wholesale optical business; there was keen competition on the East and West Coasts but little in the Midwest. Also, he already had some Hong Kong connections in the optical business. In 1983 he started an optical business with help from his wife. He described to me how he managed his business:

> When you have a product, you have to know how to sell. You have to know business management, salesmanship, and opticians. It is a small, tight community. Once you get through, you get known. I speak with accent and I look different, but I do a good job and I have a good business reputation. I was the only non-white then in optical business in the Midwest. Even on the East and West Coasts, there are not many Asians doing this business.
>
> During my typical days, in the morning I make phone calls, making appointments for the next week. In the evening, I decide what to do, whom I would go to, and what to sell. In the summer, I promote sunglasses, and I educate people. Fashionwise, we are one year behind New York, and New York is one year behind Europe. We used to order merchandise from Hong Kong and pay in 90 to180 days. Now we get products from New York and we have to pay in 30 days. By the end of the month, I send invoice to customers asking them to pay in 30 days. I have to go to Food and Drug Administration, as we are under its jurisdiction. I have to deal with customs [when merchandise is imported from overseas]. I started with a few styles [of sunglasses], now I have more than a hundred styles.[42]

Clearly, capital flow, management and marketing skills, and good connections are essential to operating an optical business. Restraints like these have probably discouraged most Chinese entrepreneurs from entering the business. But a few courageous and resourceful businessmen such as Ko have been able to broaden their business horizons and enjoy decent economic returns. Chinese entrepreneurs in nontraditional businesses are challenging the stereotype that all Chinese businessmen are restaurant owners or grocers.

Professionals

Some new immigrants worked in Chinese restaurants and grocery stores; many others entered the professions as doctors, engineers, professors, technicians, and computer experts. According to the 1980 census, of the 3,719 employed Asian and Pacific Islanders in St. Louis County, 1,699 (46 percent) were in management or the professions; 766 (19 percent) were in technical or administrative support positions, 313 (10 percent) were in sales, 549 (15 percent) were in service occupations, 126 (3 percent) were in precision, craft, and repair occupations, and 259 (7 percent) were laborers.[43] In the city itself, the job distribution was slightly different. Of the 919 employed Asians and Pacific Islanders, 252 (28 percent) were in management or the professions, 247 (27 percent) were in technical or administrative occupations, 66 (7 percent) were in sales, 246 (27 percent) were in service occupations, and 84 (9 percent) were laborers.[44] Thus about 65 percent of Asians and Pacific Islanders in St. Louis County were professionals, and about 55 percent of those in the city.

Most of the professionals were working for large organizations such as Washington University, McDonnell Douglas, Monsanto Chemical, and Ralston Purina. William Tao, Nelson Wu, Tzy C. Peng, and Dachung (Pat) Peng were quite typical among Chinese professionals in St. Louis. William Tao, one of the first Chinese professionals in St. Louis, graduated with a master's degree in mechanical engineering from Washington University in 1950 and was appointed an instructor at that university's engineering school. Five years later he started his own engineering consulting firm; however, he continued to serve as an affiliate professor at the university's engineering and architecture schools.[45]

Nelson Wu was born in 1919 in Beijing, China, and grew up in an intellectual family. He attended Qinghua University and graduated with a degree in English in 1942. After teaching for one year at his alma mater following his graduation, he wanted to study in the United States. On his way there he traveled for a month in India—an experience that inspired his later interest in art history. He entered Yale in 1945 and earned a doctorate in art history in 1954. He first taught at San Francisco State University, then at Yale. In 1967 he was recruited by Washington University to teach art history. A prolific writer in both Chinese and English, he

PHOTOGRAPH 6.3 Nelson Wu, also known as Lu Qiao, a prominent artist, writer, and professor of art history at Washington University, was representative of the post-1960 Chinese professionals in St. Louis. Wu used his own Chinese calligraphy as wallpaper in his study at home in St. Louis, 1999. Huping Ling Collection.

published works about art history in English and wrote novels and prose in Chinese. He also became an accomplished calligrapher and painter. In 1972, to promote Asian culture, he helped found the Asian Art Society at Washington University. In 1987 he was included in the "Living Treasure" program produced by the Public Broadcasting System as one of the three most accomplished artists in St. Louis—a pianist, a dancer, and a painter/calligrapher.[46]

Tzy C. Peng was born into a large family in Suzhou, Jiangsu province, in 1929. To escape his strict father, in 1947 he entered the National University of Taiwan, where he studied mechanical engineering. He graduated in 1951 and stayed on as a teaching assistant for a year. In 1952 he came to the United States to continue his studies at Notre Dame. Later he transferred to the Illinois Institute of Technology in Chicago, where he completed his master's degree in 1955. After earning a doctorate in mechanical engineering at Northwestern in 1958, he was hired by the NASA's

Ames Research Center in Moffett, California. Thus he began his career as an aerospace engineer. After nine years with NASA, Boeing, and General Electric, he came to St. Louis in 1967 to join the research laboratory at McDonnell Douglas.[47]

Dachung (Pat) Peng was born in Jinan, Shangdong province, in 1946, and migrated to Taiwan with his parents in 1949. He came to the United States in 1969 and earned his doctorate in applied mechanics at Lehigh University. In 1974 he was hired by Monsanto as a member of its technical center in Florida. Two years later he was transferred to Monsanto in St. Louis. Within five years he had been promoted to Monsanto Fellow, which broke the company record for fast promotion. In 1989 he suggested that the company start doing business with Greater China (China, Hong Kong, and Taiwan). His suggestion was accepted, and the company established a "China Insight" program to promote its business with China. Dachung Peng was appointed to oversee this program and to promote Chinese culture within the company.[48]

Since the 1950s a third employment pattern has developed among Chinese Americans that blends elements of entrepreneurship with professional skills. Basically, it involves Chinese professionals starting up their own entrepreneurial companies. William Tao was among the first. In 1955, after teaching for five years at Washington University, he left for the private sector. He began by establishing a private consulting practice with a partner. A year later, the partner died. Tao was determined to continue the practice on his own, and to that end he incorporated it in 1957. A resourceful man with keen business sense and solid professional training, he grew his company into one of the most highly respected in its field, which is electrical and mechanical engineering.[49] The route taken by Tao was not the usual one, it being a departure from the stereotype that Chinese are either restaurateurs or professionals.

Characteristics of the Chinese Economy in St. Louis

It is clear from the preceding discussion that Chinese St. Louisans have tended to enter either the restaurant business or the professions. This suggests some of the characteristics of the city's Chinese economy in the 1960s. First, the Chinese restaurant business in St. Louis depended on ethnic networks for labor, capital, and raw materials (i.e., restaurant supplies), but on the mainstream public for its market. This pattern was highly similar to that in other Chinese enclaves in North America and Southeast Asia. Bernard Wong documented how in New York City the business and political leaders of the Chinese community have controlled wealth and political power and have been linked horizontally and vertically to other members of that community.[50] Peter S. Li found that in Canada, kinship networks have been a key factor in starting traditional Chinese businesses such as food services and retailing.[51] Similarly, Linda Y. C. Lim found that in Southeast Asia, new Chinese immigrants rely heavily on ethnic networks to find housing and jobs.[52] It is fair to say that *guanxi* (ethnic networks) have enabled overseas Chinese businesses to succeed.[53] As one strand in the web of overseas Chinese businesses, the Chinese restaurant business in St. Louis in the post-1960s was caught in these ethnic networks, though it also benefited from them. Capital to start a restaurant business often came from family savings and from loans extended by members of the clan. Laborers tended to be unpaid family members or underpaid relatives or clansmen. Supplies were ordered at wholesale prices from ethnic wholesalers. Ethnic networks were thus indispensable to the Chinese restaurant business in St. Louis.

At the same time, the Chinese restaurants relied heavily on patrons of all ethnic backgrounds. Inevitably this linked the ethnic economy with the larger, mainstream one. Chinese restaurants could not survive without mainstream customers, and to tap those customers, they had to scatter themselves around the city. Geographical dispersion improved the chances of survival for individual Chinese restaurants and for the sector as a whole; however, it also meant that Chinese businesses tended not to cluster in a specific neighborhood or district. The dispersion of Chinese restaurants was partly responsible for the absence of a Chinese business district.

Second, the Chinese professionals integrated themselves completely with the larger society both professionally and economically. Their professional training enabled them to compete with European American peers in the mainstream labor market. Because most of them were employed by large and well-established mainstream enterprises, they were never buffeted by the winds of small entrepreneurship. At the same time, their careers were at the mercy of mainstream economic forces. This meant that they were more concerned about the broader economy than about the Chinese ethnic economy.

The Chinese restaurant business was "doubly dependent" on the ethnic business sector and the mainstream economy, thus resulting in the absence of large business concentrations. The economic integration of Chinese professionals did much to determine the form of the new Chinese community now taking shape in St. Louis, albeit without determining it entirely. This new community would lack physical boundaries and would be dominated by the common cultural interests of its members.

THE CAMPAIGN TO SAVE THE LAST CHINESE HAND LAUNDRY: SAM WAH LAUNDRY

Chinese St. Louisans continued to shift from laundries to restaurants, until by the late 1970s only one Chinese hand laundry—Sam Wah Laundry at 4381 Laclede Avenue—stood alone reminding St. Louisans of the past when Chinese hand laundries were a part of the city's streetscape. There, two brothers in their eighties—Gee Kee One (Gee Sam Wah) and Gee Hong—still rose early every morning and ironed and washed until late at night, just as they had for half a century. The long-time loyal customers still came to the Gee brothers to have their laundry washed and ironed manually.

In 1978, however, the last stronghold of Chinese hand laundry was about to vanish as all its counterparts had earlier. That year the Sam Wah was slated for demolition. The Station Partnership, which owned the property, had decided to sell it to the Washington University Medical Center Redevelopment Corporation.[54] The Gee brothers would be forced to move out. Aging, lonely, with limited English, and unfamiliar with the legal system, the Gee brothers had no recourse but to close the laundry without knowing what they were going to do and where they were going to go. In July, Sam Wah and Gee Hong hung a sign on their door: "We Will Accept No Laundry after July 24th, 1978. We are Closing on August 7th, 1978."

The public didn't hear this sad news until Eliot F. Porter, Jr. of the *St. Louis Post-Dispatch*, a longtime customer, went as usual to drop off his dirty laundry and pick up his washed laundry on an October day of that year. When he opened the bundle, he found a handwritten note from Gee Hong in the front pocket of a shirt: "You nice friend . . . . All time you help me . . . . Do something for me . . . . You wife both very nice . . . . Don't speak . . . . Laundry money free . . . . No charge . . . . OK thank you."[55]

Eliot Porter and his wife Jane had been customers of the laundry for ten years, and the brothers had become their friends. They had even invited the Porters to the back of the laundry on Chinese New Year's Eve. The brothers fixed a meal for them and set off firecrackers to entertain them afterwards.[56] The Porters and other customers were fond of the two old gentlemen; they also appreciated the quality of their work and their low prices. An old price list found in laundry shows that in the 1920s they charged 20 cents for washing and ironing a shirt.[57] The Gee brothers had held to that price for decades; by the 1970s they were charging only 35 cents.[58]

Porter was saddened by the news and was deeply sympathetic to the brothers' plight. He immediately went to Gary Glenn, Rebecca Glenn, Doreen Dodson, and other customers of the laundry. They soon formed the Friends of Sam Wah Appeal and hired a lawyer to handle the case.[59] Besides loyal customers, the Friends of Sam Wah Appeal included sympathetic individuals such as Austin Tao, a prominent engineer from Shanghai. On Leong was also very supportive of the brothers and involved itself heavily in the situation. Don Chin, president of On Leong and owner of a Chinese restaurant, the Dragon Inn, joined the appeal and along with Annie Leong helped interpret for the elderly brothers during the entire saga.[60]

The deal between the Station Partnership and Washington University was part of the urban renewal of the times. The university was trying to protect the neighborhood around its medical school by opening a parking lot. To bring this about, it hired a development firm called Team Four consisting of developers, lawyers, engineers, and city planners. On 13 September 1978 the Station Partnership ordered the laundry owners to move out. But where would the aging brothers go? Neither Washington University nor Team Four—except Austin Tao, a Team Four partner—cared much. There was an apartment building right across the street, and the Gee brothers could move there. But they could not afford to pay the $120 monthly rent.

Neither man had family or relatives in the United States. They had left Hong Kong for San Francisco in the late 1910s. Gee Kee One, a widower by then, left his two sons behind, and Gee Hong his wife and two children. They learned the laundry business in San Francisco and then went to Chicago to practice the business. Unaccustomed to the cold, they moved to St. Louis in 1922 to join their uncle Sam Wah, who had been running laundries in St. Louis since 1887. They inherited the Sam Wah Laundry from their uncle and continued to operate it under the same name. Since coming to America, they had never been able to visit Hong Kong. They worked in their laundry, which was equipped with a century-old washer and dryer and an antique atomizer, and they lived in the back of the laundry. Their furniture consisted of a stove, a chair, two beds, and a homemade shrine of religious figurines. During their fifty-six years in St. Louis, work had taken up most of their time. Social isolation and a limited command of English left them bewildered and confused about their future.[61]

The Friends of Sam Wah Appeal was outraged by the bureaucratic treachery. But they also knew how expensive it could be to fight the bureaucracy. They began raising funds for an appeal with the goal of saving the brothers' business. They distributed flyers calling for public support:

SAVE THE LAST CHINESE LAUNDRY IN ST. LOUIS

For fifty years Sam Wah and Gee Wong have lived and worked in their little laundry at 4381 Laclede Avenue.

For fifty years, they have paid their taxes, obeyed the law, served their customers and helped their neighbors.

Now, the city has condemned their building and Sam and Gee face eviction . . . to make way for a parking lot. They have no family, no relatives. They know no other life.

Is this any way to treat two old gentlemen who ask only to be left in peace . . . to live out their days in dignity and honest toil?

Show your support for Sam and Gee by attending the condemnation hearing. It's at 1:30 p.m. Tuesday, Nov. 14, at Room 208 in City Hall.

Give us a call if you'd like to join us in this effort.

Concerned customers of Sam Wah:

Gary Glenn, 367–4660   Rebecca Glenn, 367–4660   Eliot Porter, 726–6643[62]

Meanwhile, Robert N. Paskel, the lawyer hired by the Friends of Sam Wah Appeal suggested a strategy for fighting City Hall. He quoted the principle of "life tenancy," which basically declared that an aging tenant can live in a property until death. He was concerned that the two elderly men might not survive a relocation—a condition that lawyers called "transfer trauma." Another sympathetic lawyer had contacted social workers at the On Lock Senior

Health Center in San Francisco, an institution specializing in issues affecting elderly Asians, for more data on transfer trauma.[63]

On 14 and 28 November 1978 the Board of Building Appeals of the City of St. Louis convened. Sam Wah and Gee Hong appeared, represented by Robert Paskel and by Doreen Dodson, another attorney. Don Chin was also present to interpret for the brothers. Dodson presented their case and cited the life tenancy principle. Team Four rebutted that the building had been constructed at the turn of the century and was in violation of the city's safety codes. Richard Ward, a Team Four partner, claimed that the building was a mess and estimated that it would cost at least $10,000 to repair it to meet those codes. The board came down in favor of Team Four, ruling that the building should be fixed to meet the codes within ninety days.[64]

The campaign to save Sam Wah Laundry began raising funds. Many mainstream St. Lousians sympathized with the brothers and made donations. On Leong donated $500 at once. "Don Chin, the owner of Dragon Inn," recalled Porter, "put a roll of money in the fund." Even Team Four donated money in an attempt to repair its battered image.[65] By late 1979 the campaign had raised $12,500 cash and some donated materials and labor to repair the building. The donated fund eventually reached $20,000. Basically, there were three types of donors: Central West End developers and Washington University Medical Center Redevelopment Corporation; hardware stores; and the St. Louis Chinese community, including On Leong, the International Chinese Architect Society, the Chinese Gospel Mission, the St. Louis Chinese Society, the Organization of Chinese Americans, the St. Louis Chinese Jaycees, and the Chinese Liberty Assembly. Some individual Chinese also contributed. Austin Tao had been providing assistance from the beginning. Donald Chin and Annie Leong served throughout as interpreters, fundraisers, and best friends of the brothers.[66]

On 7 December 1979, Gee Hong handed a $1 bill to Richard Ward, who was representing Team Four, which owned the property at 4381 Laclede. In return, the Gee brothers received the deed to the property and became its owner for as long as either one lived or worked on the property. Eliot Porter, who had organized the campaign, attended the ceremony to celebrate the victory, bringing with him his dirty laundry.[67]

The Sam Wah Laundry was saved, and the Gee brothers continued to wash and iron laundry until their last days. In 1984, at ninety, Sam Wah died of a heart attack and was buried in Valhalla

Cemetery. Gee Hong, whose heart was by then failing, continued to run the business after his brother's death. In late February of 1986, he was found dead in his bed, and joined his brother at Valhalla.[68] Right after this the Washington University Medical Center Redevelopment Corporation leveled the building, giving Eliot Porter and Rebecca Glenn just enough time to rescue a box of letters in Chinese. The two learned from these letters that the Gee brothers had a safe deposit box in a bank downtown containing several thousand dollars in cash. They used part of the fund to bury Gee Hong and gave the rest to On Leong.[69] The story of Sam Wah Laundry had ended poignantly.

The campaign to save the laundry had implications worth pondering. First, European Americans had launched and led the campaign. Individual Chinese (especially Austin Tao, Donald Chin, and Annie Leong) had become involved, and some Chinese organizations (especially On Leong) had provided generous donations, but it was European Americans who had originally shown the brothers some humanity and who had fought for their rights. Eliot Porter brought a keen awareness of civil rights with him when he moved to Missouri from New England. He was used to riding his bicycle to work every day from his home on Waterman Boulevard, and along the way he would drop off his dirty laundry and pick up the clean laundry at Sam Wah Laundry. He appreciated the value of hand laundry in preserving fabric, and he especially appreciated the old men's kindness. When the brothers related their plight to him in broken English, he was outraged, and his conscience demanded that he help them. As Porter remembered it two decades later: "They came from China and they had their heads down. People had to fight for them."[70] Porter and Gary and Rebecca Glenn, owners of a hardware store near the laundry, together called public attention to the case. As a journalist, Porter was able to use the media to arouse public anger at the city planners and sympathy for the elderly men. During the campaign the *St. Louis Post-Dispatch* reported on the case extensively and told the brothers' sad story repeatedly. Robert Paskel, the lawyer who worked for the Friends of Sam Wah Appeal, utilized his legal knowledge to make a feasible case for them. Doreen Dodson conducted a vast amount of legal research to establish that the treatment of the brothers amounted to a civil rights violation, and in the end she won the brothers' day for them. At the same time, On Leong, the traditional Chinese community organization, was so used to the confined territory of Chinatown and to following Chinese practices that it lacked knowledge of the Western legal system—knowledge that would have enabled it to fight for the brothers without European Americans' help. The newer Chinese community organizations such as the St. Louis Chinese Society, the Organization of Chinese Americans, and the St. Louis Chinese Jaycee were less than a decade old and were still learning American democracy, so they were too green to provide effective leadership. Chinese St. Louisans had achieved remarkable educational and occupational success since the 1960s, yet they still lacked political skills and clout and so had none to lend the Gee brothers. This lack of political clout was still a serious problem for Chinese St. Louisans, just as it had always been.

Second, the campaign reminds us of the dark side of urban renewal. As an effort to improve the city's image and promote its commerce, urban renewal came with a cost—St. Louis was losing its cultural heritage and violating the civil rights of its disadvantaged citizens. Urban renewal too often targeted the inner city and decaying neighborhoods that were home to the poor and to ethnic minorities. In demolishing old neighborhoods, the city was destroying its ethnic heritage. Washington University's redevelopment project threatened to erase the last Chinese hand laundry, a symbol of the early years of Chinese St. Louis. Meanwhile, the relocation that redevelopment forced was deeply painful for those directly affected. And the city bureaucracy was insensitive to the individual and communal sufferings of those being relocated. Twenty years later, Porter still sounded angry: "I could see common decency. They were two old men. Why couldn't you let two old men stay there for a few years? After they die, you could do anything with the building. There was a controversy if you gave power to an agency to do the urban renewal. How did the people benefit from Washington University Redevelopment? Is that purpose justified?"[71]

Third, the campaign reveals a sharp divide between the city bureaucracy and the common citizens. "It was a war," Porter recalled, "We wouldn't have done anything if there was not a crime."[72] The campaign was a battle between bureaucratic treachery and the human decency of ordinary citizens. The city planners were trying to apply bureaucratic regulations to force the brothers out; to this, the Friends of Sam Wah Appeal responded with a fundraising campaign to repair the building so that it would meet the city codes. The fact that the campaign was able to raise $20,000 plus building materials and labor highlights the confrontation between city bureaucrats and ordinary citizens. Clearly, the city planners who implemented urban renewal cared little about whether they were hurting people.

THE VIETNAMESE REFUGEE COMMUNITY AND KOREAN CHINESE COMMUNITY

In the 1960s the Chinese American community in St. Louis was further strengthened and diversified by new immigrants from Vietnam and South Korea. The Vietnamese Chinese came to St. Louis as refugees after Vietnam fell to the communists in 1975. In the spring of that year the United States and many other countries opened their gates to many war refugees from Indochina. The first Vietnamese refugees to arrive were mainly army officers and their families. As the situation deteriorated rapidly after the communist takeover, more Vietnamese joined the waves of refugees escaping the terror. The Vietnamese refugees came from all walks of life—they included army officers and common soldiers, government bureaucrats, teachers, doctors, engineers, lawyers, students, businessmen, farmers, fishermen, Catholic priests and nuns, and Buddhist monks and nuns. By 1987, 529,706 Vietnamese had been granted refugee status in the United States.[73]

St. Louis took in its share of these refugees and has received about 10,000 since 1975. The work of settling them has been carried out by International Institute of Metro St. Louis. Founded in 1919, the institute helps newcomers from around the world become self-sufficient St. Louisans. Each year its staff and volunteers help about six thousand immigrants and refugees from more than forty countries.[74]

Most Vietnamese refugees first had to deal with the trauma of fleeing their home country. It has been estimated that at least 10 percent of these refugees died en route.[75] My oral history records suggest that about 40 percent of Vietnamese refugees died at sea.[76]

Ha's story typifies the experience of escaping Vietnam and coming to America. Ha (a pseudonym) was born in Cambodia and moved to Vietnam in 1952 when she was twenty, with her parents, who were Vietnamese Chinese. Her father worked for the Vietnamese government and her mother was a housewife. Ha received her college education in social work and nursing in Vietnam and then married to a South Vietnamese army officer. In 1975 she had to separate from her husband and leave Vietnam with her four children. She recalled how she fled Vietnam, her life in the refugee camps, and the difficulties of an immigrant's life in America:

I flew out of Saigon three days before it fell. Saigon was in chaos and we were lost. My husband was an army officer and the army provided transportation for his family. We left Vietnam at a twenty-four-hour notice. I couldn't bring anything. I had only a small bag with change clothes for each person. We flew to America, but most people came on boat. I heard many horrible stories of escaping on boat. People who organized the trip only took gold. There were many dangers, especially when the boats went through Thailand. There were pirates who robbed anything valuable including clothes. There were storms. I heard stories that people drank urine when there was no water on boat. Everyone had a terrible story. But people would rather risk their lives than live under the Communists.

We first stayed in a refugee camp in Guam Island for two weeks for security clearance. After the clearance we were moved to another refugee camp in California where refugee families were matched with American families that would sponsor them. Finally, we went to Arkansas to wait for a sponsor. We stayed for six weeks in the refugee camp in Arkansas. I didn't like the conditions in camps. We had to get in line for food. I didn't want to be in line because it was humiliating. So I only had one meal a day. There were buses bringing newcomers from time to time. I looked for friends inside the camp and found some. We were all uncertain about our future.

My sponsor was from Bay, Missouri, a farming area. We stayed with her for one year when she was responsible for our living. The government gave her $500 per person at one time. When I met my sponsor I asked her questions. How would people receive us? Is there a job for me? Is there a school for my children? During my first year in the United States, I regretted leaving Vietnam. But I don't think I had a choice. I worried a lot, especially money. I didn't have money. I cried a lot at night. But I didn't cry in front of my children, because I wanted them to be free of worry. Many of my friends had the same feelings. Survival was a problem and I had to start all over again both financially and culturally; like a child, to learn everything. First year, I didn't have a job. My sponsor provided everything. I didn't like just receiving. My sponsor is a Christian, she did it for humanitarian reason. I appreciate her very much. But I didn't want to depend on anyone, that especially was not good for my children. Because my sponsor lived in a rural area, there was no job. She was quite wealthy and had a housekeeper. I went along with the housekeeper during the day to learn to use household machines of vacuum cleaner, washer, and drier. I tried to learn to cook American food. I also spent some time to write my resume.

In 1976, I found a job in St. Louis working for Lutheran Family Service. I lived on Russell Avenue, near South Grand in south side of St. Louis, because housing was cheaper there and there was a bus line.

But I knew that being a single woman living in city was scary. Starting from 1977, I worked for the International Institute for three years. From 1980 to 1986, I worked in Columbia for [a branch office of] the International Institute. In 1986, I came back to St. Louis to continue to work for the International Institute. I am a case manager at the Institute serving the elderly in community. I saw a lot of situations and a lot of difficulties. I try to help people, especially elderly people, cope with difficulties. My clients generally are undemanding and quiet. Most clients don't speak English and I try to mainstream them.[77]

Ngoc Doan's story was very similar to Ha's. Doan worked for the South Vietnamese government before the communist takeover. In 1980, at forty-two, he left Vietnam with his wife, a Vietnamese Chinese, and their ten-year-old daughter. They boarded a boat, like most Vietnamese refugees, and spent months at sea. After arriving in St. Louis, Doan, who had learned English in Vietnam, went to St. Louis Community College for one year. After this he enrolled at St. Louis University for three years to earn a bachelor's degree in computer science. After graduation he worked for the Emerson Company for eleven years. Later he worked for the International Institute as a consultant.[78]

The International Institute of Metro St. Louis provided a variety of services and programs to help refugees. The institute's social work department had the main responsibility for refugee settlement. It met refugees at the airport, found them apartments, helped them shop, helped them enroll their children in schools, and provided orientation for life in America. It also offered free English classes. It obtained benefits from the Missouri state government for them, including food stamps and rent and utility supplements. Its social workers provided counseling to help them cope with the trauma of fleeing Vietnam and the culture shock of coming to America.[79]

With the institute's help, most Vietnamese refugees found jobs within four months of arriving. Most worked as unskilled or semi-skilled laborers in factories; however, some professionals, such as Ha and Doan, found employment in private companies and institutions as computer programmers, engineers, and social workers.

In the first years of the settlement, most of the 10,000 Vietnamese refugees rented apartments in the south end of the city, where housing was less expensive and public transportation provided access to work and to public facilities. Most Vietnamese refugee families found gainful employment with steady income and worked hard, and within two or three years were able to buy homes in the suburbs.[80]

The Vietnamese refugees who settled in south St. Louis revitalized that area. Ethnic restaurants and grocery stores opened to serve their needs. Jay International Food at 3173 South Grand Avenue stocked many ethnic foods, and was heavily patronized by Vietnamese families as well as other ethnic St. Louisans.

In the 1970s and 1980s a number of Korean Chinese families came to St. Louis. Many of them entered the food service industry. There had been a strong demand for Chinese food in the area since the early 1970s. The Chinese began migrating to Korea during the late Qing dynasty (1644–1911), to escape famine, poverty, and domestic upheaval. The second wave of Chinese immigration to Korea occurred in the late 1940s, when the communists were about to take over China. Ninety percent of these later Chinese immigrants were from Shandong province, a peninsula two hundred miles from the Korean port of Inchon. Thus Inchon became their main entry port to Korea. Many of them later moved to Seoul, making Seoul the Korean city with the largest Chinese population. The discriminatory policies of the Korean government prevented ethnic Chinese from becoming Korean citizens. Many ethnic Chinese had lived in Korea for generations yet they still had to renew their certificates of residence every five years. Korean regulations also barred Chinese from owning large businesses and properties. As a result, most ethnic Chinese in Korea ended up running restaurants specializing in Shandong cuisine. Tired of the discrimination they faced in Korea, some ethnic Chinese left the country. Of the 20,000 ethnic Chinese in Korea, about 1,000 have immigrated to the United States or Taiwan since the 1970s.[81]

Most Korean Chinese in St. Louis came from Seoul, where they had been operating restaurants. This made it easier for them to enter the restaurant business in the United States. The experiences of Sherwin Liou, owner of the Mandarin House, a well-known Chinese restaurant in St. Louis, exemplify in many ways those of the Korean Chinese in St. Louis.

> My grandfather migrated to Korea from Shandong during the Qing dynasty. He owned a store in Seoul dealing with import and export business. In 1937, Japanese occupied China. My parents were forced to leave for Seoul in 1940 to join my grandfather. I came along with my parents when I was only two or three years old. I grew up in Seoul

and I am a third-generation Korean Chinese. Later, Korean government forbade foreigners from engaging in import and export businesses and my family had to change to restaurant business specialized in Shandong cuisine.

Chinese immigrants in Korea were very conservative and traditional. We were proud of our Chinese heritage. I went to a Chinese language school in Seoul. I worked in my family restaurant and later married. My wife is also a native of Shandong.

In 1972, President Nixon visited Beijing and his visit aroused a fervent in America on Chinese cuisine, especially northern Chinese cuisine. In 1974, a big hotel in Queens, New York wanted to recruit Chinese chefs. The hotel dispatched recruiters to the chamber of commerce in Hong Kong, Tokyo, and Seoul to look for good Chinese chefs. Six Chinese chefs in Seoul were recruited and I was one of them. Before my departure from Seoul, however, the hotel changed its plan and my employment was canceled. At this point, an old friend of mine who wanted to open a Peking style Chinese restaurant in St. Louis invited me to come to help him. So I came to St. Louis with my wife and our three children, and my family became the second Korean Chinese family in the town. Now there are more than 20 Korean Chinese families in St. Louis. I helped my friend open Yen Ching, the first Peking and Szechuan cuisine restaurant in St. Louis, and later we opened second Chinese restaurant, China Garden. Finally, I opened my own restaurant, Mandarin House.

During our first ten years in St. Louis, we did not intend to stay in America. We still owned business in Korea and planned to go back there if we couldn't make it in St. Louis. But our children liked living in America. After living in St. Louis for ten years, we sold our business in Korea and decided to stay in America.

Mandarin House is one of the large Chinese restaurants in St. Louis. We serve primarily northern Chinese cuisine. We also serve popular Chinese American dishes and 95 percent of our clients are Americans. My restaurant has 11,000 square foot and it can serve 350 guests at one time. Many individual families order wedding banquets in my restaurant. Community organizations also hold large celebrations of Chinese holidays here.[82]

Mrs. Sui's story was similar. Her parents migrated from Shandong to Korea in the 1940s. Born and raised in Seoul, Sui went to a Chinese-language school for her education. Like most of her counterparts, she spoke Chinese with a thick Shandong accent. Sui and her husband, Yuansheng Sui, immigrated to the United States in the early 1970s, becoming the first Korean Chinese family in St. Louis. The Suis opened Yen Ching Restaurant with Peking and Szechuan cuisine, which appeared in restaurant critic John Heidenry's "Chinese Dining Guide" for *St. Louisan* in 1976 as one of eight important

Chinese restaurants.[83] Besides the restaurant, the Suis also own a soy sauce factory.[84]

Four-fifths of the one hundred Korean Chinese in St. Louis are like Sherwin Liou and the Suis: they run Chinese restaurants, most of which are husband-and-wife places specializing in Shangdong or northern Chinese cuisine. The Shandong Restaurant at 2021 Woodson Road is a typical Korean Chinese family restaurant. Its owners, Mr. and Mrs. Che, both had ancestors who immigrated from Shandong to Korea. The Ches came to St. Louis in 1983 and have been running the restaurant since. Its dining area is small—only about twenty seats. While Mr. Che cooks in the kitchen, Mrs. Che waits on customers. They serve northern Chinese cuisine, including dumplings, noodle soup, fried noodles, and hot bean sauce noodles, and their clients are Chinese and non-Chinese searching for authentic and inexpensive northern Chinese food.[85]

The new immigrants from Vietnam and Korea have reinforced and diversified the Chinese community in St. Louis. Most Vietnamese Chinese refugees lived at first in the southern part of the inner city and worked in assembly factories or as manual laborers. Many of them, especially the professionals, after some years of steady employment and stable income, were able to move out of the inner city and buy homes in the counties. Unlike the immigrants from Vietnam, the Korean Chinese came to St. Louis as links in an immigration chain and were helped by relatives and friends who were already in the city. Perhaps this immigration pattern influenced their career choices once they arrived, since most Korean Chinese landed in restaurant business, where they are now a significant factor in the city's Chinese food service industry.

CONCLUSION

The 1960s to the 1980s was a time of transition for the St. Louis Chinese community. Socially, urban renewal contributed to the decline of On Leong's political influence and frustrated Chinese St. Louisans' efforts to build a new Chinatown. The poignant story of Sam Wah laundry demonstrated the powerlessness of the Chinese community; it also highlighted the damage that urban renewal was doing to the city's ethnic heritage.

Demographically, Chinese St. Louisans had transformed themselves from urban Chinatown residents into suburban Chinese

Americans. The arrival of Vietnamese Chinese refugees and Korean Chinese beginning in the 1970s boosted the community's population and its social and demographic diversity.

Economically, after World War II, Chinese St. Louisans abandoned laundries for restaurants and groceries. The local Chinese economy is now characterized by a twofold dependence: businesses rely on ethnic networks for capital, labor, and material goods; but they also rely on the mainstream society for customers. Ethnic networks are crucial to starting and running a business, but it is the mainstream markets that decide whether those businesses will succeed. This has meant that Chinese restaurants have avoided clustering in one neighborhood; rather, they have spread out to keep the competition reasonable. Meanwhile, Chinese professionals have integrated themselves economically into the larger society as employees of large, established companies and institutions. Their close economic association with the larger society has determined that the Chinese community of St. Louis will no longer revolve around an inner-city enclave, or the suburban commercial strips.

7 Building a Cultural Community, 1960s–1980s

> ... individual men and women, such as scholars, teachers, journalists, industrialists, traders, entrepreneurs, and writers, who try to understand China intellectually and bring their conceptions of China to their own linguistic communities.
>
> —Tu Wei-ming, "Cultural China," *The Living Tree*

IN THE 1960s, with the disappearance of Hop Alley, the decline of On Leong, rising numbers of Chinese professionals, and the demographic shift to the suburbs, a new type of Chinese community, which I define as a "cultural community," began to take shape in the St. Louis area. The following factors contributed to the emergence of the cultural community. First, the economy of the St. Louis Chinese community changed so that a commercially based Chinatown district no longer had a reason to exist. Chinese restaurants now depended on mainstream customers and had to disperse if the industry as a whole was to prosper, and this worked against the formation of a new Chinatown neighborhood. Meanwhile, most Chinese St. Louisans were now professionals employed by large non-Chinese companies; they had integrated themselves with the mainstream economy and so had little incentive to promote a commercial Chinese district.

Second, urban renewal repeatedly frustrated the community's efforts to build a Chinese commercial district. Hop Alley, the original Chinatown in St. Louis, was demolished in 1966. The urban renewal projects of the 1970s impeded efforts by local Chinese to build a new Chinatown on Delmar Boulevard. Local Chinese feared that any action they took to build a new Chinatown would be nullified by future urban renewal schemes, and as a result they stopped making plans to build a new Chinatown. Meanwhile, the negative stereotypes associated with Chinatowns discouraged many in the community from taking steps to create a new Chinatown district.

Yet Chinese St. Louisans still felt a need for community. That need was no longer economic, since by now most Chinese in the region were professionals and enjoyed middle-class lives; rather it was based on cultural, emotional, and political aspirations. Culturally, they wanted to preserve their Chinese identity, which they feared they might lose as their population dispersed. Chinese-language schools and Chinese festivals were two results of this desire to preserve cultural identity. Most of the Chinese had by now integrated themselves professionally and economically into the larger society; even so, immigrant life had left them feeling culturally displaced, and they yearned for opportunities to discuss common issues and share common values with other members of their community. Furthermore, to protect their social and economic achievements and to make further progress, the Chinese would have to learn to speak in a louder and clearer voice; an ethnic community would serve as a means of political empowerment. These cultural, emotional, and political needs validated their efforts to build an ethnic community. But in the circumstances, this would be a cultural community rather than a physical one.

DEFINING THE CULTURAL COMMUNITY

Unlike many Chinese American communities across the country, the cultural community that developed in St. Louis had no physical boundaries. Instead it was defined by social boundaries, in terms of community organizations, Chinese churches, and Chinese language schools, as well as the city's Chinese restaurants, grocery stores, and other service businesses. Most elements of the cultural community, such as the churches and the language schools, did occupy physical structures, but these were scattered throughout the city and did not constitute a physical Chinatown. The Chinese businesses were also dispersed and thus did not constitute a physical commercial district. (For this reason, this chapter does not discuss Chinese businesses.) However, the cultural activities organized by Chinese groups generated a sense of community, and this in turn fostered a social and emotional space in which the cultural community could take root. Thus we can understand the cultural community as having two dimensions: physical, and social and emotional. Whether they were owned or rented, the facilities of the cultural institutions and community groups served as the physical space for the cultural community. The activities held at these facilities created the social space for the cultural community. The latter depended on the former but at the same time was more significant than the former in creating a cultural community.

Unlike geographically defined Chinese communities, the physical space of the cultural community was undefined and often unidentifiable, as the significant part of the community infrastructure possessed no permanent physical space. At the same time, its social space was easy to see: it was where Chinese-language classes were held, Chinese religious congregations convened, and cultural activities took place. Thus it is more relevant as well as more feasible to study the community's social space rather than its physical one. It is difficult to measure and analyze the social and emotional dimensions of a cultural community, but it is not impossible, when we focus on its key components, which may also define the community's social boundaries. These key components the community in St. Louis were three: community organizations, Chinese churches, and Chinese-language schools. An examination of these will help us understand the social and emotional dimensions of the cultural community. Although some of the community organizations and institutions discussed in this chapter existed before the 1960s, most were established during or after. All will be examined below.

New Community Organizations

The St. Louis Chinese Society

The St. Louis Chinese Society—in Chinese, *Zhonghua Xiehui*—was the first community organization for Chinese students and professionals. It was formed in 1962, by 150 families of Chinese professionals, and stated its mission as "to promote understanding and appreciation of America's culture to Chinese immigrants and students, to promote understanding and appreciation of Chinese culture to American people, and to foster fellowship and understanding between the members of the society and between members of the community in which they live."[1]

The St. Louis Chinese Society actually was founded in 1947 as a student club for Chinese attending Washington University and St. Louis University.[2] During the 1940s and 1950s most of its activities were cultural; it was a venue where Chinese students from China, Taiwan, and Hong Kong could get together for parties and to celebrate Chinese holidays. In 1955 it recast itself to include professionals. It met regularly at the International Institute.

The new St. Louis Chinese Society was more inclusive and also more ambitious. Ten years after its founding, its membership had increased to four hundred families, both Chinese and non-Chinese. Its community offerings had expanded; it now provided fellowship, cultural programs, and the celebration of Chinese holidays, especially the Chinese New Year.[3] In the early 1970s it replaced On Leong as the sponsor for the Chinese New Year celebrations in St. Louis; it also became the unofficial voice of the Chinese community in the mainstream media.[4] During the 1970s and 1980s, its peak years, its Chinese New Year celebrations and Christmas parties often attracted eight or nine hundred participants.[5]

The celebration of the Chinese New Year was not just a cultural occasion; it was also a barometer of the Chinese community's strength, and of the organizational and political clout of whichever community group sponsored it. In this regard, the St. Louis Chinese Society's sponsorship of traditional celebrations marked a sea change in the city's Chinese community. The society's growing influence, and the fact that 90 percent of its members were college graduates, highlighted three important facts: Chinese St. Louisans were evolving into a middle-class group; power in their community was shifting away from Cantonese-speaking merchants and earlier Chinese arrivals and toward Mandarin-speaking professionals and more recent arrivals; and the community was losing its insularity and becoming more open to the mainstream as well as more democratic within itself.

In its early years the St. Louis Chinese Society was a community organization without political leanings. In the late 1980s the Nationalist government in Taiwan began aggressively recruiting support from the overseas Chinese. The Overseas Chinese Affairs Commission—*Haiwai Gongzuo Weiyuanhui*—a Nationalist government agency in charge of overseas Chinese affairs, began to subsidize the St. Louis Chinese Society for its New Year celebrations. As a consequence, the St. Louis Chinese Society gradually lost its neutral stance and became a pro-Nationalist community organization.

The St. Louis Chapter of the Organization of Chinese Americans

Inspired by the civil rights movement, and encouraged by the growth of their community's population since 1965, Chinese Americans began to understand that they needed to form a national lobby group to protect the civil rights of Chinese Americans and to promote awareness of Chinese American culture. In 1973, in the national capital, representatives of Chinese Americans from Detroit, St. Louis, and Washington, D.C., convened to establish the national Organization of Chinese Americans (OCA; *Meihua Xiehui*).

A year earlier, the Chinese in St. Louis had formed the League of Chinese Americans; this group then became one of the three founding chapters of the OCA. The St. Louis OCA's mission statement indicated that it would strive "to foster American democracy, to uphold the Constitution of the United States of America, to eliminate prejudices and ignorance, to enhance the image of the Chinese in America, to promote active participation of Americans of Chinese ancestry permanently residing in the United States of America in civic and national life, and to secure justice and equal opportunity and equal treatment of Chinese Americans."[6] As a nonpartisan organization, the St. Louis OCA soon replaced the St. Louis Chinese Society as the most important community organization for Chinese American professionals.[7] Undoubtedly, the local branch of the OCA has been strengthened by the size and prestige of the headquarters group in Washington, D.C., which has a full-time staff, and its national chapters.[8]

The St. Louis Taiwanese Association

The St. Louis Taiwanese Association—*Taiwan Tongxiang Hui*— was formed in the early 1970s by speakers of the Taiwanese dialect. According to its mission statement, its mandate was to help the Taiwanese strengthen their identity and their links with the island, to foster friendships, to promote the native culture of Taiwan, and to encourage cultural exchanges between Americans and Taiwanese.[9] About a hundred Taiwanese families joined it. Because it promoted the native culture of Taiwan and because it distanced itself from the Nationalists, it was widely perceived as a lobby group for an independent Taiwan. Actually, it was not very different from other Chinese American community groups; most of its members were professionals from Taiwan who believed in promoting Taiwanese culture and identity.

The St. Louis Chinese Jaycees

The St. Louis Chinese Jaycees—*Zhonghua Qing Shang Hui*— was a chapter of the international Jaycees. Unlike other Chinese

American community groups, it was an offshoot of a mainstream organization. As the only Chinese chapter of Jaycees, it was established in 1976 with the mission to help young professionals and entrepreneurs improve their leadership skills. The official name of Jaycees was Junior Chamber of Commerce, commonly known as J.C. (Jaycees). The Jaycees' bylaws state that members must be under forty; officers of the organization must be under thirty-five.[10] One of its more popular programs was "speak-up," which focused on improving its members' public speaking skills so that they could use those skills to serve the community.

The St. Louis Chinese started a Jaycees organization for a number of reasons. First, at the time very few Chinese in St. Louis were involved in mainstream activities; this was mainly because they were unfamiliar with American political processes. As an organization rooted in its community, every Jaycee chapter took a keen interest in community affairs. The group's founders felt that a local and ethnically based chapter of Jaycees would help the Chinese in St. Louis make mainstream contacts. Second, the Jaycees made a specialty out of training community leaders. The founders of the St. Louis Chinese Jaycees realized that too many Chinese professionals and entrepreneurs had limited communication skills (in particular, English skills) and needed to improve them. Third and more importantly, as American citizens of Chinese ancestry, they knew they had to learn more about how democracy worked. The Jaycees' training programs would help them familiarize themselves with parliamentary procedures; this in turn would encourage them to involve themselves in mainstream politics.[11]

The St. Louis Chinese Jaycees had a relatively small membership and, it follows, limited influence in the community. In the 1990s they changed their name to "Asian Jaycees" to attract more members.

The Chinese Liberty Assembly

In 1979 a group of politically enthusiastic students from Taiwan formed the St. Louis branch of the Chinese Liberty Assembly (*Zhongguo Ziyouren Xiehui*). Most of its members were students attending Washington University and St. Louis University. When the U.S. government normalized diplomatic relations with China in 1979, pro-Nationalist students in St. Louis formed the organization to promote the influence of the Nationalist Party among the overseas Chinese. This organization's major activities have included the following: celebrating the National Day of the Republic of China (ROC) on 10 October ("Double Tens Day"); orienting Taiwanese students newly arrived in St. Louis; arranging activities to promote Chinese culture; and convening an annual academic conference.[12] The Chinese Liberty Assembly also published a monthly magazine, *Chinese Liberty Journal*. A number of professionals from Taiwan with interests in literature and journalism served as its editors. The magazine stayed in publication until April 1996, when an organizational change was carried out.[13]

In 1998 the Chinese Liberty Assembly changed its name to the Midwest Chinese American Science and Technology Association (MCASTA). Since then the organization has focused mainly on a flag-raising ceremony on 10 October each year and on the annual academic conference. It continues to support the Nationalist Party in Taiwan, but it has also transformed itself from a strongly political organization into a quasi-professional one. Its annual conference aims at promoting academic exchanges and communications.

The Chinese Cultural Center (St. Louis Overseas Chinese Educational Activity Center)

The Chinese Cultural Center was established in the early 1980s. After the normalization of Sino-U.S. relations, the Nationalist government in Taiwan had to adjust its policies toward the overseas Chinese. On 15 February 1979, the United States and the Nationalist government agreed that to look after Taiwan's interests, there should be an American Institute in Taipei to replace the American embassy and a Coordinating Council for North American Affairs in Washington, D.C. The Coordinating Council for North American Affairs would have consulate-like branches in nine major cities.[14] The Nationalist government at the same time directed its Overseas Chinese Program Department to establish Chinese Cultural Centers in major American cities to promote the interests of the Nationalist government among Chinese American communities. Thus the Chinese Cultural Centers in the United States were referred to as "unofficial consulates" representing the Nationalist government in America after it lost legal representation in 1979. The centers received funds from the Nationalist Party and the ROC government to support Chinese-language education in the United States and to provide publications on Chinese culture, history, and government policies.[15]

The Chinese Cultural Center in St. Louis, like its counterparts in other American cities, sponsored many cultural activities, including workshops promoting Chinese culture, seminars introducing American ways of life, and art exhibits displaying works by Chinese students from Taiwan enrolled at higher educational institutions in St. Louis. The library of the Chinese Cultural Center, with a stock of thousands of books and magazines on Chinese culture, history, literature, and politics, was open daily to the public. As an agency funded by the Nationalist Party, the center invited and entertained various delegations and individuals connected with the Nationalist Party in Taiwan. It also held the annual flag-raising ceremonies on 10 October. Nevertheless, the Chinese Cultural Center helped foster a cultural community in St. Louis, and the center itself served as important physical location for the St. Louis Chinese American cultural community.

In 1994, austerity measures compelled the Nationalist Party to stop funding the Chinese Cultural Centers in the United States. After that, the funding and management of the Chinese Cultural Centers were transferred to the Overseas Chinese Affairs Commission of the Republic of China. The names of the centers were for that reason changed to the Overseas Chinese Educational Activity Centers; they were now community organizations receiving subsidies from the Overseas Chinese Affairs Commission. Although the name was changed, the St. Louis Overseas Chinese Educational Activity Center (*Qiao Jiao Zhong Xin*) continued to sponsor the same activities as before. Because they were community organizations, the centers' funding from the Overseas Affairs Commission was challenged by the Department of the Treasury of the ROC government and was eventually cut off. The Center in St. Louis was forced to close at the end of December 2001 as a result of the budget crunch.[16]

CHINESE CHURCHES

The St. Louis Chinese Gospel Church

The earliest Chinese church was the St. Louis Chinese Gospel Mission (*Zhonghua Fuyin Jiaohui*; see Chapter 3). In October

1924, Miss Chiles, a retired missionary, gathered a group of Chinese children and started the Sunday school, thus laying the foundation for the first Chinese Christian church in St. Louis.[17]

The period from 1924 to the early 1940s was the first stage of the development of the church, when American Christian workers provided this church with leadership and organization. The Chinese Sunday school rented a room from the St. Louis Gospel Church on Washington Street, which held morning services for an American congregation. Then in the afternoons, Chiles and her enthusiastic helpers—mostly small business owners and working-class Americans—would drive Chinese children and their parents to the Sunday school. In the early years of the St. Louis Chinese Gospel Church, the congregation consisted mainly of women and children, since most Chinese men were reluctant to attend because of the language barrier and their lack of familiarity with Christianity.

After almost two decades of hard work, the small congregation began to grow. By the early 1940s it had become necessary for the Chinese congregation to find its own space. During World War II, however, the U.S. government had to ration daily necessities and most Americans lived simple and frugal lives. Despite the financial difficulties, the devoted American Christian workers donated $10,000 for the purchase of a two-story building at 4237 McPherson Street to be used as a Chinese church.[18]

The Chinese Gospel Mission's move to McPherson marked the beginning of the second stage of the church—from the 1940s to 1990, when Chinese Christians emerged as leaders of the congregation. Mr. Pond, a local Chinese tailor, became the church's organizer. Every Saturday afternoon he cleaned up the building for Sunday worship. On weekdays he and his wife Beulah visited the Chinese laundries and restaurants. Pond continued this work until his death in 1961.[19]

Four Chinese pastors served the congregation from the late 1960s to 1990. Meanwhile the church continued to expand. In the late 1960s, Fred Cheung, a youthful and energetic minister from Hong Kong, came to lead the church. His devotion and pioneering work laid a solid foundation for further development of the church. About fifty Chinese families attended the Sunday services regularly.[20] The congregation grew until in 1968 the church on McPherson had reached its capacity. Since more Chinese St. Louisans were living in the suburbs, the church decided to move to a suburban location. At this point the church was between ministers: Cheung had accepted a position in Washington, and Peter Lai, the new minister from Detroit, had not yet arrived. The church was administered by a board of elders headed by Shing Chu, a mechanical engineer and a student at Covenant Theological Seminary in St. Louis. In 1969 the church bought an old building at 644 Bompart Avenue in the suburb of Webster Groves, which would be easily accessible to most of the congregation. The board of elders decided to change the church's name to the St. Louis Chinese Gospel Church and to renovate the old building, which had been built in 1904 during the World's Fair. The renovation included raising a sign in both English and Chinese outside the church and repairing the kitchen, which the previous congregation had not used.[21]

Peter Lai led the church from 1969 to 1974. Under his ministry the church continued to grow. Many local Chinese families and senior citizens attended the services regularly. Many of the church's members were professionals. For instance, Richard Hong, an electrical engineer in Ballwin, and his brother Kenneth, a student at Kansas State University, were faithful members of the church.[22]

Stephen Liang served as minister from 1976 to 1980; he was replaced in 1982 by William Hsueh. Under Hsueh's ministry the church began to develop steadily. One significant development was the appearance of more and more young Chinese, of high school age or younger, most of whom had grown up in the church. To meet the needs of these parishioners, John People came to the church as a youth pastor. The youth ministry successfully served more youth who were attracted to the church.

By the end of 1980s the church had again outgrown its building, as new members, visitors, graduate students, and scholars from Mainland China joined the congregation. The church decided that instead of moving into an existing church, it would build a new one from scratch. With funds donated by the members, the church purchased a lot at 515 Meramac Station Road. The new building was completed in December 1990. The new structure included a sanctuary, classrooms, a kitchen, and a gymnasium.[23]

With the completion of the new church building, the St. Louis Chinese Gospel Church now entered its third stage. To accommodate the American-born youth and new members who did not speak Cantonese, the Sunday services were presented in English, and then translated into Mandarin and Cantonese for senior citizens and for those who did not understand English well. The dual-language services indicate that the church was trying to serve the Chinese community while reaching out to the larger society. As a result of its constant efforts at outreach, the membership had grown to 142 adults and 42 children by 1999, and included Chinese St. Louisans in all walks of life.[24]

The St. Louis Chinese Christian Church

The St. Louis Chinese Gospel Church was the oldest Chinese church in the area; many of its members spoke Cantonese. The St. Louis Chinese Christian Church was one of the largest; most of its congregation spoke Mandarin. It was founded in 1974 as a Bible study place for a group of Chinese students from Hong Kong, Taiwan, and Malaysia studying at Washington University. In time it grew into a congregation of more than two hundred.

This church's membership closely reflected the profile of the Chinese St. Louisans. About 60 percent of them were professionals working at Monsanto Chemical, McDonnell-Douglas, Anheuser-Busch, IBM, and Southern Illinois University at Edwardsville; 20 percent were undergraduate and graduate students at Washington University, St. Louis University, the University of Missouri at St. Louis, Maryville University, and Meramec Community College; 15 percent were elderly, parents of Chinese from Taiwan and China; the remaining 5 percent were restaurant or other small business owners. Besides weekly religious services, the church also provided many meaningful social services for the Chinese cultural community, from fundraising for emergency relief to babysitting, family counseling, and visits to hospitalized church members.[25]

The above two capsule histories indicate that the Chinese churches always tried hard to meet the spiritual, social, and cultural needs of the Chinese in St. Louis. The syncretistic attitude of the Chinese toward religions, long noted by writers of Chinese American and East Asian studies, was also undoubtedly present among the Chinese St. Louisans.[26] The practical and even secular approach of the Chinese to religions made the social and cultural functions of the Chinese churches more significant and crucial in the building of the cultural community.

CHINESE-LANGUAGE SCHOOLS

The Chinese in St. Louis had attempted to establish Chinese-language schools early in the century, but failed to sustain them.

The earliest attempt was in 1916, when the Chinese Nationalist League of America was founded in St. Louis. The league's corporation deed stated that one of its purposes was to provide for the education of boys and girls of Chinese birth or descent.[27] It was unclear whether the league sponsored a Chinese-language school for Chinese youth; no other evidence can be found that they did. However, a later effort in the 1960s by On Leong and Shien-Biau Woo and Chia Wei Woo, two doctoral students at Washington University, did succeed. Shien-Biau Woo and Chia Wei Woo taught Chinese children reading and writing in Chinese. Unfortunately, the school was forced to close two years later, when Shien-Biau Woo and Chia Wei Woo graduated from Washington University and no replacements for them could be found.[28] The school's failure has been attributed to the shortage of Chinese-language instructors and lack of interest among the Chinese children.[29]

Chinese-language schools in St. Louis were able to survive permanently only after the late 1970s. Two factors contributed to their success. First, the rapid population increase among Chinese in St. Louis beginning in the 1970s raised the issue of Chinese-language education. Unlike the earlier Chinese immigrants, most Chinese in St. Louis now were family oriented. Chinese parents generally hoped their offspring could learn the Chinese language in order to inherit the Chinese heritage, to communicate with grandparents and relatives outside the United States, and possibly to enhance future employment opportunities in China, Hong Kong, Taiwan, and overseas Chinese communities. This common desire from Chinese parents generated a public interest in establishing Chinese-language schools.

Second, the development of Chinese-language schools across the United States since the 1970s (a result of the more liberal 1965 immigration law, which brought more Chinese immigrant families to the country) provided useful models and invaluable experience for the Chinese in St. Louis. According to Him Mark Lai, the Chinese-language schools in America have experimented with different models: full-time Chinese-language schools, daily afternoon Chinese-language schools after regular public school, and weekend Chinese-language schools, with the first two models found mainly in older and more established Chinese communities and the third developing in more recent decades throughout the country.[30] Inspired by schools in other Chinese American communities, the Chinese in St. Louis adopted the weekend model, and were able to sustain and expand their Chinese-language schools. In the late 1970s, two language schools—the St. Louis Chinese Academy and the St. Louis Chinese Language School—were established in St. Louis.

The St. Louis Chinese Academy

On 8 July 1978 the St. Louis Chinese Academy (*Shengluyi Zhonghua Yuwen Xuexiao*) was established in a classroom at Washington University by Wang Yun. The classes met every Sunday afternoon for three hours from 1:30 to 4:30. Since Chinese from Taiwan comprised most of the Chinese community in St. Louis, the traditional Chinese characters (*fantizi* or *zhengtizi*) and a phonetic system of *zhuyin fuhao*, prevalent in Taiwan, were taught, and Mandarin Chinese was used as the medium. In the beginning there were about thirty students in three classes of different levels.

In the 1980s, as the population of Chinese Americans continued to grow, the St. Louis Chinese Academy developed rapidly. The classes increased from three to seven, and the curriculum expanded to include Chinese folklore, architecture, and games. Chinese-language classes were taught in the first two hours, and electives—Chinese dance, painting and calligraphy, fine arts, and martial arts—were taught in the third hour. A Board of Governors was formed to regulate and manage the school. The principals of the school in the 1980s included Patricia L. Yeh, Zongni Tong, James Yeh, and Shumei Wu, most of them professionals from Taiwan.[31]

The St. Louis Chinese Language School

In the fall of 1978, Grace Shen Lo, a biochemist from Taiwan, established the St. Louis Chinese Language School (*Shengluyi Zhongwen Xuexiao*) using space at the St. Louis Chinese Baptist Church. The school's mission was to teach the Chinese language, to promote Chinese culture, and to provide cultural services to the community. At first there were only twelve students with different abilities in written Chinese. The following year, the school opened its doors to the public and forty-six students enrolled.

Like the St. Louis Chinese Academy, the St. Louis Chinese Language School also used Mandarin and adopted the traditional Chinese characters and *zhuyin fuhao*. The school met every Sunday afternoon from 2:20 to 4:30 during each academic year. Throughout the 1980s the school expanded as enrollment increased. Besides the two-hour-long Chinese-language classes, it also offered other extracurricular activities—Chinese chess, calligraphy, painting, dance, and crafts. Grace Shen Lo, Daoxing Wang, Dachung Peng, and T. Leo Lo, most of them scientists and engineers from Taiwan, served as principals of the school during the 1980s.

The two Chinese-language schools in St. Louis shared similar successes and frustrations. Student enrollment at both increased steadily every year, matching the population growth of Chinese Americans in the city. At each school the curriculum grew more diverse and flexible in response to students' needs. A less recognizable but more significant success of these schools, however, went far beyond academic achievements. They were serving as vital community cultural and social centers, as places where parents could exchange practical information and share their common cultural heritage while their children were taking classes or participating in other activities. In this sense, the Chinese-language schools were not only transmitting Chinese heritage to the younger generation, but also providing glue to hold the Chinese community together. The social and psychological value of the Chinese-language schools must not be underestimated.

The Chinese-language schools enjoyed curricular successes and popular support from the community, but they were also confronting constant obstacles. In particular, they had great difficulty finding places to hold classes that were convenient for the students as well as affordable. Since the rents the schools paid directly affected tuition fees, this was a central concern. With rents always going up, both schools were always having to search for new locations and move once they found them, in order to satisfy both aforementioned criteria and to meet the ever-growing enrollment.

DOMINANCE OF THE PROFESSIONALS FROM TAIWAN

As noted earlier, the Chinese cultural community in St. Louis is now dominated by Chinese professionals from Taiwan. Most Chinese community organizations and churches and all of the Chinese-language schools were started by Taiwanese Chinese and are operated by them. Unsurprisingly, this reflects a national trend—Chinese American professionals from Taiwan have been entering every aspect of Chinese American life since the 1970s. This has been a direct result of the "study-abroad" wave that developed in Taiwan beginning in the 1960s.[32]

The 1965 Immigration Act allotted every country in the Eastern Hemisphere, regardless of its size, a quota of 20,000 immigrants. This has meant that more Chinese from Taiwan have been able to come to America. It has also meant that Chinese immigration has doubled. In the 1960s, with universities and colleges closed in Mainland China by the Cultural Revolution, a study-abroad craze developed on Taiwan. University and college graduates yearned to pursue graduate studies abroad, especially in the United States.[33] Between 1950 and 1974, the Taiwanese education ministry approved 30,765 students for advanced studies in the United States.[34] Over the following decades the number of Chinese students from Taiwan rose rapidly. Between 1979 and 1987 around 186,000 students came to America to continue their education.[35]

The study-abroad movement in Taiwan has had three stages: development, peak, and decline. The movement developed in the 1950s and 1960s, peaked from the 1970s to the 1990s, and has been declining since the late 1990s.[36] This movement had its roots in success of the postwar Taiwanese economy. In the 1950s and 1960s that island experienced economic growth accompanied by structural and demographic changes. The nonagricultural sector—especially the manufacturing sector—rose dramatically in importance. Industrial development required better trained and more highly educated personnel. At the same time, a demographic transition from high to low fertility, coinciding with a shift in income distribution toward greater equality, changed people's attitudes toward child-rearing; higher incomes and fewer children enabled parents to support their children's desire to obtain advanced degrees in the United States.[37]

This social and economic transformation resulted in foreign studies becoming wildly popular among Taiwanese beginning in the 1950s. A popular adage on the island at the time best illustrates this phenomenon: "Everyone desires to study in the National University of Taiwan (*Taida*) or Donghai (Tung-hai) University, and then go to America" (*lai lai lai, lai Taida, qu qu qu, qu Mei Guo; lai lai lai, lai Donghai, qu qu qu, qu Mei Guo*). The National University of Taiwan is the most prestigious public university, and Donghai University is the most prominent private institution in Taiwan. Every Taiwanese youth aspired to be admitted by one of these top universities for an undergraduate education, and then to pursue graduate studies in America.[38]

Taiwanese students came to America through three main channels. Most of them were self-sponsored. In 1950 the Nationalist government decreed that every high school graduate who had been granted a four-year scholarship from a foreign institution and who had passed the standard study-abroad test administered by the government could study abroad. This regulation was phased out in 1955 because it was too easy to finesse. A new law took its place that specified that only graduate students who had passed the governmental study-abroad examination could study overseas. Between 1953 and 1975, 25,000 university graduates passed the standardized tests. The second group of Taiwanese students were government-sponsored. To send the most talented to obtain advanced knowledge from abroad so that they could serve the island's drive for modernization, the Nationalist government had been holding Study Abroad Scholarship Examinations since 1955. About 5,000 graduate students came to America on government scholarships between 1955 and the 1990s. Visiting scholars from Taiwan comprised the third group of newcomers. In 1961 the Taiwanese education ministry drafted a regulation permitting all public and private higher educational and research institutions to sponsor qualified scholars to pursue advanced training or education abroad. Between 1961 and 1995, 5,000 scholars were selected to study abroad.[39]

In the early years, most Taiwanese students were from families with links to the Nationalist Party and its government and were self-sponsored. Dependent on American scholarships or on incomes earned in summers and during the academic year, the Taiwanese students worked diligently for their advanced degrees. Because the Taiwanese economy was still far behind the American one, most Taiwanese students elected to stay in the United States after completing their education. In 1950 the Taiwanese education ministry issued a bulletin, "Measures to Supervise Returned Study Abroad Students." In 1955 the Executive Yuan established a Committee to Supervise Returned Study Abroad Students; its main responsibility was to encourage students to return to Taiwan and arrange for their return. In 1971 this committee was placed under the Youth Supervision Commission (Qing Fu Hui) of the Executive Yuan. Qing Fu Hui's statistics indicate that between 1950 and 1971 only 2,341 Taiwanese students returned to the island (only 7.7 percent).[40]

In the second stage, four factors propelled Taiwanese students to study in the United States. First, the reconciliation between the United States and the People's Republic of China (PRC) in 1972 generated diplomatic and political crises in Taiwan. Following the lead of the United States, most allies broke their ties with Taiwan and established diplomatic relations with the PRC. Taiwan's diplomatic isolation resulted in profound political instability, which drove many Taiwanese to seek a future outside their island. Second, a relaxation of Taiwanese government policies relating to study abroad made it easier for those who wished to study in America. Since the 1970s the government in Taiwan has been simplifying its policies on study abroad. In 1976 it abolished the standardized study-abroad test; self-sponsored students could now study in a foreign country simply by providing a certificate of foreign-language proficiency. In 1979 the Ministry of Education revised its policies again to permit self-sponsored students to study abroad without letters of recommendation. In 1989 the policies were simplified even further so that self-sponsored students could leave the country without permission from the education ministry. Since then, 20,000 self-sponsored students a year have been coming to the United States. Third, economic prosperity in Taiwan enabled Taiwanese to study abroad. The economic boom in Taiwan that began the 1970s placed Taiwan among the industrialized countries. The earning power of the Taiwanese greatly increased; per capita income reached $2,000 in the 1980s and $10,000 in the 1990s. This meant that more parents could afford to send their children to study overseas. Many college graduates would work for a few years after graduation while studying English and applying to an American institute. Once admitted by a graduate school in America, a Taiwanese college graduate could use the money he or she had saved to support advanced studies in the United States. Fourth, the more diverse and advanced graduate programs at American universities attracted many Taiwanese students. Even at the National University of Taiwan, the most prestigious school on the island, there was a shortage of qualified faculty and less choice among academic programs.[41]

During this stage, most Taiwanese students still chose to stay in the United States after completing their education or training.

Many of them were employed by research and higher educational institutions and by private companies; a few became entrepreneurs. At the same time, a steadily increasing number of students returned to Taiwan. Between 1971 and 1991, 24,981 students—20 percent of the total Taiwanese students in the United States—returned to Taiwan. Since 1992, the figure for Taiwanese student returnees has increased annually: from 5,157 in 1992, to 6,172 in 1993, to 6,150 in 1994, to 6,272 in 1995.[42]

Since the late 1990s the study-abroad movement in Taiwan has declined, for three main reasons. First, graduate education in Taiwan improved tremendously and is now internationally competitive. Beginning in the late 1980s, many graduate schools in Taiwan began requiring students, before they could graduate, to produce an essay publishable in a reviewed international journal. This helped lift graduate education in Taiwan into the international class and made study abroad less desirable. Second, the Internet, and the electronics industry as a whole, became widely accessible from Taiwan, which reduced the importance of study abroad. Third, young Taiwanese (i.e., those born after 1980) were now accustomed to their material comforts and were no longer interested in the long-term studies abroad. Many were now choosing to attend foreign summer programs to improve their foreign-language skills or to obtain specialized training.[43]

During the first two stages of the study-abroad movement, the Taiwanese Chinese in St. Louis were mainly students turned professionals. They were determined settlers; having found employment in St. Louis, they committed themselves to the local community. Professionals from Taiwan invested tremendous amounts of time, energy, creativity, and money to build a Chinese cultural community in St. Louis. Their contributions have made them the dominant force in the community's infrastructure.

ASSESSMENT OF THE CULTURAL COMMUNITY

Between the 1960s and the 1980s the Chinese in St. Louis made a strong effort to establish and develop a cultural community. From the very beginning this community had some unique characteristics.

First, regarding the community's geography, it is clear that it had no physical concentration in terms of buildings or neighborhoods. None of the community organizations owned or rented its own meeting place or activity center. Instead, these organizations convened in facilities provided by the mainstream society or at the homes of board members, and rented space from private or public facilities as they required it for large-scale cultural activities. The Chinese churches were either rented or owned by the congregations, but they were also scattered throughout Metro St. Louis. The Chinese-language schools, like the Chinese churches, required at least semipermanent locations for their weekend classes, but these spaces were always rented from schools or churches. This absence of any geographical concentration of cultural facilities was partially a result of the residential pattern of Chinese St. Louisans; by now they were spreading out into suburban middle-class or upper-middle-class neighborhoods. In part this was because they rejected the idea of inviting racial profiling by developing an ethnic enclave.[44]

Second, the Chinese cultural community in St. Louis was dominated by professionals, who were also the demographic majority. These professionals were the community's power brokers. It was they who established and operated most of the community organizations and institutions. It was they who took charge of the community's cultural activities. Their motives for becoming so involved in the community were cultural rather than economic. As professionals, they had already integrated themselves with the larger society and had little vested interest in exploiting an ethnic community for their economic benefit. Yet they still yearned for an ethnic community, for their own cultural welfare and that of their children.

Third, there were no class divides or tensions within the community, as there so often were among the Chinese in other major American cities. The community's members belonged to the same social class as its leaders. A working class did exist in Chinese St. Louis, but it was dispersed throughout the city, in the kitchens of Chinese restaurants and in the stockrooms of Chinese grocery stores, and thus it was unable to develop into a strong and visible social force (see Chapter 8).

Yet even without physical boundaries, this cultural community was strong, cohesive, and tightly knit. Together, the community organizations and cultural institutions succeeded in creating a visible and indispensable ethnic community. By offering a wide array of activities and events, the cultural community bound its members together and rendered them vital social and emotional support. In this way it constituted an alternative model for ethnic communities—one in which there was no physical concentration and no discernible enclave.

8 Development of the Cultural Community, 1990s–2000s

AFTER ITS BUILDING PERIOD from the 1960s to 1980s, the Chinese American cultural community in St. Louis entered a stage of rapid development. Demographically, it embraced a more diverse population, including a large number of Chinese students and professionals, who had been arriving from Mainland China since the late 1980s. Their presence led to a structural realignment within the cultural community—one characterized by the increasing numbers of business owners and professionals from China, the teaching of simplified Chinese characters in the Chinese-language schools, and the growing influence of the St. Louis Chinese Association, a community organization whose members are mostly Mainland Chinese.

The emerging Chinese-language press in St. Louis has done a great deal to promote the Chinese ethnic economy, to preserve Asian American ethnic heritage, and to link the cultural community to the larger society. The new ethnic economy is now more diversified than the previous one, which centered on the traditional service industries of laundry and restaurants. It now embraces not only a growing and more competitive food service industry, but also rapid expanding nontraditional service industries such as real estate, health, insurance, construction, architecture and design, legal consultation, accounting, auto repair, and computer services.

At the same time, the cultural community has become more politicized than ever before. Because of the community's complexity, its members have divided along various lines reflecting dialect, places of birth, occupations, political leanings, religious beliefs, and cultural interests. Yet even while divided in this way, Chinese St. Louisans are at the same time united by common interests and by their commitment to preserve and promote the Chinese American culture and to protect and improve their place in America through social and economic integration and political empowerment.

STRENGTHENING THE CULTURAL COMMUNITY:
CHINESE STUDENTS AND PROFESSIONALS FROM
MAINLAND CHINA

New demographic changes have been taking place in St. Louis. According to U.S. censuses, since 1980 the Chinese population of St. Louis has more than tripled, from 2,484 in 1980 to 4,658 in 1990, to 9,120 in 2000.[1] Various unofficial estimates, however, give a figure between 15,000 and 20,000.[2] Mainland Chinese, estimated to be about 5,000 strong in the area, have contributed greatly to this growth.[3] Since most Mainland Chinese came to the United States as students pursuing higher education or professional training, a brief history of study-abroad programs in Mainland China would be useful to understand recent demographic changes in St. Louis.

The Study-Abroad Movement and Tiananmen Incident

The study-abroad movement first emerged in China as a result of China's response to Western aggression against China in the wake of the Opium Wars of the 1840s and 1850s. The Self-Strengthening Movement (1861–94) was an attempt by the Chinese Qing government to modernize China militarily and technologically in order to cope with the Western powers and in order to control the countryside, which was afflicted with domestic turmoil in the decades following the Opium Wars. It was this movement that spearheaded the study-abroad movement in China. Between 1872 and 1881, 120 Chinese students studied in the United States, supported directly by the Qing government's scholarships.[4] In 1884, Li Hongzhang (Li Hung-chang), one of the chief engineers of the Self-Strengthening Movement, sent seventeen students to study shipbuilding in Britain, France, and Germany, and nine students to Britain to learn navigation.[5] In the following two decades the number of Chinese students entering colleges and universities in the United States totaled 32.[6] There were still only 50 Chinese students in America in 1903.[7] After 1909, however, the number of the Chinese students in the United States began to increase rapidly. There were 239 by 1909, 292 by 1910, and 650 by 1911.[8] This rapid increase was partly due to China's Westernization movement and partly due to the Boxer Indemnity Fellowship, which provided scholarships for selected Chinese students to study in the United States.[9]

After the Republic of China was established in 1912, the new government continued to send students abroad to study. Besides national scholarships, there were provincial and private ones. As a result, by 1922 the number of Chinese students in America had increased to 1,446, including 135 women.[10]

In the 1930s and early 1940s the study-abroad movement was interrupted by the Sino-Japanese War (1937–45). To further the reconstruction and modernization of China, the postwar Nationalist government continued the study-abroad program; thus many more students came to America in the immediate postwar period. According to a survey by the China Institute in America, the number of Chinese students in America increased from 706 in 1943 to 3,914 in 1948.[11]

The Chinese Communist Party founded the People's Republic of China (PRC) in 1949. The new government, like its predecessors, relied on foreign countries to train its specialists. For the next few decades, however, the Soviet Union was the only foreign power friendly to China; for this reason the Chinese government kept sending students there until the 1960s, when relations between Moscow and Beijing deteriorated. At that point, Mao Zedong placed China on a reclusivist course and began promulgating policies of self-sufficiency and self-reliance. During the Cultural Revolution (1966–76), international exchange programs were essentially suspended and no one was sent abroad to study, except for 1,629 students, most of whom studied foreign languages.[12] Following the Sino-American reconciliation in 1972, the PRC government again began to view study abroad as a shortcut to acquiring advanced scientific and technical knowledge. The decision to begin scholarly exchanges was made in 1978, even before relations with the United States were normalized in 1979. Since then these cultural exchanges have been vital to relations between the two countries.

The study-abroad movement has been highly popular in China since 1979; people are simply better off with an American degree. For middle-aged and established scholars, study abroad became a prerequisite for promotion. For young university or college graduates, an advanced degree from a foreign institution—especially one in the United States—marked the beginning of a promising career in China. For many of these people, studying overseas meant not only academic advancement but also material gain, in terms of the savings they could build from their meager scholarships and stipends and from income earned while abroad. Although these savings were small by American standards, many Chinese were able to buy their families modern appliances and electronics once these savings were converted into Chinese currency at a highly favorable exchange rates. Many other Chinese wanted to study in the United States so that they could find a way to stay there.[13]

Motivated by their own personal dreams and expectations, more and more Chinese students and scholars entered the United States after 1979. According to Chinese government records, between 1979 and 1988, 36,000 Chinese students studied in the United States.[14] The U.S. government has placed the figure even higher than this. Jesse Chain Chou found that that there were 63,000 students and scholars from the PRC over the same years.[15] The Immigration and Naturalization Service estimated that there were 73,000 Chinese students in the United States in 1989.[16] In a statement on 2 December 1989, President George Bush stated that "as many as 80,000 Chinese have studied and conducted research in the United States since these exchanges began."[17]

Chinese students and scholars came to America holding one of two visas: J-1, for government-sponsored students and scholars, and F-1, for self-supporting students. The J-1 visa was designed to slow the "brain drain," a problem faced by sending nations: students were coming to the United States for their education and then finding ways to stay permanently. American immigration policies required a J-1 visa holder to return to the home country for at least two years before re-entering the United States with a "green card" (signifying permanent resident status). Most government-sponsored students and scholars were issued J-1 visas, which meant that both the American and Chinese governments required them to serve the PRC after completing their education or training in the United States. Before 1989, almost two-thirds of Chinese students and scholars held J-1 visas.[18] In contrast, self-supporting students (F-1 visa holders) were financed either by American institutions of higher education or by relatives in the United States; this meant that the two-year home residence requirement did not apply to them.

The student democracy movement in China in the spring of 1989, and the crackdown on that movement by the Chinese government on 4 June 1989 at Tiananmen Square in Beijing—generally remembered as the Tiananmen Square Incident—provided new and unexpected opportunities for Chinese students and scholars with J-1 visas. After 4 June the Chinese government unleashed harsh persecution on supporters of the movement. Chinese students and scholars in the United States feared that the Chinese government would punish them when they returned to China, so they petitioned the U.S. Congress for a waiver of the two-year home-residence requirement for J-1 visa holders. On 30 November 1989, under pressure from the U.S. Congress and the general public, President Bush issued "Administrative Measures for PRC Nationals". to protect Chinese students involved in the democracy movement. This order waived the two-year foreign residence requirement for any Chinese national living in the United States on 1 December 1989, as well as employment restrictions on all Chinese nationals living in the United States on 5 June 1989.[19] In effect, the order lifted virtually all restrictions on J-1 visa holders from the PRC by allowing those living in the United States prior to 1 December 1989 to stay and work. Many Chinese students and scholars made the most of this order, and chose to stay in the United States permanently and to look for employment opportunities upon or even before completing their education or training. No official statistics are available, but unofficial sources indicate that after the Tiananmen Incident, as a result of the presidential order, more than 90 percent of Chinese J-1 holders arranged for permanent residence and became holders of the "June 4th green card," as it was commonly called. They found work—often professional work—in the United States, thus transforming themselves into professionals.[20]

Employment Patterns: Professionals and New Entrepreneurs

An unofficial estimate shows that in St. Louis there are about 5,000 Chinese from the PRC, including both professionals and students and their families. Most of the PRC professionals are employed by universities and private companies as professors, engineers, computer programmers, technicians, and administrators. Some of the city's larger employers—Monsanto Chemical, Washington University, and the University of Missouri at St. Louis—have hired many PRC professionals. Most students from the PRC are enrolled at Washington University and St. Louis University.[21]

The interviews and individual cases discussed below provide useful information on the experiences of Chinese professionals. Bin Sun came to the United States from Hubei, China, in 1992 to join her husband, a doctoral candidate in biochemical genetics at the University of Texas–Galveston. In 1993 she began her master's program in the same program at the same university; she graduated in 1995. In 1997 she moved to St. Louis with her husband, who had been hired by St. Luke's Hospital. She immediately found work at Monsanto Chemical. She described her work there:

I was hired by Monsanto in June 1997. First I was a contract technician. Monsanto hires a contract worker through an employment agent. Monsanto pays the contract worker at $21 per hour, of which the agent gets $7 and I get $14. After four months of being a contract worker, I became a regular employee. In addition to an annual salary I also get pension plan, 401K, paid vacation, and other benefits. My title is research biologist, studying molecular biology to enhance crop yield or nutritional traits of crops by biotechnology.

If you want a promotion and high bonus, you have to work hard. I have two supervisors. One is the personnel manager, who decides your wage, bonus, and project. The personnel manager usually sees you once a year, talking about your work and giving you feedback. A personnel manager normally has several projects. For every project, there is a Ph.D. holder as a project leader. The project leader has daily contact with employees. Usually there are three to five persons in a project. Some big projects have ten employees. The size of a project varies depending on the project and market. If a project has no market value, the company will stop the project. If a project is canceled, employees often change to other projects. Sometimes the company might dismiss some employees. An employee with a master's degree has a starting salary of $41,000. The pay varies according to personal experiences, fields, and market. Recently, the company is developing and has hired many Ph.D.s, many Asians. Asian Indians joined the company earlier and many are holding high-ranking positions. Many of the employees are from Mainland China, and the masters degree holders are mostly Chinese females. The company hired them because the Chinese women are obedient, diligent, and organized. They work very hard and make very few demands. American employees are usually very demanding. After a few years of employment, they would demand promotion and their own projects. Ph.D. holders usually are males and they are mostly project leaders.[22]

Bin Sun's description indicates the working conditions for most Chinese professionals at Monsanto. By working for a larger private company, a Chinese professional can receive competitive income and benefits, with only the remote possibility of unemployment. The company's hierarchy reflects cultural, racial, and gender differences. Asian employees, especially female ones, are perceived as model workers—obedient, disciplined, and effective. Asian Indian employees, as the company's more senior members, have joined the administrative hierarchy; Chinese professionals, the latecomers, serve as the front-line staff. In particular, female employees from China have been relegated to the base of the corporate ladder.

In recent years, professionals from the PRC have been climbing the ladder in the corporate world. Jingyue Liu's success exemplifies this progress. Liu graduated from the Science and Technology University of Beijing in the 1980s; in the early 1990s he earned his doctorate in physics from the University of Arizona. In 1994 he joined Monsanto as a researcher. Having been acknowledged as the first to recognize important characteristics of a particular catalyst, he tirelessly pursued detailed spectroscopic characterization to qualify his observations. Liu was among several scientists who discovered, developed, and successfully implemented a new catalyst technology for manufacturing glyphosate, the active ingredient in Monsanto's Roundup herbicide, which is revolutionizing some sectors of American agriculture. His research in microscopy and surface science was essential to this success. In recognition of his contribution, Monsanto promoted him to Science Academician—one of only twenty in the company as of 2000. In January 2002, Liu was selected as one of the five recipients of the 2001 Edgar M. Queeny Award for science and technology; this award came with a $50,000 grant.[23]

Compared to large corporations, academia provides Chinese professionals with more job security and professional freedom. Haiyan Cai's case is illustrative. Cai's mother was born in the United States in 1925; she and her family returned to China in the 1930s. In 1981 she immigrated to the United States as an American citizen; thus Cai was able to come to the United States as an immigrant in 1982. During his first year in America, Cai worked as a waiter in a Chinese restaurant in Washington, D.C. A year later he brought his wife to America and enrolled in the graduate program in mathematics at the University of Maryland at College Park. At first he had no scholarship, and his wife worked in a Chinese restaurant to support him. With the help of a professor from Taiwan, he obtained a research assistantship to work on a computer program for the U.S. Department of Agriculture. Five years later, in 1988, he completed his doctorate in mathematics. His wife enrolled in the bachelor's program in computer science at Maryland–College Park in 1984 and graduated in 1988.

After graduation, Cai was hired by the University of Missouri at St. Louis (UMSL). UMSL was not his top choice, but he and his wife enjoyed living in St. Louis and decided to stay. Six years later he was granted tenure and promoted to associate professor. He has spent much of his time conducting research and writing academic papers, which weigh heavily in tenure and promotion decisions in academia. He also enjoys teaching mathematics, although he is sometimes frustrated by students' lack of interest in statistics. Cai is fascinated by ancient Chinese philosophy, especially Daoism, and has become a highly active member of the cultural community. In 1997 the St. Louis Chinese Association (discussed in the following section) launched a literary journal, *The Chinese*. With the help of his wife, who had earned a bachelor's degree in Chinese literature at Xiamen University, Cai served as the journal's editor-in-chief.[24]

Cai's case typifies those of self-sponsored Chinese students; Xiaolong Qiu's represents those of government-sponsored students and scholars. Qiu was born in Shanghai in the 1950s. His father had been a factory owner in pre-1949 China, and because of this Qiu himself suffered discrimination during the Cultural Revolution, like most young Chinese from "bad families"—those of landlords, capitalists, and Nationalists. After the Cultural Revolution, Qiu established himself as a poet, literary critic, and translator in China and became a member of the prestigious Chinese Writers' Association. In 1988 he came to Washington University as a visiting scholar under a Ford Foundation fellowship. At first he planned to stay in the United States for only a year to complete his manuscript on T. S. Eliot at Washington University—an institution that Eliot's grandfather had established. The Tiananmen Incident of 4 June 1989 changed that plan. In the summer of 1989 he was shocked to discover, from a Voice of America broadcast, that he was on the Chinese government's list of supporters of the June 4th movement. Afraid that he would be persecuted if he returned, he immediately changed his status from visiting scholar to student; this was possible because of the presidential executive order protecting PRC nationals from retaliation by the Chinese government. Thus he was able to stay in the United States. Now he enrolled in the comparative literature program at Washington University, where he completed his doctoral degree in 1996. Since then he has been teaching Chinese literature at that university. During his years at Washington University, Qiu's literary career has flourished. He received the Missouri Biennial Award in 1994 and the Prairie Schooner Readers' Choice Award in 1996. He published his first novel in English, *Death of a Red Heroine*, in 2001, and a second novel, *A Loyal Character Dancer*, in 2002.[25]

By this time, Chinese were entering not only academia but also the highly competitive legal profession. While still in China, Zhihai Liang received advanced training in English; he earned a bachelor's degree in English and American literature from Shandong University and a master's degree in diplomatic English from the Foreign Affairs College—China's diplomatic training school in Beijing. A good command of English and a strong academic background earned him admission to the graduate programs of several prestigious universities in the United States, which also offered generous financial-aid packages. Instead, in 1987, he chose the St. Louis University Law School. Liang recalled his first experiences there:

> The second day after I arrived in St. Louis, barely beginning the process of overcoming the thirteen-hour time difference between Beijing and St. Louis, class started. This was by no means the only thing that made my adjustment to new life in America challenging. The $200 I brought with me from China did not get me very far after $140 for rent, $30 for a week supply of food, and the rest for textbooks. I soon found myself logging books in the law school library 15 to 20 hours a week to make a pre-tax $250 per month. This work schedule plus a full load of 15 credit hours per semester made the first few weeks of my life in America quite hectic. Law was a completely new subject to me—it was not particularly difficult as promised by some of my friends. But it was my part-time job necessitated by a scholarship that paid only my law school tuition that made me work hard every single day including holidays.[26]

Liang's experience reflected that of many Chinese students in American graduate schools. The academics were challenging, and unfamiliarity with American culture made them even more difficult. Liang had already been exposed to Western cultures through short-term tours with the United Nations in Europe, and he had a solid command of English, yet he still had to struggle with both. But the greatest challenge confronting him—and so many other Chinese students—was a lack of money. Like so many others, he was forced to spend much of his time working to make ends meet instead of concentrating on his studies. Liang's experience of beginning to practice law was also illustrative:

> Following my graduation in 1990, I worked for two years with the big law firm that I clerked for the previous summer before striking out on my own in 1992. In the early days of my practice, I took in all kinds of cases involving immigration, domestic matters, personal injuries, civil litigation, and even some criminal defense. My philosophy was that I ought to try and prove that I was every bit as good as a native-speaking lawyer. I filed lawsuits seeking damages and defended my clients in criminal matters. My English with foreign accent sometimes worked in my favor in court, in that some of the opposing counsels would not take me seriously and were not well prepared. However, my litigation victories did not come without comparable shares of scary moments and extra hours of work that I put in, for which I could not bill my clients.
>
> Being the first Chinese-speaking attorney in town gave me a leg up in tapping into a ready market. Today my practice concentrates on immigration, personal injuries, general corporate matters, international business, and some domestic matters, most of which can be done in office. I enjoy a very high rate of success in every category of cases I

handle, and sometimes achieve results that even surprise my colleagues. In the early nineties many immigration attorneys were counseling their clients to have a Nobel Prize or its equivalent to think about a Green Card based on outstanding achievement. An accomplished Chinese scientist in Illinois was shunned by prominent immigration lawyers in Chicago due to his employer's refusal to sponsor [him] for his Green Card application and his lack of a Nobel Prize. Following a thorough study of the law and meticulous documentation of his academic accomplishment, I filed my first case of self-petition under outstanding achievement category. He got his Green Card in 1992 and ended up working for a national research institution. I felt I won a Nobel Prize myself.

I have found my profession to be rewarding yet emotionally quite draining, in that you are happy to achieve the results your clients have desired, but those moments of accomplishment feeling are very brief, as there are always some problems waiting for you to solve and many of them are very challenging. In one case a student couple's four-year-old daughter was injured at the playground of a daycare center and their request for reimbursement of a meager $800 in medical expenses met with repeated denials. They went to a number of lawyers but were dismissed—the chance of proving negligence by the daycare center was too slim, plus the amount of damages was negligible. I took the case because I myself have a daughter who was not much older than the little girl at that time, and I myself was once a poor student and could very much appreciate the significance of a $800 bill. Several rounds of serious negotiations with the parties involved finally generated a five-digit settlement for the little girl. It is this kind of putting yourself in the shoes of your clients that motivates me to get the best result for them. At the same time, the quality of your personal life may take a toll for this level of emotional involvement in your clients' cases.

I am involved in OCA and the St. Louis Chinese Association, and volunteered to write articles on legal matters for these organizations.[27]

Tony Gao is another successful Chinese lawyer. He came to the United States in 1988 to study law at the St. Louis University Law School. He had already earned a master's degree in comparative law and foreign legal history from the East Chinese University of Political Science and Law in Shanghai, and had taught for three years at his alma mater. Although his scholarship covered his tuition and fees, he had to work to meet his living expenses. During his two years at law school he worked at the university library and on research projects. In 1991 he completed his studies, passed the bar exam, and joined a law firm, where he stayed for more than two years. In 1994 he opened his own legal practice:

> When I graduated, there was a local law firm that needed a lawyer to do immigration law. I sent my résumé and was hired. I couldn't get into big firm because I didn't know how to sell myself. I worked there for two and a half years. Then I opened my own office in April 1994. By

then I already had some trusted clients, but I still had some challenges. When I started, I had only one case. Now I have more than 500 cases, most of them in immigration. How you were initially involved becomes a routine, it is hard to change. About a half of my clients are Chinese. Other clients are companies. I have clients from all over the country representing all nationalities of China, Russia, India, Pakistan, Spain, Australia, New Zealand, Albania, Bulgaria, Kenya . . . . They are all immigrants. Many are from outside of St. Louis by referral.

The difficult part of the job is that I am too busy. I have to balance my time with family. My business has expanded threefold since 1994. I have a full-time associate and have to hire a part-time associate. Usually I arrive in my office at 9 am. I am on the phone for most of the time. I first deal with leftover work. Then e-mails and phone calls roll in. My associate does preliminary work. For some complicated cases, I have to handle them myself. I work till six or seven P.M. I go home for dinner and then come back to work till midnight. I used to work seven days, now I work six days. I often come to work on Sundays, because cases are time sensitive and there are deadlines to meet. Technically, clients would contact me and then we discuss their situation in detail. I will also review their documents and provide my analysis and pre-liminary opinion. I will tell them what I can do and what I cannot do. If I am hired, my associate will prepare various forms and letters, and I will review them. I have a lot of cases that I can't take, because I can't be expert in every field. If I were in China, I would have bigger practice and higher social status.

I am also involved in the St. Louis Chinese Association as a secretary. I participate in its board meeting every month and I took care of its legal preparation free of charge. I also took care of the Modern Chinese Language School's legal issues. Whenever there is a show, I donate money to it.[28]

Some Chinese in St. Louis established medical practices. Xinsheng Jiang's story is a testament to the initiative and ingenuity of doctors from Mainland China. Jiang graduated from Beijing Medical University in 1970 and for fourteen years was a physician in the neurology department of that university's hospital. In 1988 she came to the United States as a postdoctoral fellow in the department of neurology at the Ohio State University Hospital, where she conducted research related to musculoskeletal disease. Three years later she came to St. Louis and continued that research in the biology department at Washington University. While there she became acquainted with the local community and noticed a need for a traditional Chinese medical practice. In 1997 she decided to start an acupuncture practice in the back of the Oriental Ginseng and Gift Shop on Olive Boulevard. Jiang believed in the traditional Chinese medical theory of restoring the balance between *yin* and *yang*, the two opposing forces in the human body. Soon, several hundred patients were seeing her regularly. For each treatment of thirty to sixty minutes she charges $35 to $40—much less than her American counterparts. Her patients affectionately call her "Dr. Ginger" to show their appreciation of her skill and care.[29]

Most Chinese professionals were hired by larger employers, and many others settled into small or medium-sized companies. Because of the risks involved, few entered business as entrepreneurs. Some who had courage and energy, however, ventured on their own into the business world. Two of them were James Zhang and Chris Lu.

James Zhang came to St. Louis from China in 1987. Born in Chongqing, Szechuan province, in 1956, he was raised in a well-off and respected family, as both his parents were government officials. Before coming to America he earned his bachelor's and master's degrees in American literature and taught for two years as an assistant professor at Sichuan University. He entered Washington University on a scholarship, and graduated three years later with a master's in comparative literature. He had planned to return to China after completing his graduate education, but after the Tiananmen Incident he chose to stay in America instead. He spent a year exploring career opportunities in St. Louis. In 1990, realizing that he could not easily find a job with the degree he held, he enrolled in the MBA program at the UMSL. In summer of that year a friend in the real estate business invited him to join her company. Zhang decided to give it a try, and went to the American Real Estate School for a month. Having passed its test, he received his license as a real estate agent. While still a full-time student at UMSL, he began working as a part-time real estate agent for Fortune Realty. In 1992 he completed his MBA and found himself again at a crossroads: he could apply for a position in a company, or he could continue to be a real estate agent. By that point he was doing very well in real estate, so he decided to continue with it. He kept working for Fortune Realty until 1995, when he decided to strike out on his own. He later discussed the difficulties and joys of starting his own business. His recollection provides us with a detailed picture of the operation of the real estate business:

> I knew it was hard, but I thought, I have training and ability. This country provides opportunities for you. I applied for a license for setting up a real estate company. Then I rented office space and bought furniture. I had a couple of agents who were willing to work with me: a Chinese and an American. I set up my business in 1996.
>
> Initially, I bought a national real estate franchise and went into business with another partner. Not too long after that, the partnership

broke up. Later, I bought another franchise with myself as the sole owner. To have a franchise, you operate under their rules and pay a franchise fee that is a one-time charge to get started. Then there is a percentage charge per transaction. All the fees will add up close to 10 percent of our gross income. Recently, I decided to come out of that franchise deal. I felt that what I was paying for I was not getting much from. So I dropped the franchise and changed my company's name to Better House Realty in mid-1998.

Now I am a broker and have eight agents, some full-time and some part-time. There are two kinds of licenses in real estate: sales agent and broker. After you pass the test for agent, you have to have two years of experience before getting a broker license by Missouri real estate law. A broker can operate independently, having managing responsibilities and taking responsibility for all transactions; whereas an agent has to operate under a broker. The benefit to owning a business is that you work for yourself, and you have freedom and independence. Another benefit is that there is no limit to your income. A drawback is working irregular hours on weekends and evenings. You have to develop a high degree of communication skills, a lot of patience, and persistence. I enjoy the status the job provides me. Although my income fluctuates, it is better to own my own business than to be an engineer or a professor.

My typical day is working between two responsibilities of being an agent and a broker. As an agent, my day begins with checking the market by opening a computer database. There are multiple listing services to provide information regarding the St. Louis real estate market. I also have lists for buyers and sellers with different pricing ranges. If a currently listed property is sold, I would call my buyer, contact the title company, inspection company, and lenders which all provide services to my clients. Because of my experience and the trust of the clients, most of my business comes from referrals. People come to me because of my excellent service. Although advertising is important, reputation is more effective.

As a broker, I have to check on what the office is doing. If my agents have problems, I sit down with them and find solutions to their problems. I have to plan for marketing, and to see if there are ways to improve the company. Most time I am on the phone talking to them.

My week is divided between weekdays and weekends. During weekdays, I stay in my office, doing paperwork for transactions, and spending half of my time talking to people. In some evenings, I have to call clients. They are always my top priority. Sometimes, people (both clients and agents) even call me at midnight if they need to talk. During weekends, I work with buyers or hold open houses. I take off one week a year for vacation.

I am thinking of expanding my business. It's good to form partnerships, because you can use capital and management more effectively. Most of my clients are Chinese; 95 to 97 percent of my clients are from referrals. I emphasize doing a good job for my clients. The average of yearly transactions is 40 houses. My commission is 5 to 6 percent since most of my clients are immigrants. Bigger companies usually charge 7 percent.

With a dozen other Chinese professionals, I founded the St. Louis Chinese Association in December 1996. We thought we had needs for our organization such as sponsoring cultural and social events for the community.

My wife is a mechanical engineer and she is doing well. She is now a chief engineer in her company, Progressive Recovery Inc., a company that designs and manufactures industrial equipment.[30]

James Zhang's story highlights the difficulties and uncertainties of owning a business. The risks and the long working hours are challenging, but with initiative, courage, and perseverance, an entrepreneur has more opportunities for personal development and prosperity.

Chris Lu's story in a number of ways resembles James Zhang's. Lu was born in 1957 in Nanjing and grew up on a government-owned farming company in Jianagxi province. He majored in political science as an undergraduate and then took a master's degree in modern Western philosophy from Nanjing University. After graduation he taught for two years as an assistant professor at Nanjing University. In 1987 he came to St. Louis on a scholarship to study philosophy at Washington University. As the first Chinese student in the department, he encountered many difficulties; for example, he had to write his first term paper by hand because he had never used a computer. On completing his master's, which took two years, he had to decide whether to stay in America— something that was now possible for him since the Tiananmen Incident. He chose to stay and get a more "practical" degree to help him find a job. In the fall of 1989 he enrolled in the MBA program at the Southern Illinois University at Carbondale. After graduating in 1992, his landlord, the owner of Diagraph, a packaging company, hired him as a management trainee. In 1994 he was sent to work in branch companies in Hong Kong and Beijing for two years while his wife and daughter stayed in St. Louis. Missing his family badly, he returned to St. Louis in 1996 and decided to start his own business. In the interview I conducted with him, he discussed how he turned himself into an entrepreneur:

> I saw that the Chinese population in St. Louis grow gradually and realized there were business opportunities. I contacted American Family Insurance to set up an agency. The company provided me with no-interest loan to get started, and I took care of everything else. My office started with only a rented desk space in the basement of the *St. Louis Chinese American News*, where I did business transactions and marketing. Marketing is the primary activity of my business. I

advertise my business in the *St. Louis Chinese American News*. Most Chinese entrepreneurs in St. Louis are in the restaurant business, but American Family Insurance does not have good policy on restaurant business insurance, which affects my business. I also sell auto, home, life and health insurance policies. The insurance business is very competitive and I have to try very hard to satisfy the needs of clients. Although the company decides the rates of policies, I can use my advantages, such as an ability to speak English, Chinese, and Cantonese, to attract more clients. For the agencies with the same price, clients prefer me to others. So my business has grown rapidly. I have several hundred clients, 70 percent of whom are Chinese, the rest being white Americans, black Americans, Korean Americans, and people from Middle Eastern countries. I have sold 700 policies in the past two and a half years. I now have my own office and have hired a part-time employee to work in the morning.

My working day is mostly filled with phone calls. Most of the callers ask prices, some want to change a policy or want to make appointments. During an appointment, I help a client fill application forms, explain the policy, and answer questions. Some restaurant owners are too busy to come to my office, and I drive to their restaurants to make it easier for them. So my working hours are very irregular. On Sundays I try not to work, and I take my daughter to Chinese-language school. But on Saturdays, I work for half a day in my office, taking care of business transactions, banking transactions, and paying bills and taxes.

When the business grows more, I will hire a full-time employee to free myself from some of my daily responsibilities. I enjoy being my own boss and the flexibility and freedom I have. I also like meeting different people. The disadvantage of having your own business is that there are too many things to take care.

My business is good enough to support my family. My wife works at Washington University's Medical School as a senior technician. Her job pays her well and she gets pension, medical insurance, and vacation benefit as well.

I am the vice-president of the St. Louis Chinese Association. When it was founded in 1996, I was in charge of fundraising because I have more social connections.[31]

James Zhang's and Chris Lu's stories point to the risks and benefits of owning one's own business. It is worth noting that their wives both work in larger institutions or companies that provide pension benefits and health and life insurance. This serves as a safety net for their families.

Jerry Li and Jenny Lu provide another example of a married couple combining self-employment with steady employment. Before immigrating to the United States, Jerry Li was an associate professor of engineering at Tongji University in Shanghai. In 1990 he came to St. Louis to pursue a doctorate at Washington University's Engineering School. To support himself, he worked in a Chinese restaurant. The following year, Jenny Lu came to St. Louis to join him. Although she held an economics degree from Tongji University, the only work she could find was in a Chinese restaurant, where she earned $500 a month washing dishes and vegetables and doing odd jobs. After earning his master's in 1992, Li decided not to go on to a doctorate. He was hired by Madison Madison International of Missouri Inc., a small engineering consulting company. Having noticed that the company was not making much money, Li and his wife bought a Chinese restaurant in downtown St. Louis in 1994. They replaced the Chinese cook with a Mexican who would work for less. Lu managed the restaurant. Business was brisk during the day, when downtown workers came in for lunch, but slow in the evenings and on weekends, when the downtown emptied out. The restaurant made them some money, but more importantly, it taught them how to manage a Chinese restaurant. They realized they would need to find a niche if they were to succeed in the highly competitive food service industry. The niche they found was *dim sum*. In the early 1990s only one Chinese restaurant in St. Louis, China Royal, was serving *dim sum* on weekends, and they noticed that it was the busiest Chinese restaurant in St. Louis.

In 1996 they sold the downtown restaurant and bought Great Chef Garden. Before making the purchase, they did careful homework. Great Chef Garden was in a business plaza on a major road, Manchester Road, easily accessible to the many Chinese living in the West County. The restaurant was well maintained and would need little remodeling. Its kitchen was spacious and suitable for making *dim sum*. Fortunately for them, a *dim sum* cook was looking for a job and they were able to hire him. Li decided to make *dim sum* buffet a special feature of the restaurant. This strategy worked beautifully, and the restaurant was soon packed on weekends. Later on, to stay competitive, Great Chef Garden began offering hot pot buffet, and the business continued to grow.[32]

The above cases illustrate that most newcomers from Mainland China were professionals before immigrating and became students-turned-professionals in St. Louis. Most PRC professionals work for the region's big employers, but a few have become entrepreneurs. These new entrepreneurs are equipped with advanced degrees, a good command of English, a keen sense of the market economy, and a strong drive for success; clearly, they are a departure from the earlier Chinese, who mainly owned laundries, grocery stores, and restaurants.

Realigning the Cultural Community: The St. Louis Chinese Association and the St. Louis Modern Chinese Language School

Employment in the United States has enabled some PRC Chinese professionals to apply for an adjustment in their status from temporary visitor to permanent resident. The "green card" signifies permanent residency; an individual who holds it is entitled to apply for a citizenship after five years. Theoretically, then, it takes five or six years for an immigrant to become a citizen if he or she so chooses. Following this standard route, by 1996 many Chinese professionals had obtained citizenship. Besides becoming citizens, Chinese professionals also established themselves in their respective professions. Having obtained legal rights as citizens and having achieved financial security, many are now looking beyond their personal and family needs and seeking ways to benefit the larger community.

It was in this context that the St. Louis Chinese Association was established at the end of 1996. A nonpartisan and nonprofit community organization, it strives to promote Chinese culture, to protect the legal rights of Chinese, and to encourage cultural

PHOTOGRAPH 8.1   The buffet counter at Great Chef Garden restaurant at 17 National Way Shopping Center, Manchester, Missouri, 1999. Restaurants serving buffet are attracting more diners. Huping Ling Collection.

exchanges between Chinese and Americans.[33] The profile of
the organization well illustrates the characteristics of Chinese professionals. Since its founding, about one hundred Chinese families
have joined it. They represent Chinese from almost every province
in China; most, however, are from Beijing, Shanghai, Guangzhou,
and various provincial capitals. Most worked in professional fields
in China before coming to the United States. Having finished their
training in America, most found employment in universities or private corporations as professors, researchers, engineers, computer
programmers, technicians, and administrators; or they are now self-
employed as attorneys, insurance agents, physicians, real estate
brokers, and restaurateurs. Most of them were married in China
and have one or two children who have grown up in America
(whether born in China or the United States).

That such an organization exists indicates three factors. First,
the Chinese professionals who have arrived since the 1990s feel a
strong sense of belonging and are determined to stay and become
naturalized citizens; in this they are profoundly different from those
who preceded them more than a century ago. Though they embrace
both Chinese culture and American values, they clearly have committed their lives to America. They do not view America as a temporary and convenient place to make and save money, but as their
home. Second, the Chinese professionals want to embrace democracy, and now that they are citizens, they feel compelled to learn
how it works. In this regard, the St. Louis Chinese Association
serves as a testing ground for Mainland Chinese to learn and practice democratic processes. In establishing itself, the association followed legal procedures meticulously when filing its papers to obtain
status as a nonprofit corporation. At its meetings and in carrying
out its activities, it carefully follows parliamentary procedures.
Third, the association has brought new energy to the community
and forces the old power structure to reform and rebalance itself.

The organization's impact is being increasingly felt. In 1997 it
established the St. Louis Modern Chinese Language School. The history of the Chinese diaspora tells us that all over the world, Chinese-language schools have been a powerful force: they instill Chinese traditions and values in the children of Chinese immigrants; they
promote cultural exchanges between China and host countries; and
they bind Chinese communities together. Like all immigrant parents, Mainland Chinese parents are eager to pass their heritage on
to their children, and they understand that they can do so only if
their children learn the Chinese language. By 1997 there were

already two Chinese-language schools in St. Louis, both founded and operated by Taiwanese Chinese, who taught classical characters. In the 1950s, as part of its literacy campaign, the PRC government had begun strongly promoting simplified Chinese characters and establishing them as the standard. At the same time, it began promoting *pinyin*, a phonetic system that utilizes the Roman alphabet to pronounce Chinese characters. Yet the Taiwanese Chinese and the overseas Chinese continued to prefer the traditional, classical Chinese characters. The Mainland Chinese are now accustomed to simplified characters and want their children to learn them; that system is also easier for beginners. This preference for simplified Chinese characters and *pinyin* led the Mainland Chinese to start a third school, the St. Louis Modern Chinese Language School.[34]

The new school accomplished more than its founders expected. It opened in the fall of 1997 with two classes of about forty students, who were taught only simplified Chinese characters. Enrollment since then has doubled every semester. By 1999 the school's curriculum had expanded to include electives such as Chinese arts, dance, and drumming.[35] By 2001 it had three hundred students in sixteen classes. The school expanded its curriculum again to incorporate mathematics, Chinese martial arts, and Chinese literary composition.[36]

The St. Louis Modern Chinese Language School is more than a place for Chinese children to learn their language and culture. It is also as a cultural center for Chinese parents. To ease parents' culture shock and help them assimilate, the school now sponsors lectures on practical matters such as tax filing, immigration law, and Chinese American history. The school has also arranged displays of the parents' art and photography and has organized aerobics and martial arts classes for them.

Though it is a cultural institution, the school is beginning to exert political influence among Chinese St. Louisans. Its achievements are obvious and are being recognized by the Chinese community as a whole. To compete with it, the two older Chinese-language schools have themselves adopted simplified Chinese characters and *pinyin*, along with the traditional characters and *zhuyin fuhao*. The drum dance team of the St. Louis Modern Chinese Language School has been invited to perform at many important cultural activities sponsored by Chinese organizations and by those of the larger community.

The St. Louis Chinese Association and St. Louis Modern Chinese Language School have brought about a realignment of the community's power structure. Along with the OCA, the largest Chinese community organization, which is dominated by Taiwanese, the St. Louis Chinese Association is seen as highly influential in the community. Relations between the two groups have been harmonious; they have cooperated in many community activities, and some Mainland Chinese belong to both and are active in both. Although the number of Chinese professionals from Taiwan has stopped growing since the 1990s as a result of the decline of the study-abroad movement in Taiwan (see Chapter 7), the ranks of the professionals from Mainland China have been growing. The latter will eventually replace Taiwanese professionals as the dominant force in the Chinese cultural community. Signs of this are already apparent. The St. Louis Chinese Association is now a presence at all important community activities, and the activities it sponsors are now the most heavily attended.

PRESS IN THE CULTURAL COMMUNITY: *ST. LOUIS CHINESE AMERICAN NEWS* AND *ST. LOUIS CHINESE JOURNAL*

With the Chinese American cultural community in St. Louis growing rapidly, its need for a Chinese-language newspaper became evident. In 1990 the *St. Louis Chinese American News* was founded to meet that need. In 1996, as the community continued to develop, another Chinese newspaper, the *St. Louis Chinese Journal*, entered the local market. These two weeklies reflect a resurgence of the Chinese press in North America since the 1970s.[37]

The St. Louis Chinese American News

Before the *St. Louis Chinese American News*, there was only one news publication in Chinese in St. Louis: a monthly magazine called the *Chinese Liberty Journal*, launched in 1979. That same year the PRC and the United States normalized their diplomatic relations. In response to this, a group of Taiwanese students at Washington and St. Louis universities started the *Journal* with the goal of promoting democracy in Taiwan and drawing attention to that island. In 1988, Francis Yueh, a computer programmer, graduated from the University of Illinois at Springfield and came to St. Louis to work for a computer software company in Earth City. Born in Taichung (Taizhong), Taiwan, he had written articles for magazines and newspapers in Taiwan and was strongly interested in journalism. In 1989 he began to help edit the *Chinese*

Liberty Journal. The same year, he also became the St. Louis correspondent for two Chinese-language newspapers, the *China Post*, based in San Francisco, and the *Central Daily*, based in Taipei. Unfortunately, the *China Post* survived for only six months. Having noted that the community enjoyed this newspaper, in September 1990 a Chinese couple, George and Sandy Tsai, who were entrepreneurs and had always been interested in community affairs, decided to start a Chinese-language paper in St. Louis. They invited Yueh to work as a reporter.[38]

The newspaper struggled in its early years. As a free newspaper, it relied on advertisements for its survival. Local Chinese businesses were uncertain whether it would survive and so were reluctant to support it financially. The Tsais had to finance the paper themselves, and its staff worked as volunteers. Dachung Peng, an engineer at Monsanto Chemical, was its editor for the first few months.[39] Later, he was replaced by Francis Yueh. Although a computer programmer, Francis Yueh and his wife May were committed to the paper's success. After several years of hard work, the newspaper began attracting more financial support from the community, and its position stabilized. In 1997, May Yueh became the paper's director, while Sandy Tsai continued as publisher.[40]

The Yuehs decided that the newspaper should focus on the local community and should "promote Chinese culture, bridge between the Chinese community and the larger society, and voice community needs and development." So reads its mission statement. It operates as an independent local newspaper to maintain its freedom and community orientation. The front page features Chinese community news; the rest of its twenty-six pages are divided into various sections: news features, community news, business news, columnists, interviews, literary prose, and reviews of movies made in China, Taiwan, and Hong Kong. The paper's print run has increased from its original 1,000 copies to 5,000. Every Thursday the newspapers are delivered to about fifty distribution points— mainly grocery stores, restaurants, churches, and language schools. By the end of the 1990s the staff has grown to six: a director, an editor-in-chief, an editor, an advertising manager, a part-time reporter, and a full-time delivery person.[41]

In 1997 the *St. Louis Chinese American News* launched a website, www.scanews.com. This made it the first Chinese newspaper in St. Louis to establish a Web presence. In 1998 it signed a contract with Sinanet.com, the largest website in Chinese in North America, and in this way began reaching out to Chinese readers throughout the cyber-world. In 1999 it began a partnership with Hunchnet.com, which brought local newspapers from more than ten of the largest cities in the United States together as a Web hub. These developments point to an important transition: the *St. Louis Chinese American News* is transforming itself from a traditional local newspaper into a cyber-newspaper.

In November 2001 the paper began to publish a special English section, *St. Louis Chinese American*, which it inserted inside the regular weekly Chinese paper. The English section is appreciated by non-Chinese readers, including second-generation Chinese Americans, Asian Americans, and St. Louisans in general.

The St. Louis Chinese Journal

In 1996 the *St. Louis Chinese Journal* was founded by Wen Hwang. Hwang graduated from the Chinese Cultural University in Taiwan in 1983 with a major in home economics. She soon married and went to North Carolina with her husband, who was doing graduate studies. In 1989 she came to St. Louis with her husband, who had found work there. A year later she became involved in the Chinese community and became the editor of its monthly magazine, the *Chinese Liberty Journal*, sponsored by the Chinese Liberty Assembly of Greater St. Louis. Through the magazine she made many friends who shared her passion for literature. She also learned how to run a magazine. She was also a reporter from 1995 to 1996 for the *World Journal*, the largest Chinese-language newspaper in North America.

After the *Chinese LibertyJournal* shut down in April 1996 due to lack of funding, the Southern Chinese News Group—a newspaper chain established in 1978 that owns Chinese newspapers in ten American cities—invited Hwang to join their company. She did, and established *St. Louis Chinese Journal*. The paper receives news items from the chain's headquarters and provides broad coverage of myriad topics. The news section of the thirty-two-page paper offers local, national, and international news. The paper also features literary, sports, health, and entertainment sections with quality articles.

Like the *St. Louis Chinese American News*, the *Journal* struggled at first. It relied heavily on advertisements, yet when Hwang approached local Chinese businesses, they often turned her down. Several of the paper's original partners withdrew when they saw that it was losing money. Hwang did not give up, however. She and her husband worked on the newspaper in their spare time.

This perseverance eventually paid off, and the paper survived. Its staff expanded until it included Hwang and three part-timers. By 1999 the paper had stabilized and Hwang began looking for opportunities to expand it.

In 1999, as a sideline, Hwang published the first Chinese Yellow Pages in St. Louis. In 2000 she launched a sister newspaper, the *Kansas Chinese Journal*.[42]

In different ways, both Chinese-language newspapers have served the St. Louis Chinese community well. The *St. Louis Chinese American News* focuses on the Chinese community of Greater St. Louis and has contributed to the community's cultural pride. The *St. Louis Chinese Journal* provides the community with news from around the country and the world. Both papers promote local Chinese business and have strengthened links among individuals, enterprises, organizations, and the Chinese cultural community and the larger society. In this way, both are indispensable to the community, especially to those of its members who have difficulty with English.

COMMERCE IN THE CULTURAL COMMUNITY: A NEW ETHNIC ECONOMY

Since the 1990s the economy of the St. Louis Chinese has become more diversified. The food service industry has grown rapidly and is still the primary sector of the Chinese American economy, but other, nontraditional Chinese service businesses have now joined it and have further expanded it.

Dispersion of the Food Service Industry

At the end of the 1990s, 126 Chinese restaurants were listed in the *St. Louis Chinese Yellow Pages*.[43] By 2003 there were 306.[44] Obviously, the Chinese food service industry is growing rapidly. An analysis of where these restaurants are, what they offer, and who runs them tells us even more about developments in the community. Most Chinese restaurants are along major highways or in the shopping centers and plazas of the area's suburbs. This is a repeat of the pattern followed by Chinese restaurants a few decades earlier. This geographic dispersion reminds us again that the industry depends on mainstream customers and on those of other ethnic groups. To reach and serve this clientele, the Chinese food industry has had no choice but to spread itself out.

There are three basic categories of Chinese restaurants: formal, buffet, and takeout. Most of the formal restaurants are well established and have better reputations. Their owners are more active in the community, and they often host Chinese wedding banquets and dinners for Chinese community groups. The buffet restaurants range in size from large to medium. They are usually found along commercial roads and cater to both Chinese and non-Chinese diners. Takeout restaurants are more likely to be found in shopping malls, the inner city, and ethnic neighborhoods, where they serve a wide range of customers. Remember, though, that there is no clear-cut distinction between the different categories and that their services often overlap. For instance, some formal restaurants offer both buffet and table service. Many takeout restaurants also provide dinning areas.

Concentration of the Wholesale Grocery Business

The wholesale grocery business is the second-largest traditional Chinese business after restaurants. In 2003 there were twenty- one Chinese wholesale groceries in St. Louis. Unlike Chinese restaurants, wholesale groceries have always tended to concentrate in one place, and they still do. Five of them are now found on Olive Boulevard, a main road running east to west through University City, a suburb northwest of the city. Along this road, between 79th Street and Interstate 170, there is a mile-long stretch along which are scattered thirty-three Chinese businesses, including an architect's office, an attorney's office, two auto repair services, a bakery, two beauty salons, a dental office, two medical clinics, five groceries, a health products store, four herb and gift shops, three insurance agencies, a jewelry store, two Chinese-language newspaper offices, six restaurants, and a phone card sales office.[45] Since the 1980s we could almost call this a Chinatown, except that these businesses constitute only 6 percent of the Chinese businesses in greater St. Louis (see Table 8.1). The Chinese wholesale groceries rely on the Chinese American population and do not have to disperse in order to survive. In this they are different from Chinese restaurants.

Chinese grocery and other businesses came to cluster along Olive Boulevard probably for a number of reasons relating to urban renewal and urban sprawl. In 1979, when Chinatown was forced to move a second time—from the 1500 block of Delmar—Chinese business owners noticed that Olive Boulevard, a main road north of Delmar, was easily accessible for Chinese residing in the inner city as well as for Chinese suburbanites. Olive Boulevard was a natural place to relocate.

Nine food product factories have emerged in the St. Louis area to "feed" the region's restaurants and wholesale groceries. These constitute the third-largest traditional sector in the Chinese ethnic economy. The restaurants, wholesale groceries, and food producers together comprise 63 percent of the Chinese American economy (see Table 8.1).

Laborers in Traditional Service Industries

Those who have read Chinese American history will already be familiar with the clash between labor and capital in Chinatowns, with the conflicts between elites and the masses, and with the sharp divide between "uptown" well-off Chinese Americans and "downtown" working-class new immigrants. More and more excellent studies are documenting and analyzing the social and economic fissures in Chinese American communities.[46] At first glance, these sharp dichotomies seem absent in St. Louis: most of the city's Chinese are middle- or upper-middle-class professionals

PHOTOGRAPH 8.2 Central Trading Center, a shopping center with a number of Chinese businesses, on the 8200 block of Olive Blvd., St. Louis, 1999. A number of Chinese businesses have clustered on Olive Blvd.; however, they account for only 6 percent of all Chinese businesses in St. Louis. Huping Ling Collection.

TABLE 8.1 Chinese American Businesses in St. Louis, 2003

Type of Business	Quantity	Type of Business	Quantity
Accountancy and tax	7	Electric repair	4
		Florists	4
Acupuncturists and herbalists	4	Food production	9
		Funeral homes	3
Air conditioning and heating	2	Furniture	3
Architects and design	7	Gift shops	5
		Wholesale groceries	21
Attorneys	7	Health products	6
Auto dealers (representatives)	2	Insurance	16
		Jewelry	5
Auto repair	5	Newspapers	2
Bakeries	2	Optical goods	1
Beauty salons	4	Printing	1
Bridal shops	1	Realtors	52
Computer training	2	Restaurants	306
Computer–Internet	4	Restaurant supplies	3
Counselors	1		
Construction	10	Tailors–alteration	2
Dentists	4	Travel agencies	5
Physicians	23	Total:	533

Sources: Tabulated according to the *St. Louis Chinese Yellow Pages* 2003 and the *St. Louis Chinese American Yellow Pages* 2003.

and entrepreneurs who live in the suburbs. Closer investigation, however, provides a less rosy picture than this.

In the kitchens of many Chinese restaurants, scores of Chinese—most of them recent immigrants and college students—are employed as laborers. They wash dishes, prepare vegetables and meats, and do whatever odd jobs are demanded of them. They also work in dining rooms as busboys, gathering dishes and cleaning tables. It is estimated that these laborers earn around $1,100 a month, typically for a seven-day, eighty-four-hour week similar to that in other urban Chinese communities. The servers, who are usually college students or immigrants with better English skills and longer experience in the business, receive the same or even less pay but are entitled to keep the customers' tips. A waitress at a prominent Chinese restaurant in St. Louis vividly described the life of laborers in Chinese restaurants:

> I came to St. Louis two years ago from Shanghai. I first earned an MBA at Maryville University. The MBA program at Maryville is not very prominent, so my degree didn't help me much in finding a job. Then I enrolled in computer information science for a master's degree at Southern Illinois University at Edwardsville.
>
> A half year after I came to the U.S., my husband joined me. He had a degree in computer science. He has been working for American firms since he came here, but the pay is not very good. So this semester he is taking one class in computer science at Washington University, hoping to get a graduate assistantship so he can be a full-time student and earn a degree from Washington University.
>
> During Saturdays and Sundays, I work at this restaurant. It is the second Chinese restaurant I have been working for. The owner is pretty nice and that's why I have been working here. The other waitresses and I come here at 10 A.M. to prepare food. The restaurant opens at 11 A.M. and closes at 10 P.M. After closing, we have to take all the food away and do cleaning. We work about twelve to thirteen hours a day. The waitresses are paid $15 a day; after taxes, it is only $7.50. So our income mainly comes from tips. Each evening, we would have about fifty to sixty groups of guests. We have to share some tips with busboys. After that, I can have about $100 a night, which makes my hourly pay about $10. So it is not bad. But the work is hard. We have to work all the time. My husband also worked in a Chinese restaurant for a month. He said he would never work in a restaurant again unless he had to.
>
> The busboys (mostly Mexicans) are paid by a fixed salary of $1,100 to $1,200 a month. They work twelve hours a day and seven days a week. Our guests are primarily Americans.[47]

A few Chinese students are able to work as maitre d's or cashiers. These are important positions in Chinese restaurants and are usually monopolized by the owner. Lee, a graduate student from Shanghai with fluent English and a charming smile, came to St. Louis to major in finance at Washington University. Having already worked for foreign companies in Shanghai, she was able to find a weekday job at an American company. On weekends she works at a large Chinese restaurant as a maitre d and cashier.[48]

Workers in Chinese grocery stores, including cashiers and stockroom clerks, have an equally hard time. Most cashiers can speak Cantonese, Mandarin, and some English and have been with the business longer. They wait on customers and stock goods, or prepare fresh vegetables when business is slow. Most of the stockroom workers are newly arrived immigrants with fewer language skills. They pack and sort dry goods, prepare fresh vegetables and seafood, and cut meats. Mr. Yang is a new immigrant in his sixties from Henan province who came to St. Louis to join his son, a white-collar professional. Because he speaks neither Cantonese nor English, the only job he could find was in a Chinese grocery store as a stocker and packer.[49]

Chinese come to St. Louis with different work experiences and language skills and from different parts of China. This "complicates" Chinese workplaces and helps create and strengthen hierarchies in them. Furthermore, the class distinction between labor and capital in traditional Chinese business settings is often blurred, in that the owners themselves often started as workers in their businesses and routinely participate in all aspects of those businesses.[50] Chinese business owners are both bosses and workers, and this makes it difficult to draw a class line between employees and employers. Therefore, it would be oversimplistic to portray owner/employee relations in Chinese businesses as based on class. It would also be inaccurate to compare the differences between workers and owners in St. Louis with the class cleavages that are apparent in the Chinatowns of New York City and San Francisco. This is not to say that class conflict does not exist in St. Louis or that workers are not exploited in the city's Chinese businesses. On the contrary, the city's traditional Chinese service industries are as capitalist as any other, so that exploitation is rife. Employees and employers in Chinese businesses certainly have different interests, which often conflict. Restaurant workers are often paid less than the minimum wage, and this is blatant exploitation of labor, although it is currently legal. The owners of traditional Chinese businesses don't pay their employees' health insurance and benefits; this, and the usually poor working conditions, compound the difficulties faced by Chinese workers. Inevitably, these workers come to resent the owners. However, because the working-class Chinese are dispersed through kitchens and stockrooms throughout the city, they have never been able to organize any sort of open and united protest. It is more difficult to assess the extent of class conflict in St. Louis than in larger Chinese communities such as those on the coasts, where Chinese laborers are more numerous, and many are even unionized.

Rapid Growth of the Nontraditional Service Industries

The traditional food, sales, and service industries continue to dominate the Chinese ethnic economy; however, nontraditional serv-

PHOTOGRAPH 8.3 The food-service sector continues to drive the ethnic Chinese economy; however, nontraditional service businesses are emerging and are expanding rapidly. Light Speed Motorsports at 8314 Olive Blvd., St. Louis, 2001. Huping Ling Collection.

ice businesses are beginning to emerge and are rapidly expanding. The most important new Chinese service businesses in St. Louis are as follows (see Table 8.1): real estate (52 businesses), physicians (23), insurance (16), construction (10), accountancy (7), architecture and design (7), law (7), health products (6), auto repair (5), gift shops (5), jewelry (5), and travel agencies (5). Most of these businesses are located in mainstream professional buildings, shopping centers, or plazas.[51] The diversification of the Chinese American economy in St. Louis mirrors the overall changing social and economic profile of Chinese Americans and of new immigrants from Asian countries. These new elements constitute a departure from traditional business patterns among Chinese Americans. Thus they deserve more scholarly attention and interpretation.

The rapid increase in the new Chinese service businesses and the pattern of ethnic business distribution in St. Louis parallel those in suburban Los Angeles. In Monterey Park, a suburb eight miles east of L.A.'s downtown with a large Asian American population, the new Chinese immigrants from Taiwan and Hong Kong have since the 1970s been speculating in real estate; they have even been establishing businesses or subsidiaries for funneling money from their home countries to the United States. The new Chinese investors are opening banks in Los Angeles that are making Monterey Park "a focal point for Pacific Rim investment," observed Timothy P. Fong.[52] According to Yen-fen Tseng's study, between 1979 and 1992, twenty-two Chinese-owned banks opened in the San Gabriel Valley. The new immigrants from Taiwan, Hong Kong, and China to Los Angeles include many individuals with executive experience. In 1985, 30 percent of Taiwanese immigrants, 23 percent of Hong Kong immigrants, and 5 percent of PRC immigrants to that city had executive experience.[53]

According to Wei Li's 1996 study of the ethnic Chinese economy in Los Angeles County, Chinese businesses there followed a pattern similar to the one in St. Louis. In Los Angeles the restaurant business is still among the top ones in the ethnic Chinese economy, but many new service businesses—medicine, dentistry, insurance, law, real estate, auto repair, accountancy, travel agency, loans and mortgage brokering, computer services, and banking—have overtaken the traditional businesses (i.e., trading and food services).[54]

In St. Louis since the 1990s, the new ethnic economy has been characterized by the continued dominance of the dispersed restaurant businesses, along with the rapid increase in new service businesses. The Chinese ethnic economy is still built around a dispersed restaurant industry, which still accounts for 60 percent of the Chinese economy. The new types of service businesses, scattered as they are across the city in high-rises and commercial plazas and along commercial roads, have blended into the mainstream economy. Thus the physical dispersion of the Chinese American businesses makes the cultural community an ideal alternative community structure.

POLITICIZING THE CULTURAL COMMUNITY

The cultural community in St. Louis is politically fragmented, just as in other Chinese American communities. Its members have formed various cultural institutions and social organizations based on dialects, national origins, occupations, political leanings, religious beliefs, and cultural interests. All of them vie for the community's attention, but at the same time, all of them draw on one another to promote Chinese cultural heritage, to bridge cultural gaps between the Chinese American community and the larger society, to protect the civil rights of Chinese Americans, and to participate in mainstream politics.

Political Fragmentation

The Chinese American community in St. Louis is more complex now than it ever was. During the Hop Alley era, most Chinatown residents were Cantonese-speaking laborers and small entrepreneurs. The postwar arrivals—especially after 1965, when the U.S. immigration laws were loosened—were mainly Mandarin speakers from big cities in China and Taiwan and from Hong Kong. These later arrivals integrated themselves professionally with the larger society and took up residence in middle-class suburbs. Beginning in the 1970s, ethnic Chinese from Vietnam, Korea, and Southeast Asia further diversified the community. In the 1990s more and more students and academics from China joined the ranks of Chinese American professionals. All of this reinforced the community while contributing to its diversity.

While Chinese St. Louisans share a collective ethnic identity, they differ in nation of birth, dialect spoken, professional training and experience, religious and ideological beliefs, political orientation, and personal interests. All of these differences divide people even while linking them. The dividing lines are drawn not only along the above categories, but also crisscross within the categories. Meanwhile, within each major division emerge some subdivisions. Broadly speaking, it can be said that there are two main communities: the older, Cantonese-speaking immigrants from Guangdong (*lao qiao*), and the newer, Mandarin-speaking immigrants from Taiwan and other parts of China (*xin qiao*). These two groups can be further divided as follows.

Politically they are either pro-Nationalist or pro-Communist—in recent decades, this is roughly equivalent to pro-Taiwan or pro-PRC. This divide is reflected in the following community organizations: the St. Louis Chinese Society (mainly for professionals from Taiwan); the St. Louis Organization of Chinese Americans (for American-born and naturalized Chinese Americans); the St. Louis Taiwanese Association (for natives of Taiwan and for those who are promoting the independence of Taiwan); the St. Louis Taiwanese American Citizen League (for naturalized Chinese from Taiwan); the Kuomingtang chapter in St. Louis (for members of Nationalist Party); the Midwest Chinese American Science and Technology Association (MCASTA, which evolved from the Chinese Liberty Assembly, and which is mainly for the pro-Nationalist Chinese professionals from Taiwan); and the St. Louis Chinese Association (mainly for professionals from

China). In addition, some residents have organized the St. Louis Alliance for Preserving the Truth of the Sino-Japanese War (St. Louis APTSJW) to preserve the history of that war and to protest the Japanese government's efforts to cover up the war atrocities it committed during that war.

Occupationally, Chinese St. Louisans are represented by various trade and professional groups: the St. Louis On Leong Chinese Merchants and Laborers Association (for the older generation of Cantonese-speaking restaurant owners); the St. Louis Asian American Business Association (an incarnation of Chinese Jaycees, for the younger generation of Cantonese-speaking small business owners); the St. Louis Chinese Chamber of Commerce (for Mandarin-speaking Taiwanese, Mainlander, Korean Chinese, and Vietnamese Chinese business owners); the Midwest Chinese American Science and Technology Association (mainly for the Chinese professionals from Taiwan); the Missouri Asian-American Bar Association; a chapter of the St. Louis North American Taiwanese Professors Association; and the St. Louis North American Taiwanese Medical Association.

Regarding religion, the Chinese embrace many denominations, including the following: the St. Louis Chinese Gospel Church, the St. Louis Chinese Christian Church, the Taiwanese Presbyterian Church, the St. Louis Chinese Baptist Church, Lighthouse Chinese Church, the St. Louis Chinese Lutheran Church, the Lutheran Asian Ministry in St. Louis, the Lutheran Hour Ministries, the Light of Christ Chinese Missions in St. Louis, the St. Louis Tabernacle of Joy, the Mid-America Buddhist Association, the St. Louis Tzu-Chi Foundation, the St. Louis Amitabha Buddhist Learning Center, the St. Louis International Buddhist Association, and the St. Louis Falun Dafa.

Chinese St. Louisans also join, according to gender and age preferences, social organizations and clubs such as the St. Louis Chinese Women's Club, the St. Louis Formosan Women's Club, the St. Louis Senior Chinese Club, and the St. Louis Taiwanese Senior Association. Many Chinese St. Louisans are recruited into clubs that represent different cultural interests: the St. Louis Cai's Classic Kung Fu, the St. Louis Chinese Bridge Club, the St. Louis Chinese Opera, the St. Louis Chinese Painting Club, the St. Louis Chinese Writers Association of North America, the St. Louis Formosan Salon, the St. Louis Music and You, the St. Louis Chinese Choir, the St. Louis Chinese Volleyball Club, and the St. Louis Chinese Ping Pong Club. In addition, American families with adopted children from China have formed the St. Louis

Families with Children from China (FCC), which has been an integral part of the cultural community.[55]

There are more than forty Chinese community organizations; together, they reflect the kaleidoscopic diversity of the cultural community. These organizations have fragmented the community and compete with one another for funds, human resources, political influence, and audiences for their separate and often overlapping cultural events. Many community activists and leaders are worried about this disunity. Wen Hwang, the founder and director of the *St. Louis Chinese Journal* and a community activist, noted: "There are too many community organizations and activities in St. Louis. The supplies of activities exceed the demand; we have to beg people to come to the activities."[56] Patricia L. Yeh, who has been involved in the St. Louis Chinese Academy, the St. Louis OCA, and Chinese Culture Days, and who in 1996 was the first Chinese American president of Zonta International, voiced her frustration over the disconnection between the Taiwanese and Mainland Chinese: "I believe the Taiwanese Chinese and Mainland Chinese should collaborate in the community events. There are many talented people among the Mainland Chinese, but they have less English-language skills and cultural exposure than the Taiwanese Chinese. The two groups should compliment each other. We should not always hold the attitude that the larger group ought to dominate the smaller ones, and that the senior members are superior to the junior ones."[57]

Political Unity

Chinese St. Louisans have divided into myriad community organizations, but they also come together for major community affairs and significant national and international events. One of these, the Chinese Culture Days deserves a closer look.

The Chinese Culture Days were started by Grace Shen Lo and a group of community activists. Lo was born in China in the 1940s and went to Taiwan with her family after the Communist takeover. She came to the United States in 1964 to attend the University of Texas, Austin. After earning a bachelor's degree, she began work on her master's and doctoral degrees in biochemistry. In 1976, having earned her doctorate, she came to St. Louis to join her husband, T. Leo Lo, a mechanical engineer from the Texas Institute of Technology, who had been hired by McDonnell-Douglas the previous year. Since then Lo has been working for

Ralston Purina as a group director. The Los have been active in the community; they established the St. Louis Chinese Language School in 1978. They saw that Chinese American children, most of them American-born, were having a difficult time learning Chinese characters, so they decided to begin holding a "China Day" to help them learn about Chinese culture. The Los were also hoping that this event would unite all the community organizations through one activity.[58] The China Days were initially celebrated on Chinese New Year during the early 1990s. Chinese New Year usually falls in early to mid-February, and the cold weather discouraged participation. So the organizers decided to move it to the spring, change its name to "Chinese Culture Days," and hold it at the Missouri Botanical Gardens. The first Chinese Culture Days were celebrated in 1995, with Grace Shen Lo as the chief coordinator. Since then they have been a big hit every year among the many cultural activities in greater St. Louis. The celebration is normally held for two days in May or June and features a dragon dance, acrobats, traditional Chinese dance, Beijing Opera, stage plays adapted from traditional folktales, a martial arts demonstration, displays of Chinese artifacts, and the sale of Chinese food of various sorts. The event draws thousands of St. Louisans each year.

The significance of the Chinese Cultural Days goes far beyond the promotion of Chinese culture. It has been a testimony to the community's political unity. No individual or organization could single-handedly sponsor such a comprehensive set of activities. The annual affair, from planning to execution, requires a great deal of money and labor. Its preparation usually starts in October of the previous year and continues until opening day. The organizing committee includes representatives from the major community organizations, and divides itself into various subcommittees: fundraising, financial control, food, display booths, public relations, entertainment, and costume and design.[59] Hundreds of volunteers help with the long and exhausting preparations, and many more contribute on the day itself. The event was started by the Taiwanese Chinese, who still dominate it, but it has gained the participation of other big community organizations, such as the three Chinese-language schools, the St. Louis OCA (representing American-born and naturalized Chinese Americans), the St. Louis Chinese Association (representing Chinese Mainlanders), and the St. Louis Asian American Business Association (representing Cantonese-speaking business owners). The event could not possibly succeed

PHOTOGRAPH 8.4 Michael Shun, twelve, defies the dragon as he entertains the crowd celebrating the Chinese New Year (Year of the Dragon) at West Port Plaza, 2 February 1976. *St. Louis Globe-Democrat* photo by T. V. Vessell. From the collections of the St. Louis Mercantile Library at the University of Missouri-St. Louis.

without this cooperation. This event demonstrates that the community as a whole is committed to working together to promote Chinese culture and to achieving organizational unity. This is reflected in the theme of 2002 Chinese Cultural Days: "Diversity in Culture; Unity in Action."[60]

Important national events have also united the community. After the terrorist attacks of 11 September 2001, St. Louis Chinese community organizations got together to sponsor fundraising activities. On Leong Merchants and Laborers Association and the St. Louis Asian American Business Association took the lead in these activities.[61] Other organizations contributed, such as the St. Louis Chinese Association and all the Chinese churches.[62] By Thanksgiving of 2001 the community had raised $12,094 to be sent to the St. Louis chapter of the International Red Cross to aid the 9/11 victims and their families.[63]

The political unity of the St. Louis cultural community is also reflected in the composition of the various community organizations. The officers and members of the different organizations often draw from the same group of individuals, most of whom are community activists. The officers of community organizations are often active members of the Chinese-language schools and Chinese churches. The same community activists

PHOTOGRAPH 8.5 A mock Chinese wedding demonstrated at Chinese Cultural Days, Missouri Botanic Gardens, 5 June 1999. Huping Ling Collection.

and leaders often help out at different social functions. This overlap has created a political elite that controls most community affairs.

From Marginal Politics to Mainstream Politics

Scholars have generally categorized Asian American political participation as follows: electoral politics, mass protest politics, and coalition politics.[64] Electoral politics can be traced back to the 1920s, when James Hamada, a Hawaiian Republican Nisei, ran for a seat in the territorial legislature.[65] Since the 1960s, Asian Americans have become more visible in electoral politics. According to Gordon H. Chang, by 2001 three hundred Asian Pacific Americans had been elected to public office; they included 2 U.S. senators, 5 U.S. representatives, 2 governors, 49 state representatives, 89 city council members, 26 city mayors, 133 school board or higher education board members, and 210 judges. In addition, more than two thousand appointed officials at the state, federal, and territorial levels also are of Asian Pacific background.[66]

Mass protest politics emerged in Asian American politics in the 1980s. Two events are worth noting here. In Detroit in June 1982, Vincent Chin, a twenty-seven-year-old Chinese American draftsman, was killed by two European American men, Ronald Ebens and his stepson Michael Nitz. They had mistaken Chin for a Japanese at a time when many Detroit auto workers were being laid off as a result of competition from Japan's auto industry. A Wayne County Circuit judge sentenced both to three years' probation and a fine of $3,000 each plus $700 in fees. Asian Americans in Detroit and around the country were outraged by the light sentence and organized a campaign to demand a retrial. The ensuing retrials failed to put the murderers behind bars; even so, the lessons the Asian American community learned from this case were used in a later protest. In late July 1989, Ming Hai Loo (also known as Jim Loo), a twenty-four-year-old Chinese American, was murdered in Raleigh, North Carolina, in circumstances similar to those of Vincent Chin. Loo was mistaken for a Vietnamese by two European American brothers, Robert and Lloyd Piche, who had lost a third brother in Vietnam. Lo died of head injury after the brothers attacked him. Chinese Americans in the city immediately organized a Jim Loo American Justice Coalition to represent Loo's parents, who could speak little English. Lloyd, the younger brother, was sentenced to only six months for assault and disorderly conduct; as a result of the campaign, however, Robert Piche was sentenced to thirty-seven years.[67]

Scholars who specialize in studying coalition politics often tell us that "protest is not enough"; coalitions between ethnic minorities and whites have become a necessary component of urban politics.[68] Asian Americans began joining multiracial coalitions as early as 1949, when Edward Roybal, a Mexican American, was elected the first Latino member of the Los Angeles City Council in the twentieth century; for victory he depended on an alliance of Latinos, African Americans, Asian Americans, and European Americans.[69] According to scholars such as George Lipsitz and Leland T. Saito, racialized government policies have forced African Americans, Asian Americans, Mexican Americans, and Native Americans into similar occupational, residential, and political urban spaces; this in turn has created common interests and concerns among these minority groups and made multiracial political coalitions possible.[70]

The political participation of Chinese St. Louisans generally mirrors national trends in Asian American politics. They began participating in elections after Word War II. By that time, American-born Chinese were reaching voting age and foreign-born Chinese were being allowed to become American citizens. In the decades after the war, the Chinese in St. Louis tended to vote Republican; that party's traditional message resonated with the Chinese belief in working hard and accepting individual responsibility. Later, however, the civil rights movement awakened the racial consciousness of Chinese Americans, who have now grown more sympathetic to the Democrats, who tend to favor the interests of minorities and the unprivileged. Since the 1960s, Chinese St. Louisans have largely supported Democratic candidates—this, in a state where the legislature has generally been dominated by the Democrats.

By the early 1980s, Chinese St. Louisans were entering coalition politics. Some Chinese community activists and business leaders dropped their nonpartisan stance and began campaigning actively for mainstream candidates. James Yeh, a mechanical engineer and community activist, threw his support behind John Ashcroft's campaign for the Missouri governorship. A strongly conservative and deeply religious Republican, Ashcroft was not the choice of many Chinese St. Louisans. Yeh, however, thought differently: "Since we are not powerful enough to have an Asian American candidate, we should be actively involved in the campaign."[71] Yeh, his wife Patricia, and a few other Chinese American business owners organized fundraisers for Ashcroft at the Mandarin House and Chongqing restaurants.[72] Although most Chinese St. Louisans voted for the Democratic candidate, Ashcroft was elected governor in 1984, and again in 1988.

After 2000, other Chinese American professionals, entrepreneurs, and community leaders began involving themselves in federal politics. In 2002, Jim Talent, a Republican congressman from 1992 to 2000, ran for the U.S. Senate against Democrat Jean Carnahan, widow of the late governor, Mel Carnahan, who died in a plane crash during his campaign for the senate in October 2000 and had been elected posthumously. Jean Carnahan was appointed to the seat for two years by the Democratic governor, Bob Holden, the man elected to replace her late husband. In November 2002, Jean Carnahan ran for reelection to complete that senate term. Talent aggressively courted the state's small business owners, making much of his strong record as member and past chair of the U.S. Congress's Small Business Committee. On 18 March 2002, President George W. Bush came to the St. Louis suburb of O'Fallon to speak at a fundraiser for Talent that was being sponsored by the state's business owners. A ticket for the event cost $1,000, and about seventy Chinese St. Louisans attended, most of them entrepreneurs but some of them professionals and community leaders. To court support from Asian American voters, Talent and his wife Brenda—whose mother Hatsue "Katy" Lyons is a Japanese American—had their pictures taken with the Chinese American donors during the dinner.[73]

In April 2002, encouraged by their growing political influence, a group of Chinese American business owners and community leaders established the Pacific-American Campaign Coalition (PACC), with the goal of achieving greater Asian American political representation in urban politics. At a PACC fundraising dinner for Talent held on 28 April 2002, Thomas Cy Wong, the organization's president and past president of the St. Louis OCA, explained the purpose of the group:

> After attending President George W. Bush's recent visit to St. Louis and witnessing such a strong representation of Asian-Americans, PACC co-founder and Vice-President, Mr. Francois Ho and myself foresaw a unique opportunity to expound upon this need for a political outreach from and for our community. Thus, the Coalition was born, to bridge our community and to speak as one collective voice; a voice that has been relatively quiet, if not silent in the past; a voice that can now be raised as one for our community; a voice that shall take on the depth and spirit of a multi-ethnic coalition, gathered together to summon greater awareness for our community concerns.[74]

With the founding of PACC, Chinese St. Louisans have committed themselves to engaging in mainstream politics by joining with other groups of Asian Americans and with European Americans. It indicates the community's commitment to engaging the mainstream political process and to seeking political empowerment. The rise of Thomas Cy Wong and Francois Ho—both young small-business owners—indicates that political leadership in the Chinese community is shifting away from the older generation toward a younger generation that is eager to participate in mainstream politics and able and willing to work within the multiracial and multiethnic environment.

Chinese St. Louisans are also being appointed to state commissions. In May 2001, Missouri lieutenant governor Joe Maxwell appointed two Chinese American women, Ching-ling Tai and Lily Ko, to the Missouri Community Service Commission (MCSC) for three-year terms.[75] Ching-ling Tai is from Taiwan. She obtained her master's in Asian studies from Washington University in the early 1970s and went on to teach in Singapore at Nanyang University and the National University. She later earned her doctorate in sociology from the University of Hull in England and then came back to St. Louis with her family in 1984. She taught Chinese at Washington University as a part-timer. In 1987 she began teaching Chinese at the St. Louis University High School. A strong community activist, she has served the community for nearly two decades as vice-president of the National OCA, president of the St. Louis OCA, vice-president and treasurer of the *Chinese American Forum*, vice-president of the St. Louis Nanjing Sister City Committee, and board member of the St. Louis Center for International Relations and the Greater St. Louis/China Business.[76] Her long-time commitment to serving the community culminated in this appointment.

Like Tai, Lily Ko had been involved in the community for many years, in the area of health care. Born in Hong Kong, she came to the United States in 1978 to marry Walter Ko (see Chapter 6), her classmate back in Hong Kong. Before the birth of her two children, she had worked in Hong Kong, England, and the United States as a registered nurse in hospitals, nursing homes, and residential homes. When her children grew older, she returned to school. She received her bachelor's degree in health information management in 1993 and later a master's degree in health care administration from St. Louis University. A licensed nursing home administrator and registered health information administrator, she has been employed as a residential service coordinator at the Gladys & Henry Crown Center for Senior Living. She is also heavily involved in community activities such as Village of Many Colors Festival, an annual event sponsored by the government and nonprofit agencies to promote the awareness of health, social services, and resources for minority senior citizens. She has established a bilingual English/Chinese class for the Chinese seniors in St. Louis. During the 2000 presidential election, with other volunteers, she organized Chinese senior citizens to become active and informed voters and helped them register to vote. Her dedication to community services, especially those for the Chinese seniors, led to her appointment as a commissioner.[77]

CONCLUSION

The decades around the new millennium witnessed the growth and maturity of the cultural community. Newcomers from Mainland China have contributed not only to the population increase but also to the community's complexity and diversity. They have joined the earlier

PHOTOGRAPH 8.6 Members of the Asian American Business Association with Brenda L. Talent, wife of Jim Talent, Republican candidate for Missouri Senator, at the dinner fundraiser, 18 March 2002. Courtesy of *St. Louis Chinese American News*–SCANews.com.

arrivals in obtaining professional employment, operating private enterprises, celebrating cultural diversity, and, more importantly, developing the cultural community. The emergence of two Chinese-language newspapers indicates that the cultural community has expanded and matured and is demanding a community press through which it can express its cultural, social, economic, and political concerns.

The new ethnic economy of the cultural community in St. Louis relies on the traditional food service industry but also on nontraditional service industries of the sort that require more professional training and capital investment. Both sectors of the Chinese American economy are dispersed among the urban and suburban communities. Even so, the Chinese American cultural community is visible to both insiders and outsiders, largely through cultural events and celebrations.

The community has been fragmented by its own diversity; Chinese St. Louisans now differ in the dialects they speak, their national origins, their social and economic backgrounds, their educational attainments, their professional training, their political affiliations and religious denominations, and their cultural interests. Despite all these differences, Chinese St. Louisans share much common ground: the desire to preserve their cultural identity, to integrate with the larger society, and to participate in mainstream politics. These desires have been strong enough to unite the community into single, strong political voice when necessary.

9 Cultural Community in Retrospect and Prospect

CULTURAL COMMUNITY IN RETROSPECT

Members of an ethnic group deliberately congregate in social organizations and cultural activities to foster their ethnic identity. For example, in eighteenth- and early-nineteenth-century Boston, one of the earliest multiethnic urban centers in the United States, newcomers to the city included Armenian, Chinese, English, French, German, Irish, Italian, Polish, Russian, Scotch, Scots-Irish, Spanish, Swedish, and Swiss immigrants. It is estimated that twenty-seven different languages were spoken in Boston in that era.[1] Irish immigrants, the largest of these ethnic groups, numbered 72,065 and constituted one-third of Boston's population in 1865.[2] During his early career, Oscar Handlin studied the Boston immigrants, especially the Irish communities. Economically, the city's Irish were at a disadvantage and concentrated on two occupations: 65 percent worked as laborers and domestic servants.[3] Consistent with this lower placement in the labor market, they lived in tenements carved out of old mansions, abandoned warehouses, factories, and even barracks. In these crowded dwellings, there was usually no sewage system or sanitation of any kind.[4] Despite the city's poor infrastructure, the immigrants were able to find comfort through their strong sense of coherent identity. Handlin observed: "The yearning for familiar pleasure, for the company of understanding men, and the simple sensation of being not alone among strangers, drew immigrants together in tippling shop and *bierhaus*, and in a wide variety of more formally organized social activities."[5] Consequently, different immigrant groups formed their own ethnic social organizations in Boston: "Canadians gathered in the British Colonial Society while Scotsmen preserved old customs, sported their kilts, danced to the bagpipe, and played familiar games, either in the ancient Scots Charitable Society, the Boston Scottish Society, or the Caledonian Club (1853). Germans, who felt that Americans lacked *Gemuthlichkeit*, established independent fraternal organizations that often affiliated with native ones. Thus Herman Lodge was Branch 133 of the Independent Order of Odd Fellows, and Branch 71 of the Independent Order of Redmen was known as the Independent Order of Rothmanner."[6] These social groups enhanced ethnic identity and eased the daily struggles of uprooted peoples.

St. Louis was the second-largest city in the Midwest (after Chicago) and had a significant ethnic population. There, the early immigrant groups, such as the Germans—the largest immigrant group in the city— underwent a similar identity-forging process. Audrey L. Olson has questioned conventional perceptions of immigrant communities as "ethnic ghettos." In her study of the Germans in St. Louis from 1850 to 1920, she contends that "there was no homogenous physical community" of Germans.[7] Instead, in the late nineteenth and early twentieth centuries they established scores of *vereine* or societies. Olson observes that these many diverse societies shared a common trait: "They were carriers of *Gemuthlichkeit*, an untranslatable term connoting conviviality, camaraderie and good fellowship, love of celebrations, card playing, praise of this so-called German way of life, and all of these washed over by flowing kegs of good lager bear."[8] She discusses the reasons for the flourishing *vereine* life: "First, diversity of purpose demanded a multiplicity of *vereine*. Second, the lack of a physical community and the mobility patterns led to the establishment of *vereine* of the same kind in different neighborhoods; and third, dissension among Germans prompted a diversity of societies."[9] Although they never formed a coherent physical settlement, the heterogeneous Germans were able to hold their community together by sharing common cultural habits and customs, celebrating traditional holidays, playing games, and, unquestionably, drinking beer. A community that focuses largely on cultural unity is thus defined by Olson as "a gemutlich community."[10]

Even the smaller immigrant groups in St. Louis, such as the Japanese, enjoyed a comparable experience a half century later. Miyako Inoue studied recent Japanese Americans in St. Louis and found that that community lacked a physical concentration, as most Japanese Americans by the 1980s were living in white neighborhoods, belonged to white churches, and associated with white friends. Unlike the Germans, however, the Japanese had assimilated with mainstream society as a result of the widespread residential pattern.[11]

A Chinese cultural community similar to the one in St. Louis is found in Kansas City, Missouri. Prior to War II about four hundred Chinese were living there. Most of them were bachelors from the *Siyi* district or "four counties" in Guangdong province (Taishan, Xinhui, Kaiping, and Enping). They were concentrated in the laundry, restaurant, and grocery businesses and in traditional Chinese medicine as well. More than thirty hand laundries, over twenty restaurants, three grocery stores, and three doctors of Chinese medicine were protected by the chief community organization, On Leong. The Chinese population of Kansas City fell drastically after the war, when most Chinese moved to the coasts or returned to China.

By the early 1950s a few Chinese students and resident physicians at St. Joseph Hospital and St. Luke's Hospital and two Chinese restaurant owners constituted the entire Chinese population of Kansas City. More Chinese arrived there in the 1960s; most of them were employed as scientists and technicians at the Kansas University sity Medical Center or at the Midwest Research Center at the University of Missouri–Kansas City. Other Chinese professionals (architects, engineers, professors, and accountants) and entrepreneurs eventually joined the community. In 1966 about 150 Chinese in Kansas City gathered to celebrate the Chinese New Year; at that point they decided to establish the Kansas City Chinese Association; most of its members were professionals.[12] Since then that association has been the dominant community organization, responsible for the Chinese New Year celebrations and other cultural activities. By the 1970s most of the Chinese in Kansas City were Taiwanese professionals; this group formed the Kansas City Chinese Liberty Assembly. In 1973 the Greater Kansas City Chinese Language School was established to teach the language to Chinese American children.[13] Two decades later, in 1993, Chinese restaurateurs founded the Kansas City Chinese Restaurant Association.[14] A second Chinese-language school, the Kansas City Modern Chinese Language School, was established in 1999 to teach simplified characters and *pinyin* to serve the growing population of Mainland Chinese.[15] The same year, a group of professional musicians started the Kansas City Chinese Musicians Association.[16] The diverse cultural events sponsored by the community's cultural institutions and organizations have generated a cultural community in Kansas City.[17]

The above cases indicate that throughout American history, on the coasts and in the hinterlands, in big cities and small towns, most ethnic groups, whatever their size, yearn for ethnic cohesion and establish a broad range of ethnic social and cultural organizations. Where a physical ethnic community exists, its social and cultural organizations become vital to the community. Where a physical ethnic community is absent, social and cultural organizations emerge as the community structure, thus constituting a cultural community or the local variant of a cultural community.

CULTURAL COMMUNITY IN PROSPECT

The previous chapters have testified that the Chinese American cultural community in St. Louis is not an "imagined community," a term used by Benedict Anderson;[18] rather, it is a real community with both a physical space and a social space. It lacks distinct physical boundaries but has clear social boundaries. The myriad community organizations and cultural institutions serve as the community's infrastructure and constitute the physical dimension of the cultural community. The wide array of cultural and political activities that takes place within the community provides many opportunities for substantial and meaningful interpersonal and intergroup interactions, which together constitute the social space of the cultural community. The postmodern approach to social science favors the notion of communities that have flexible and even overlapping boundaries; thus a nation can be conceived of as a "community" where its members share a strong "fraternity" or "comradeship."[19] A nation can also be understood as a "symbolic universe" consisting of "individual men and women" who intellectually preserve their ethnic identity within their "linguistic communities."[20] In the United States, a nation of nations, especially in the recent decades, the concept of cultural community probably best illustrates the nature of a given ethnic group in most cities.

Two factors have contributed the most to the emergence of a cultural community: social and economic integration, and the preservation of ethnic identity. Social and economic integration naturally dissolves an ethnic physical community and in doing so makes room for different forms of community. As demonstrated by American ethnic history in general and by Chinese American history in particular, when the overall social and economic climate discriminates against a minority group, that group must develop a self-sufficient physical/commercial as well as residential community in order to survive economically. Within such a community, the members survive in the alien land through internal mutual reliance. Once the larger environment becomes more receptive to the minority group, the physical boundaries of its community gradually vanish. In St. Louis, when the Chinese enclave disappeared as its members economically and residentially integrated with the mainstream society, a cultural community emerged to take its place. It is social and economic integration that dismantled the ethnic enclave and helped forge a cultural community. Therefore, the more integrated a minority group is, the more likely it is that a cultural community will emerge among its members.

However, social and economic integration alone does not explain how a cultural community forms. This sort of integration causes an ethnic population to disperse. As a result the physical ethnic community vanishes, but it does not necessarily follow that a different form of ethnic community is created. Integration has historically led to assimilation of different ethnic groups into the larger or "white" society, and even to the disappearance of ethnicity. Only when an integrated ethnic group makes a deliberate effort to preserve its ethnic identity can a cultural community emerge. Fearing that it could lose its ethnic identity as a result of integration, the ethnic group may strive to create a community to preserve that identity. If a physical community is unfeasible or undesirable, a cultural community or its variant develops instead. This is precisely what has happened with the Chinese Americans in St. Louis. Because the Chinese ethnic economy has merged with the mainstream one, and because Chinese professionals have integrated with the mainstream economy, there is no longer a Chinese community in the physical sense—neither commercial nor residential. Nevertheless, Chinese St. Louisans maintain a strong sense of "Chineseness," and they keenly desire to preserve their Chinese identity. This has motivated them to build a social infrastructure consisting of Chinese community organizations, Chinese churches, and Chinese language schools. In the process, a cultural community has been born.

This history of the Chinese St. Louisans has not been simply another case study of a Chinese American community, and the model of cultural community it provides is not limited to ethnicities in St. Louis. The model is applicable to communities where there is no physical concentration of the ethnic minority group. It is also applicable to communities in which ethnic minority groups have integrated themselves economically and professionally with the larger society, while culturally remaining distinct from that society. The model is especially applicable to communities in which the members of ethnic minority groups are overwhelmingly professionals.

The cultural community in St. Louis provides an alternative model for understanding the diversity and complexity of Chinese American communities. The earlier theories of Chinese communities were less than adequate when they came to explaining ethnic communities that are blended with and geographically dispersed throughout the majority society, but that make a point of congregating at cultural events that distinguish them from the larger society. For these communities, the cultural community model offers an appropriate and satisfactory interpretation.

The cultural community as a variant of ethnic community also reflects the social advancement of ethnic minority groups in a society that integrates them to some extent but continues to "class" them and racialize them. The transformation of the St. Louis Chinese community from a Chinatown to a cultural community hails the social, economic, and political progress that Chinese Americans have achieved since the 1960s. In other words, the presence of a cultural community indicates that Chinese St. Louisans as an ethnic minority have made social and economic progress.

The cultural community model suggests that an ethnic community follows a certain path in its journey toward social and economic integration, but never ceases to yearn for a cultural identity. As long as the United States remains a multicultural and multiracial society, we will expect to find various cultural communities. Meanwhile, it is important to note that cultural communities do not advocate cultural separatism; rather, they celebrate multiculturalism and cultural pluralism in a multicultural and multiracial society.

Conclusion

Chinese St. Louisans have evolved from Chinatown residents to become Americans who happen to belong to a Chinese cultural community. The story of Hop Alley testifies that Chinatowns and other physical ethnic enclaves were necessary for ethnic groups whose members could survive only by extending one another mutual aid, in the form of ethnic social networks and other forms of self-governance. This, especially at a time when the social climate was less than accommodating to ethnic minorities. Many Chinese St. Louisans were re-migrants from the larger Chinese communities of San Francisco, New York, and Chicago, so it should not surprise us that the economy in St. Louis Chinatown closely resembled that of other Chinese enclaves. Occupational segregation was the predominant feature of St. Louis's Chinese economy, just as it was in other Chinese American economies. Most Chinese in the United States were heavily involved in the traditional Chinese economic activities—the laundry, grocery, and restaurant businesses. Although characterized by isolation, drudgery, and meager income, these economic activities enabled the Chinese to survive in the United States.

In addition to occupational segregation, another dominant feature of the Chinese economy was the central importance of ethnic networks. At the various stages and aspects of ethnic business operation, the ethnic networks were essential. Chinese business owners acquired their capital through mutual aid and also through loans from relatives and clansmen. They ordered their supplies from ethnic wholesalers in the larger Chinese American communities, and they relied on unpaid family members or low-paid laborers found through ethnic networks to operate their businesses.

The social life of Hop Alley was much like that of other Chinese communities in America. Besides providing sustenance for most Chinese, Chinese businesses served as cultural and social facilities on Sundays and traditional holidays. They were where Chinese went to rest, socialize, and entertain themselves. On the other hand, without a large Chinese population, even during the heyday of Hop Alley, Chinese St. Louisans integrated with the larger society more quickly than their counterparts in the larger Chinatowns, with most celebrated cases being four merchant wives and daughter.

The political structure of St. Louis Chinatown mirrored that of other Chinese communities, except that it was On Leong (i.e., not the Six Companies) that served as the community's self-governing mechanism. Like its counterparts on the East Coast and throughout the Midwest, St. Louis On Leong played a generally positive role: it provided mutual aid, mediated community disputes, sponsored social services, and organized cultural celebrations. But at the same time, it was generally powerless to protect Chinese St. Louisans from discrimination and prejudice. A case in point is that it could not prevent the demolition of Hop Alley. It could not even save the Sam Wah Laundry. On Leong's general failure to protect its members against mainstream society reflected the lower placement of the Chinese in America prior to the 1960s, more than it reflected the organization's inherent limitations.

Although Hop Alley was demolished during urban renewal, the upward mobility of the Chinese Americans was already beginning to weaken the district as an ethnic enclave. Long before the demolition of Hop Alley, the younger Chinese wanted to leave Chinatown behind and join the larger economy. It is safe to say that Hop Alley would eventually have dissolved on its own if urban renewal had not happened first. However, the destruction of St. Louis's historical Chinatown in 1966 shifted the demographics of Chinese St. Louis. Lacking a physical center, the Chinese had no choice but to join the larger economy. Consequently, most of the newcomers to the city were American-trained professionals, who took jobs with the region's big mainstream corporations. They were less likely to be new immigrants from Taiwan, Hong Kong, and China with significant capital to be invested in areas of large ethnic population concentrations. They were also less likely to be working-class immigrants with limited English and few marketable skills who could only find work in ethnic businesses. Thus the foreign-born but American-educated Chinese professionals constituted the cohort of the post-1966 Chinese American population in St. Louis.

From the 1960s to the 1990s, Taiwan-born Chinese Americans dominated almost every aspect of community life in St. Louis. They provided the leaders for all the big community organizations, especially the OCA. They established the first two Chinese-language schools and the Chinese churches, and they coordinated the Chinese Cultural Days and celebrations of various traditional holidays. Since the 1990s the dominance of Taiwan-born Chinese Americans has been challenged in St. Louis; professionals from Mainland China are settling in the region, and their influence in community affairs is growing. This power realignment of the community mirrors a nationwide demographic trend for the Chinese Americans. While the study-abroad waves in Taiwan has abated and reverse migration has occurred among the Taiwanese students studying in the United States in the 1990s, the newcomers from China have quickly joined their compatriots already in the country, gradually making Mainland Chinese the majority of the foreign-born Chinese American population in St. Louis as well as in the United States.

These Chinese American professionals have developed a cultural community in St. Louis. They work mainly for big corporations, and they live mainly in middle-class suburbs. However, they have also felt the need to establish their own community through Chinese-language preservation, spiritual worship, cultural celebrations, and other activities of cultural solidarity. In this way a cultural community has emerged.

Unlike the old Chinatown, which was physically situated in the St. Louis downtown district, the new Chinese cultural community physically does not contain either a commercial or a residential concentration. The cultural community operates through the permanent cultural institutions of the Chinese-language schools, Chinese religious institutions, and community organizations, and through a variety of cultural, social, and political activities sponsored by these institutions. Even though lacking significant physical concentration, the social space created by these activities is quite visible, recognizable, and identifiable; within it, the sense of community is effectively forged.

Cultural communities are developing in other American cities besides St. Louis, and among other ethnic groups as well. The cultural community model, with all its local variants, will continue to be found in the United States wherever ethnic communities have integrated economically with the larger society while remaining culturally distinct. The development of cultural communities demonstrates that minorities in America are enjoying economic integration and social advancement.

Notes

1. *M-R*, 31 December 1869; Louisville *Courtier-Journal*, 30 December 1896; Cohen, 86–87; *Kennedy's, 1859–1863; Edward's,1864–1871; Gould's, 1872–1879*; 1860 Census; and Blake, "There Ought to be a Monument to Alla Lee."

2. This claim is based on the author's tallies of Chinese laundries and non-Chinese laundries in St. Louis in the last decades of the nineteenth century and the first decades of the twentieth, the census data, and information from newsreports.

3. The definition of St. Louis has been changing historically. Before 1876 the city of St. Louis was within St. Louis County. That year it became an independent city. The terms St. Louis area and St. Louis region have generally corresponded to the city of St. Louis and St. Louis County. According to the1990 U.S. Census, however, St. Louis Metropolitan Statistical Area consists of St. Louis City and eleven other counties, of which seven are on the Missouri side and five on the Illinois side (The city of St. Louis is counted as both a city and a county.) Since the overwhelming majority of Chinese Americans reside in St. Louis (city) and St. Louis County in Missouri, the term "St. Louis region" in this study refers to St. Louis (city) and St. Louis County, Missouri. All statistics are drawn accordingly.

4. Profile of General Demographic Characteristics: 2000 Data Set: Census 2000 Summary File 2 (SF 2) 100-Percent Data Geographic Area: St. Louis, MO-IL MSA Race or Ethnic Group: Chinese alone.

5. The Chinese in Metropolitan St. Louis include American-born Chinese and Chinese from Mainland China, Taiwan, Hong Kong, Korea, Vietnam, and Southeast Asian countries. Community estimates of St. Louis's Chinese population range from 15,000 to 20,000.

6. Robert Park.

7. Philip Q. Yang, 85.

8. Gordon.

9. Gjerde,1.

10. Handlin, *The Uprooted*.

11. Bodnar, xx.

12. Roediger; Jacobson, 14; Ignatiev; and Kolchin.

13. Two excellent studies have discussed the "oriental problem" from different perspectives. Tchen's *New York before Chinatown* examines the

evolution of American perceptions of Orientals—perceptions that ranged from admiration to cruelly Darwinian racism. Yu's *Thinking Orientals* investigates the rise and fall of the Chicago school of Asian American studies known as the studies of the "Oriental Problem."

14. Gyory, 5.
15. Coolidge.
16. Miller.
17. Salyer.
18. Gyory.
19. Siu, "The Sojourner;" and *The Chinese Laundryman.*
20. Barth, *Bitter Strength.*
21. Wang Gungwu, *Community and Nation;* and *China and the Chinese.*
22. Glick, 102–25.
23. Lydon, *Chinese Gold,* 156–61; Sucheng Chan, *This Bittersweet Soil,* 390–99; Minnick, 246; Laura Wang, "Vallejo's Chinese Community"; Lee, *The Growth and Decline,* 234–39; Beesley; and Mason, "Liang May Seen."
24. Census, 1870–1970; Ling, *Surviving,* 115, Table 4.1.
25. Lee, *The Growth and Decline.*
26. Lyman, "Marriage and the Family;" and *Chinese Americans.*
27. Ling, "Family and Marriage."
28. Schiller, Basch, and Blanc-Szanton, eds., ix.
29. Renqiu Yu; Haiming Liu; M. Hsu; and Yong Chen.
30. McKeown.
31. Ling-chi Wang.
32. Wang Gungwu, "Among Non-Chinese," in *The Living Tree,* 81.
33. Tu Wei-ming, "Cultural China," in *The Living Tree,* 13–15.
34. Percentage computed according to *U.S. Census of Population: 1950,* Vol. IV, *Special Reports,* 3B-19.
35. Coolidge, 402.
36. Lee, *The Growth and Decline,* 147.
37. Lee, *The Chinese in the United States of America,* 52.
38. Bernard P. Wong, *A Chinese American Community,* 18; Anderson, 9.
39. David Lai, "Socio-economic Structures."
40. Lee, "Decline of Chinatowns," 423.
41. Lee, *The Growth and Decline,* 34.
42. Nee. For other works on San Francisco Chinatown, see, for example, Cather; Dicker; Lee, "The Recent Immigrant Chinese Families"; Riddle; and Tchen, *Genthe's Photographs.*
43. Chinn.
44. Loo, 3.
45. Chen, *Chinese San Francisco.*
46. Shah.
47. Wong, *A Chinese American Community.* For other works on New York Chinatown, see Julia I. Hsuan Chen; Chia-ling Kuo; Sung, *Gangs in New York's Chinatown,* and *The Adjustment Experience.*
48. Wong, *Chinatown: Economic Adaptation,* 107.
49. Wong, *Patronage, Brokerage, Entrepreneurship.*
50. Kwong, *Chinatown, New York; The New Chinatown.*

51. Kwong, *The New Chinatown*, 5, 175.

52. Zhou, *Chinatown*, xvii.

53. Hsiang-shui Chen, ix.

54. Jan Lin, xi.

55. Renqiu Yu; Bao.

56. Xinyang Wang.

57. Fong, *The First Suburban Chinatown*. For other works on Chinese communities in suburban Los Angeles, see Joe Chung Fong, "Transnational Newspapers"; Horton; Saito, *Race and Politics*; Yu Zhou, "Ethnic Networks"; Tseng, "Suburban Ethnic Economy"; "Chinese Ethnic Economy."
For comparative studies of Chinatowns in Canada, see Kay Anderson; David Lai, *Chinatowns*; and Thompson.

58. Horton, 8.

59. Tseng, "Chinese Ethnic Economy."

60. Saito.

61. Wei Li, "Spatial Transformation"; "Anatomy of a New Ethnic Settlement"; "Los Angeles' Chinese *Ethnoburb*"; and "Building Ethnoburbia."

62. Li, "Anatomy of a New Ethnic Settlement."

63. Tseng, "Chinese Ethnic Economy."

64. Lin, 107–20.

65. Hsiang-shui Chen, 31; Tseng, "Chinese Ethnic Economy," 170; Jan Lin, 39; Peter S. Li "The Consumer Market of the Enclave Economy"; "Self-Employment"; "Unneighborly Houses or Unwelcome Chinese"; and "Chinese Investment and Business in Canada."

66. Examples supporting such a pattern could be found in ample works. See, for example, Handlin, *Adventure in Freedom*; Berthoff; Birchall; Cardoso; Clark; Daniels, *A History of Indian Immigration*; and Diner.

67. See Barton; Chen, *Chinatown No More*; Cutler; and Tamura.

68. Handlin, *Adventure in Freedom*.

69. Fujita and O'Brien, 4–5.

70. Park.

71. Võ and Bonus, 6.

72. See "100 Chinese Americans Will Be Speakers and Resources," *New York Times*, 10 June 1991, A1.

73. *1990 Census of Population, Social and Economic Characteristics, Missouri*, Section 1of 2, Table 160, Social Characteristics for Selected Racial Groups: 1990, and Table 161, Labor Force Characteristics for Selected Racial Groups: 1990, 473, and 476.

74. Washington University, *A Partial Bibliography*. This lists 201 studies relating to the history of St. Louis ethnic cultures, divided by ethnic groups, yet no work on Chinese was listed. For works on Chinese in St. Louis, see Blake, "The Chinese of Valhalla"; Ling, "Hop Alley" and *Chinese St. Louisans*; St. Louis Chapter of the Organization of Chinese Americans, *Ironing Out the Fabric* (hereafter cited by title only).

75. *1990 Census of Population, Social and Economic Characteristics, Missouri*, Section 1of 2, Table 160, Social Characteristics for Selected Racial Groups: 1990, and Table 161, Labor Force Characteristics for Selected Racial Groups: 1990, 473, and 476.

CHAPTER TWO

1. *M-R*, 31 December 1869; *Kennedy's, 1859–1863; Edward's, 1864–1871; Gould's, 1872–1879;* 1860 Census about Alla Lee.

2. *Marriage Register*, Book 9, page 40, recorded 9–21–1858, Recorder of Deeds.

3. Blake, "There Ought to Be."

4. Ibid.

5. Allen, *Ellis Island,* 20.

6. *M-R*, 31 December 1869; Hyde and Conard, 357–58.

7. Blake, "There Ought to Be."

8. *M-R*, 31 December 1869; Louisville *Courier-Journal,* 30 December 1896; Cohen, 86–87.

9. *M-R*, 23 January 1870.

10. Daniels, *Asian America,* 9.

11. Chan, *This Bittersweet Soil;* Chinn; Chiu; Lydon; Minnick; Saxton.

12. Daniels, *Asian America,* 70.

13. Chan, *Asian Americans,* 46.

14. Ibid.

15. Chan, *Asian Americans,* 48; Locklear; Sandmeyer, 48, 97–98.

16. Cohen, 82–83.

17. *M-R*, 30 December 1869; Cohen, 86–87.

18. Hyde and Conard, 357–58.

19. Chinese Exclusion Cases Habeas Corpus Petitions, Case File 103.

20. *United States Ninth Census: 1870, Vol. I,* 386

21. Primm, 273–75.

22. U.S. censuses 1870–90.

23. Lipsitz, *The Sidewalks,* 34–37.

24. Comments by Diana Ahmad at the 44th Annual Missouri Conference on History, 18–20 April 2002, Kansas City, Missouri.

25. *Annual Report of the St. Louis Board of Police Commissioner,* 1896.

26. "50 Years Ago-Wednesday, August 26, 1925," *G-D*, 26 August 1925.

27. "Highbinder" was the name given to members of certain oath-bound Chinese secret societies in American cities by American police and the press. It was believed that these secret societies originated in the Great Hung League, or *Hung-men,* a political organization aimed at overthrowing the Manchu Qing Dynasty in China. The terms "Highbinders" and "tongs" were often used interchangeably.

28. Hyde and Conard, 1024.

29. "75 Years Ago—Thursday, June 8, 1892," *G-D*, 9 June 1967.

30. The 1882 Chinese Exclusion Act banned laborers for ten years. It was renewed in 1892 and 1902 and made indefinite in 1904.

31. "75 Years Ago—Wednesday, August 25, 1897," *G-D*, 25 August 1972.

32. Chinese Exclusion Cases Habeas Corpus Petitions.

33. K. Scott Wong; Tam.

34. Letter from Orville Spreen to Miss Douglas.

35. Dreiser.

36. "75 Years Ago—Wednesday, August 25, 1897," *G-D*, 25 August 1972; Chung Kok Li, interview.

37. *U.S.A. vs. Jeu Lime; U.S.A. vs. Jeu Young; U.S.A. vs. Chu Dock Yuck.*

38. Claudia Rhodes to Huping Ling.

39. *Gould's, 1873,* 1036.

40. *Gould's, 1874,* 1106.

41. *Gould's,* 1875–89.

42. *Gould's,* 1873–89.

43. Note that many of the surnames mentioned here are probably not real Chinese surnames, as non-Chinese might refer to individual Chinese by the name of the store, or confuse the Chinese given name with the surname. Kee, for instance, is the Cantonese pronunciation of *ji,* which means "store" or "brand."

44. Chung Kok Li, interview. According to Sue Fawn Chung, the restriction was established by the Chinese laundry associations in the 1860s in San Francisco and Virginia City.

45. Nee; Renqiu Yu, 9; Siu, *Chinese Laundry man;* Jew, 33.

46. Ibid.

47. Hyde and Conard, 357–58; *M-R,* 23 January 1970; numerous newspaper articles in *G-D, P-D, M-R,* and *S-P.*

48. Siu, 58.

49. Porter, "Papers."

50. *Gould's,* 1887–1952; *Polk's,* 1955–80.

51. John M. McGuire, "Chinese Laundry Being Pressed," *P-D,* 12 November 1978, 3G.

52. *Ironing Out the Fabric,* 2.

53. Porter, "Papers."

54. Hong, interview.

55. *Business Directory and Mercantile Register of St. Louis, 1903–1904; Gould's,* 1905–10.

56. Hong, interview.

57. *Ironing Out the Fabric,* 1, 5.

58. Ibid., 2, 5.

59. McGuire; Porter, interview.

60. Dick Wood, "The Chinese Colony of St. Louis," *S-R,* 29 July 1900 (Mag. Sec.), 2.

61. Hong, interview.

62. *Ironing Out the Fabric,* 6.

63. Hong, interview.

64. *Ironing Out the Fabric,* 7.

65. *Gould's,* 1888.

66. *Gould's,* 1889.

67. *Gould's,* 1890–1910.

68. *Gould's,* 1912–14.

69. *Gould's,* 1919–29.

70. *Gould's,* 1906–10.

71. Wood.

72. Ling, *Surviving,* 64–70.

73. Wood.

74. Sit, *My View,* 24–25.

75. Leong, interview.

76. Chow, interview.

77. Connie Young Yu, 37.

78. Lily Chan, "My Early Influences," 25 October 1926, Smith Documents, MK-2.

79. Ho, letter to Huping Ling, 3 August 2002.

80. Ling, *Surviving*, 65–67.

81. Dreiser.

82. Tchen, *New York before Chinatown*, 264–65.

83. Ibid., 266.

84. Wong Chin Foo, "The Chinese in New York," *Cosmopolitan* 5 (March–October 1888): 297–311, 305.

85. *U.S.A. vs. Jeu Lime.*

86. "2 Sisters Arrested in Chop Suey Raid," *S-R*, 22 August 1910.

87. Liu Bo-ji, 297.

88. Wood.

89. "Housekeeping in St. Louis Chinatown," *S-R*, 14 August 1910 (Mag. Sec.), 4.

90. Leong, interview.

91. Ho, letter to Huping Ling.

92. Leong, interview.

93. Ho, letter to Huping Ling.

94. *St. Louis Directory*, 1859.

95. *Kennedy's*, 1860; *Edward's*, 1864–71; *Gould's*, 1872–80.

96. Hyde and Conard, 357–58.

97. "Gradual Disappearance of the Chinatown of St. Louis," *P-D*, 25 September 1902.

98. *Gould's*, 1899.

99. *U.S.A. vs. Hop Hing.*

100. *U.S.A. vs. Leong Choey.*

101. *U.S.A. vs. Sing Lung.*

102. *U.S.A. vs. Wong Lung.*

103. "Gradual Disappearance of the Chinatown of St. Louis."

104. *St. Louis Police Annual Report*, 1896.

105. According to author's conversations with an African–American community preservationist, 28 November 2000, and 16 March 2001, St. Louis, MO.

106. Dreiser; Wood.

107. Dreiser.

108. Cortinovis, 59–66.

109. *P-D*, 3 July 1903; Bennitt, 289.

110. Cortinovis, 63.

111. Ibid., 63–64.

112. Ibid., 66.

113. Iglauer.

114. *P-D*, 3 July and 18 October 1903; *G-D*, 5 December 1904.

115. *G-D*, 5 December 1904.

116. Cortinovis, 63.

CHAPTER THREE

1. Daniels, *Asian America*, 17; Lyman, *Chinese Americans*, 86–92.

2. Chan, *Asian Americans;* Ling, *Surviving,* 25–39.

3. Chan, *Asian Americans,* 104.

4. Cases 19571/18-5, 14282/4-4, RG 85, National Archives, Pacific Sierra Region, San Bruno, CA.

5. Tang.

6. Peffer.

7. Chan, *Entry Denied,* 94–146.

8. Hyde and Conard, 357–58.

9. *M-R,* 23 January 1870.

10. Classified advertisement, *S-R,* 29, July, 1900 (Mag. Sec.), p. 9.

11. "Housekeeping."

12. Primm, 166.

13. "Housekeeping."

14. Ibid.

15. "Only Four Chinese Women in St. Louis," *S-R,* 4 October 1908, pt. 5, p. 4.

16. Ibid.

17. Ibid.

18. Ibid.

19. "Housekeeping."

20. Ibid.

21. Ling, *Surviving,* 61–72.

22. Tchen, *Genthe's Photograph,* 106.

23. Lee, *The Growth and Decline,* 252.

24. "Life History," by a Chinese girl at McKinley High School, Honolulu, 20 November 1926, Smith Documents.

25. Leong, interview.

26. Hong, interview.

27. Primm, 339.

28. *New York Times,* 13 March 1966, Sec. 4, p. 12; Harper and Skolnick, 96–105.

29. *California Statutes,* 1880, Code Amendments, Ch. 41, sec. 1, p. 3.

30. *California Statute,* 1905, Ch. 481, sec. 2, p. 554.

31. Tenth Census, 1880, New Orleans, Louisiana, population schedules, as cited in Cohen, 147.

32. Mason, "Family Structure," 163.

33. Tchen, "New York Chinese," 176–77.

34. *M-R,* 31 December 1869; *Kennedy's,* 1859–63, *Edward's,* 1864–71, *Gould's,* 1872–79; 1860 census; and Blake, "There Ought to Be."

35. The 1890 Census; Rhodes to Huping Ling.

36. "Hop Alley to be Invaded," *S-R,* 1 May 1910 (II), p. 16.

37. "Hop Alley Census Adds 300," *S-R,* 2 May 1910, p. 14.

38. "2 Sisters Arrested in Chop Suey Raid," *S-R,* 22 August 1910.

39. Ling, "Family and Marriage."

40. Jew.

41. Wong.

42. Lui.

43. Hyde and Conard, 357–58.

44. Ibid.

45. *Ironing out the Fabric,* 12.

46. Hong, interview.
47. "70th Anniversary, 1924-1994," St. Louis Chinese Gospel Church, November 1994, 3.
48. Hong, interview.
49. "70th Anniversary," 3.
50. Hong, interview.
51. Hyde and Conard, 357–58.
52. Ibid.
53. "Housekeeping."
54. Hong, interview.
55. *Ironing Out the Fabric*, 12.
56. Hong, interview; Wood.
57. Leong, interview; Wood; "Housekeeping."
58. Wood.
59. "Hop Alley to Be Invaded."
60. Leong, interview; "Housekeeping."
61. Leong, interview.
62. "Hop Alley to be Invaded."
63. *Ironing out the Fabric*, 3.
64. *S-R*, 10 February 1880.
65. "Chinese Grand Lodge of Free Masons of the State of Missouri," *Corporation Book* 18, page 499 (11-3–1899), Recorder of Deeds.
66. Ibid.
67. I. Hsu, 408–412.
68. "Chinese Empire Reform Society of Missouri," *Corporation Book* 24, page 296 (1-5-1903), Recorder of Deeds.
69. *Gould's*, 1910–27.
70. Ibid.
71. Ibid.
72. I. Hsu, 408.
73. I. Hsu, 408–12.
74. "Chinese American Educational Association," *Corporation Book* 30, p. 59 (5-25-1905), Recorder of Deeds.
75. "Chinese Nationalist League of America," *Corporation Book* 53, p. 554 (7-18-1916), Recorder of Deeds.
76. "Chinese Nationalist Party," *Corporation Book* 97, p. 467 (12-7-1928), Recorder of Deeds.
77. Dreiser.
78. "The Late Wong You," *G-D*, 25 October 1879; "A Celestial Funeral," *G-D*, 26 October 1879.
79. Dreiser.
80. Ibid.
81. Chung.
82. Dreiser.
83. "Bones of Chinese to be Sent Home," *P-D*, 17 November 1928.
84. Blake, "The Chinese of Valhalla."
85. "Chinese-American History Reflected in Cemetery," *Kirksville Daily Express and News*, 10 August 1999.
86. Blake, "The Chinese of Valhalla."

87. According to the author's field study of the Chinese burials in Valhalla Cemetery.

88. Blake, "The Chinese of Valhalla," note 9.

89. Blake, "The Chinese of Valhalla."

CHAPTER FOUR

1. "Charles Quinn New Mayor of Chinatown," *G-D*, 1 February 1948; "Chinatown Mayor Speaks at Dinner Marking New Year," *G-D*, 11 February 1948; and "Daughter of Mayor Weds," *G-D*, 14 July 1949.

2. Ashbury.

3. Gang and Grant, 157; *G-D*, 1 April 1949; Kuo-lin Chen, 42–43. Presently, On Leong has more than twenty branches in eastern and midwestern states.

4. Li, interview.

5. "On Leong Tong Chinese Merchants Association," *Corporation Book* 43, page 543 (4-6-1912), Recorder of Deeds.

6. Chu.

7. "Housekeeping."

8. Reynolds.

9. Chu, 23–24.

10. Chen, 35–37.

11. Chu, 27; for the development of Chih Kung in North America, see Chung, "Between Two Worlds."

12. Chen, 42–43.

13. "Hop Alley Makee Feast Like B. M. L.," *S-R*, 11 October 1914.

14. Hoy; Lai, "Historical Development;" Ling, *Surviving*, 47–50.

15. The reasons the CCBA did not spread in the Midwest may be associated with its failure to challenge immigration authorities in the 1890s.

16. "On Leong Tong Chinese Merchants Association," *Corporation Book* 43, page 543 (4-6-1912), Recorder of Deeds.

17. Ibid.

18. "On Leong Chinese Merchants and Laborers Association," *Corporations Book* 60, page 537 (3-4-1919), Recorder of Deeds.

19. Li, interview; Don Ko, interview.

20. "Chinese in St. Louis," *G-D*, 19 November 1956; "Chinese Cook Up Tasty Convention," *G-D*, 19 April 1962.

21. Li, interview.

22. Lai, "Historical Development;" Chinese General Correspondence, 1898–1908, RG 85.

23. Lai, "Historical Development," 19–20.

24. Li, interview.

25. Leong, interview.

26. Lai, "Historical Development;" Ling, *Surviving*, 96.

27. Don Ko, interview.

28. "On Leong Chinese Merchants and Laborers Association," *Corporations Book* 60, page 537 (3-4-1919), Recorder of Deeds.

29. Leong, interview; *G-D*, 8 February 1959, 19 April 1962, 25 January 1963, 14 February 1965, and 4 August 1966.

30. Julia I. Hsuan Chen, 38.

31. Hoy, 21–22.

32. Lai, "Historical Development."

33. Kwong, *The New Chinatown*, 86–90.

34. Chung, 222.

35. Lai, "Historical Development."

36. Kwong, *The New Chinatown*, 81–106.

37. Riordon.

38. Lee, *The Chinese in the United States of America*; Kwong, *Chinatown, New York*; and Loo.

39. "Hop Alley Makee Feast Like B. M. L.," *S-R*, 11 October 1914.

40. "50 Years Ago—Saturday, Dec. 15, 1917," *G-D*, 15 December 1967.

41. *Gould's*, 1897–1914.

42. Wood.

43. Ibid.

44. Ibid.

45. "Bones of Chinese to be Sent Home."

46. *Gould's*, 1939–1952; "Chinese Here Aiding Homeland," *G-D*, 14 October 1937.

47. "Chinese Nationalists Here Split on House Government," *S-T*, 12 March 1930.

48. "Chinese Here Aiding Homeland;" *G-D*, 11 August 1939.

49. "250 Attend St. Louis Tea for Benefit of Chinese," *P-D*, 18 June 1938.

50. "Chinese Here Aiding Homeland."

51. "All Limousines in City hired for Mourners," *G-D*, 23 December 1947.

52. Ibid.

53. "Charles Quinn New Mayor of Chinatown," *G-D*, 1 February 1948; "St. Louis Chinese Denounce the Reds," *P-D*, 14 December 1950.

54. "St. Louis Chinese Denounce the Reds;" "Daughter of Mayor of Chinatown Weds," *G-D*, 14 June 1949.

55. Note that Charles Quinn's term (1938–48) as president of the National On Leong Association overlapped with that of Joe Lin (1937–47), perhaps due to error in newspaper articles.

56. "St. Louis Chinese Denounce the Reds."

57. Ibid.

58. "C. H. Quin Chu Dies," *P-D*, 1 February 1976.

59. McKeown, 198–223.

60. *Gould's* for 1914–52.

61. Ibid.

62. "Chinese Here Search For 'Kung Hsi Fa Tsai'," *G-D*, 27 January 1957.

63. "Chinese Group Buys a $100,000 Building Here," *G-D*, 12 September 1948; "Chinese Pay $100,000 for Building Here," *P-D*, 12 September 1948.

64. "National Convention of On Leong Opens Here Monday," *G-D*, 1 April 1949; "14-Course Chinese Banquet Served Tong Parley Delegates," *G-D*, 3 April 1949.

65. Leong, interview.

66. "Chinese Here Welcome 4650th New Year," *G-D*, 28 January 1952.

67. "St. Louis Chinese Wishing You 'Kung Hsi Fa Tsai'," *G-D*, 8 February 1959.

68. "Chinese Cook Up Tasty Convention."

69. "Chinatown Going Down—Maybe Chop Chop."

70. Ibid.

71. "Chinese to Vacate Old Quarters as New Year Begins," *G-D*, 21 January 1966.

72. "Chinatown Changes Quarters."

73. "Demise of Old Chinatown," *G-D*, 20–21 August 1966.

74. Ling, *Surviving,* 107.

75. "Chinese Here Aiding Homeland."

76. "250 Attend St. Louis Tea for Benefit of Chinese."

77. *G-D*, 11 August 1939.

78. Li, interview.

CHAPTER FIVE

1. Hong, interview.

2. *Ironing Out the Fabric*, 2.

3. Ibid., 5.

4. Hong, interview.

5. Leong, interview.

6. "Story of a Chinese College Girl," 1 August 1924, Smith Documents, A-54.

7. "Life History," 29 November 1926, Smith Documents, MK-26.

8. Yans-McLaughlin, 71.

9. Mormino, 109.

10. Lynch, 79–90.

11. Chris L. Murray, "Americanization is Easy for Chinese Children in St. Louis Public Schools," *G-D*, 4 September 1927.

12. *Ironing out the Fabric*, 14.

13. Murray.

14. Ibid.

15. *Ironing out the Fabric*, 16.

16. Ibid., 15.

17. Ibid.

18. Murray.

19. Ibid.

20. Leong, interview.

21. Murray.

22. Leong, interview.

23. Hong, interview.

24. *Ironing out the Fabric*, 16.

25. "Interview with Mrs. Machida," 2 July 1924, Smith Documents.

26. *Forbidden City, U.S.A.*, 12/8/89, videocassette.

27. Adalyn Faris McKee, "Chinese Girl Student Talks," *G-D*, 27 May 1934.

28. McKee.

29. On 10 October 1911, a republican revolution overthrew the Qing dynasty and established the Republic of China. Since then the Tenth of October (Double 10) had been reserved as the national holiday. "St. Louis

Chinese Will Celebrate Historic Day of the Double Tens," *S-T*, 6 October 1938.

30. Ibid.

31. Primm, 441.

32. Hong, interview.

33. Ibid.

34. Ho to Melissa M. Szeto; Ho to Huping Ling.

35. Chow, interview.

36. Chan, *Asian Americans*, 121; Daniels, *Asian America*, 187; and Ling, 113–35.

37. Burnett, 2.

38. Ibid., 2–3.

39. Chinn, 147–50.

40. *Ironing Out the Fabric*, 1.

41. Margaret Maunder, "The Chinese Speak," *G-D*, 6 November 1943.

42. Maunder.

43. Ho, letter to Huping Ling.

44. Sit, 41–47.

45. Nash, 869.

46. Edna Warren, "Woman Reporter," *G-D*, 31 July 1942.

47. Warren.

48. Ibid.

49. Maunder. For Chinese women's participation in World War II, see Zhao, 48–77.

50. Ibid.

51. Isaac, xviii-xix.

52. "Act of Congress Lets Chinese Woman Stay with Family Here," *G-D*, 28 December 1942.

53. Daniels, *Asian America*, 192.

54. Riggs, 43–183.

55. 57 Stat. 600–1.

56. Maunder.

57. Ibid.

58. Ibid.

59. Ibid.

60. Burnett, 2.

61. Hong, interview.

62. U.S. Censuses, 1940–60.

63. Tao, interview; Ted Schafers, "William Tao Is Living Proof," *G-D*, 2–3 December 1967, p. 8G; and Lan Shi, "Hope More People Would Get to Know William Tao," *Chinese*, No.1 (1999): 3–9.

64. Tai, interview; Andrew Lu, interview.

65. Andrew Lu, interview.

66. Wubing Zong and T.C. Peng, "Prominent People in Public Service," in *Chinese American Forum*, Vol. 14, no. 3 (January 1999): 2–6.

67. Zong and Peng.

68. Zong and Peng.

69. Leong, interview; "New Chinatown Springing Up in the 1500 Block of Delmar," *P-D*, 21 July 1966.

70. Ibid., 454–56.

71. Ibid., 457, 468.

72. Ibid., 468–69.

73. Schacht, "Chinatown Going Down—Maybe Chop Chop."

74. Gottschalk, "Chinese Community Mourns Passing of Its Tradition."

75. Ibid.

76. Ibid.

CHAPTER SIX

1. "Their Background Is Chinese, But Now They Are St. Louisans," *G-D*, 14 February 1972.

2. Beulah Schacht, "New Chinatown Here Opens with a Bang," *G-D*, 26 September 1966.

3. "Chinatown Just a Memory," *G-D*, 1 February 1978.

4. "'Year of the Sheep' Begins for 450 Here," *G-D*, 9 February 1967; "St. Louis Chinese Mark New Year With Ceremony," *P-D*, 9 February 1967.

5. Margie Wolf Freivogel, "St. Louis's Chinese Community," *P-D*, 14 November 1971.

6. "Chinatown Just a Memory."

7. Edward L. Cook, "City's Chinatown Must Move Again," *G-D*, 19 September 1978.

8. Ibid.

9. "Chinatown Granted a Reprieve until May 1," *G-D*, 25 January 1979.

10. Edward L. Cook, "A Little Bit of China Joins Folks 'Down by der Gravois'," *G-D*, 6 September 1979.

11. Ibid.

12. *Census of Population: 1960, Vol. 1 Characteristics of the Population*, Part 27, Missouri, 153; *1970 Census of Population, Vol. 1 Characteristics of the Population, Part 27, Missouri*, 155–56; and *1980 Census of Population, Vol. 1 Characteristics of the Population, Chapter B. General Population Characteristics*, Part 27, Missouri, 14.

13. INS, *Annual Report*, 1945–49.

14. INS, *Annual Report*, 1948.

15. INS, *Annual Report*, 1945–54.

16. Tung, 39

17. *The U.S. Census of Population, 1960.*

18. *Statutes at Large*, 1965, V. 79, 912–13.

19. *1980 Census of Population, Supplemented Reports*, and "Foreign-Born Immigrants: Chinese-Tabulations from the 1980 U.S. Census of the Population and Housing," mimeographed report, 1984.

20. Loo, 62–71.

21. Kwong, *The New Chinatown*, 175–76.

22. Zhou, 86.

23. *1980 Census of Population and Housing, Census tracts, St. Louis, MO-ILL. Standard Metropolitan Statistical Area*, Section 2, 490–93.

24. Zhou, 167.

25. Ibid., 84.

26. *Gould's*, 1920–31.

27. Renqiu Yu, 138–42.

28. *Gould's*, 1931.

29. INS, *Annual Report*, 1965–75.

30. John Heidenry, "Chinese Dining Guide," *St. Louisan* (April 1976): 52–54.

31. Ibid.

32. *Polk's*, 1976–77, 136–37.

33. Don Ko, interview; Ann Ko, interview.

34. Kwong, interview.

35. Chen Pen-ch'ang, 9.

36. *Gould's*, 1930–40s.

37. Leong, interview.

38. While *Polk's St. Louis City Directory* listed one Chinese grocery store in 1980, oral history interviews reveal at least three Chinese groceries during the same time period.

39. Jean Chiu, interview.

40. Ibid.

41. Ibid.

42. Walter Ko, interview.

43. *1980 Census of Population and Housing, Census Tracts, St. Louis, MO-ILL. Standard Metropolitan Statistical Area*, section 2, 490.

44. Ibid., 493.

45. Tao, interview; *Washington University Magazine*, Vol. 47, No. 4 (Summer 1977).

46. Wu, interviews; Ling, "Lu Qiao Qi Ren"; Patricia L. Yeh, "Asian Art Society," *W-J*, 7 November 1993; and "The 25th Anniversary of the OCA," *C-N*, 3 December 1998.

47. Tzy C. Peng, interview.

48. Dachung Peng, interview.

49. Schafers; and *William Tao & Associates Consulting Engineers* (pamphlet in author's possession).

50. Wong, *Patronage, Brokerage, Entrepreneurship*.

51. Peter S. Li, "Chinese Investment and Business in Canada."

52. Linda Y.C. Lim.

53. For more discussions on Chinese ethnic networks, see Chan Kwok Bun.

54. Porter, "Papers."

55. Porter, interview.

56. Ibid.

57. Porter, "Papers."

58. Porter, interview.

59. Ibid.

60. Ibid.

61. Ibid.; Porter, "Papers"; McGuire.

62. Porter, "Papers."

63. Porter, interview; McGuire.

64. Porter, interview; Porter, "Papers"; McGuire.

65. Porter, interview.

66. Porter, "Papers."

67. Fred W. Lindecke, "Chinese Laundry Isn't Washed Up," *P-D*, 8 December 1979.

68. "Gee Hong, 88," *P-D*, 27 February 1986.
69. Porter, interview.
70. Ibid.
71. Ibid.
72. Ibid.
73. *Refugee Reports*, 18 December 1987: 10.
74. IIMS, brochure.
75. Freeman, 7.
76. Doan, interview; Ha, interview.
77. Ha, interview.
78. Doan, interview.
79. IIMS, *Annual Report*; LeLaurin, interview; Crosslin, interview.
80. Doan, interview.
81. Young-Rok Cheong, "Evolution of Economic Status of Chinese in Korea," paper presented at ISSCO Seoul Conference 2000, 12–13 June 2000; Sheena Choi, "Educational Choices of Ethnic Chinese Minorities in Korea," paper presented at ISSCO Seoul Conference 2000.
82. Sherwin Liou, interview.
83. Heidenry.
84. Yuansheng Siu, interview; Mrs. Siu, interview.
85. Mrs. Che, interview.

CHAPTER SEVEN

1. International Folklore Federation of Greater St. Louis, *Nationalities of Greater St. Louis.*
2. Margie Wolf Freivogel, "St. Louis Chinese," *P-D*, 14 November 1971.
3. Freivogel.
4. Freivogel; *G-D*, 14 February 1972; *P-D*, 27 January 1976; *G-D*, 17 February 1977; and *G-D*, 1 February 1978.
5. Dachung Peng, interview.
6. Mission Statement, St. Louis OCA, 1974.
7. The presidents of the St. Louis OCA included William Tao (1973), William Chang (1974), Ruby Chiang (1975), Alberto Ng (1976), Tony Shen (1977), S. K. Liu (1978), Austin Tao (1979), Howard Young (1980), Nora Wong (1981), T. Leo Lo (1982), Warren Der (1983), Roberto Lee (1984), Grace Shen Lo (1985), Howard Young (1986), Tony Huang (1987), Dachung Peng (1988), George Wang (1989), Dennis Soung (1990), Tzy C. Peng (1991), Warren Hu (1992), Ching-ling Tai (1993), Leo Hong (1994), Harold Low (1995, 1996), Grace Yin Lo (1997, 1998), Tom To (1999), Thomas Cy Wong (2000), Jimmy Chu (2001), Matthew Yu (2002), and Jason Tang (2003).
8. Grace Yin Lo, interview.
9. *C-J*, 10 January 2002.
10. Dachung Peng, interview.
11. James Yeh, interview.
12. Ibid.
13. Hwang, interview.
14. I. Hsu, 792.
15. Liangwu Yin; Dachung Peng, interview.

16. *C-N*, 29 November 2001.

17. For studies of Chinese Christian churches in America, see, for example, Fenggang Yang.

18. Harold Law, "The History of CGC"; Hong, interview.

19. Law.

20. Wayne Leeman, "Chinese Congregation Remodeling Webster Church," *P-D*, 25 June 1969.

21. Leeman.

22. Ibid.

23. Law.

24. Hong, interview; St. Louis Chinese Gospel Church program, 31 January 1999.

25. Pan, interview.

26. Lyman, *Chinese Americans*, 46–48; Ling, *Surviving*, 102; and Joy Hendry, *Understanding Japanese Society* (London and New York: Routledge, 1995), 115–16.

27. "Chinese Nationalist League of America," *Corporation Books 3*, page 554 (7-18-1916), Recorder of Deeds.

28. Freivogel.

29. Leong, interview.

30. Lai, "Transmitting the Chinese Heritage."

31. St. Louis Chinese Academy, "St. Louis Chinese Academy History," 1998, 15.

32. For the study abroad movement in Taiwan, see Ling, "A History of Chinese Female Students" and "The Changing Patterns."

33. Ling, *Surviving*, 150, and "A History of Chinese Female Students."

34. John T. Ma, "Chinese Americans in the Professions," in Yuan-li Wu, 67.

35. Chou, 1, 87.

36. Ling, "The Changing Patterns."

37. Ng.

38. Ling, "The Changing Patterns," 182.

39. Ibid., 184–85.

40. Baorui Li, "The Study to Attract Study Abroad Students back to the Country;" *Qin Fu Hui Report*, 3.

41. Ling, "The Changing Patterns," 189–93.

42. Ibid., 198.

43. Ibid., 200–3; Joyce Lin, "Summer a Language Opportunity," *Taipei Journal*, 7 July 2000; Joyce Lin, "Graduate Flock to European Schools," *Taipei Journal*, 12 January 2001; and William Chou, "Taiwan Teens Saddle Up for Overseas Studies," *Taipei Journal*, 21 June 2002.

44. Tao, interview; Walter Ko, interview.

CHAPTER EIGHT

1. *1980 Census of Population Vol. 1, Characteristics of the Population, Chapter 13, General Population Characteristics*, Part 27, Missouri, PC80-1-B27, Table-15, 27–14; *1990 Census of Population, General Population Characteristics, Missouri*, Table 6 and Table 79; Profile of General Demographic Characteristics: 2000 Data Set: Census 2000 Summary File 2 (SF 2)

100-Percent Data Geographic Area: St. Louis, MO-IL MSA Race or Ethnic Group: Chinese alone.

2. According to the author's discussion with leaders of various Chinese community organizations.

3. James Zhang, interview.

4. Wing.

5. I. Hsu, 286.

6. Chinese Institute in America, *A Survey*, 26.

7. Y. C. Wang, 158.

8. Ibid.

9. When the Boxer Uprising began in 1900, the Western powers invaded China and forced the Qing government to pay an indemnity of 450 million taels. In May 1908 the U.S. Congress passed a law to return part of the indemnity to China, stipulating that the refund must only be used to improve education. Beginning in 1909 the Qing government used the sum to send students to the United States under the Boxer Indemnity Fellowship.

10. Chinese Institute in America, 27.

11. Ibid., 18.

12. Shiqi Huang, "Contemporary Educational Relations with the Industrial World," in Hayhoe and Bastid, 226–27.

13. Ling, "A History of Chinese Female Students."

14. *China Daily*, 15 February 1988.

15. Chou, 61.

16. "Chinese Students Win Waiver."

17. "Bush Veto of Chinese Immigration Relief."

18. *China Daily*, 15 February 1988; *Consular Reports: 1979–1986*.

19. According to a cable sent to all the U.S. Immigration and Naturalization Service field offices on 4 December 1989.

20. Ling, "A History of Chinese Female Students."

21. James Zhang, interview.

22. Sun, interview.

23. *C-J*, 31 January 2002; *C-N*, 7–13 February 2002.

24. Haiyan Cai, interview.

25. "Death of a Red Heroine," *Chinese American Forum*, vol. 15, no. 3 (January 2002): 40; Youzhen Su, "When Asked about the Justice: Introducing Xiaolong Qiu's New Book *Death of a Red Heroine*," *C-J*, 8 March 2001; Xiaolong Qiu, "Interpreting 'Overseas Chinese'," *Joint Currents*, vol. 2 ed., Chinese Writers Association of North America–St. Louis Chapter (St. Louis: Chinese Writers Association of North America–St. Louis Chapter, 2002): 36–40; and *C-J*, 5 September 2002.

26. Liang, interview.

27. Ibid.

28. Gao, interview.

29. Repps Hudson, "Acupuncturist Puts Fine Point on Helping Patients Feel Better," *P-D*, 17 May 1999; "Acupuncture: Qi in the Balance," *St. Louis* (May 1999): 32; *C-N*, 18 February 1999.

30. James Zhang, interview.

31. Chris Lu, interview.

32. Jerry Li, interview.

33. The St. Louis Chinese Association, "Mission Statement," June 2000 www.stlchinese.org/org.htm (27 February 2001).

34. James Zhang, interview.

35. Zhu, interview.

36. Jin Yi, "For Our Children, For Our Future," *C-N*, 25 January 2001, S11.

37. Lai, "The Chinese Press."

38. Francis Yueh, interview.

39. Dachung Peng, interview.

40. Francis Yueh, interview.

41. Francis Yueh, interview; May Yueh, interview; "An Introduction of *St. Louis Chinese American News*," *C-N*, 14 March 2001 www.scanews.com/introduction 14 March 2001.

42. Hwang, interview.

43. *St. Louis Chinese Yellow Pages 2000*.

44. Ibid.

45. Ibid.

46. See works on Chinese American communities discussed in Chapter 1.

47. Anonymous, interview.

48. According to the author's conversation with Lee, 12 June 1999.

49. Mr. Yang, interview.

50. Don Ko, interview; Ann Ko, interview; and Jean Chiu, interview.

51. Zhang, Lu, Gao, and Liang, interviews.

52. Fong, 48–49.

53. Tseng, "Chinese Ethnic Economy."

54. Li, "Los Angeles' Chinese *Ethnoburb*."

55. *St. Louis Chinese American Yellow Pages 2003* and *St. Louis Chinese Yellow Pages 2003*.

56. Hwang, interview.

57. Patricia L. Yeh, interview.

58. Grace Shen Lo, interview.

59. *C-N*, 1 November 2001.

60. "Chinese Culture Days Feature Acrobats, Dragon Dance, Opera," *St. Louis Chinese American*, 9–15 May 2002.

61. *C-J*, 11 October 2001.

62. *C-N*, 20 September 2001.

63. *C-N*, 29 November 2001.

64. Chan, *Asian Americans*, 171; Lien; Saito, "Asian Americans and Multiracial Political Coalitions," in Gordon H. Chang, 383–408; Browning, Marshall, and Tabb; Lipsitz, *The Possessive Investment in Whiteness*.

65. Chan, *Asian Americans*, 171.

66. Gordon H. Chang, 1.

67. Chan, *Asian Americans*, 176–79.

68. Browning, Marshall, and Tabb.

69. Underwood.

70. Lipsitz, *The Possessive Investment in Whiteness*; Saito, "Asian Americans and Multiracial Political Coalitions"; and Browning, Marshall, and Tabb.

71. James Yeh, interview.

72. Ibid.

73. *C-N*, 21 March 2002; "Talent for Senate," www.talentforsenate.com.

74. "The Pacific-American Campaign Coalition Dinner for Congressman Jim Talent," *St. Louis Chinese American*, 2–8 May 2002.

75. *C-J*, 5 July 2001; and "Governor's Appointment in the State of Missouri," *Chinese American Forum*, vol. 17, no. 2 (October 2001).

76. Tai, interview; and "Governor's Appointment in the State of Missouri."

77. Lily Ko, biographic note; "Governor's Appointment in the State of Missouri."

CHAPTER NINE

1. Handlin, *Boston's Immigrants*, 29–30.

2. Ibid., 233.

3. Ibid., 62, 237–38.

4. Ibid., 106–16.

5. Handlin, *Boston's Immigrants*, 159.

6. Ibid., 160.

7. Olson, 280.

8. Ibid., 134.

9. Ibid.

10. Ibid., 281.

11. Inoue.

12. Guogan Wu, "An Overview of the Chinese Community in Kansas City," *Kansas City Chinese Journal*, 1, 8 March 2001.

13. *Kansas City Chinese Journal*, 7 December 2000.

14. *C-N*, 14 December 2000; and *Kansas City Chinese Journal*, 7, 28 December 2000, 1, 8 March 2001.

15. *Kansas City Chinese Journal*, 9 August 2001.

16. *Kansas City Chinese Journal*, 28 December 2000.

17. *Kansas City Chinese Journal*, 14, 28 December 2000, 4, 18 January, 1 February, 10 May, 9 August 2001; *C-N*, 14 December 2000.

18. Benedict Anderson.

19. Ibid., 7.

20. Tu, "Cultural China," 13–14.

Selected Bibliography

PRIMARY SOURCES

Censuses, Directories, and Manuscripts

Annual Report of St. Louis Board of Police Commissioners, 1873–1950s.

Business Directory and Mercantile Register of St. Louis, 1903–4.

Chinese Exclusion Cases Habeas Corpus Petitions: 1857–1965. U.S. District Court for the Eastern District of Missouri, St. Louis, Records of the District Courts of the United States, RG 21, National Archives–Central Plains Region, Kansas City, Missouri.

Chinese Herb Remedy Company. *The St. Louis Free Press* advertisement of Chinese Herb Remedy Company, 1010 Olive Street, St. Louis, 1892. Missouri Historical Society, St. Louis.

Dreiser, Theodore. "The Chinese in St. Louis." In *Journalism, Vol. 1: Newspaper Writings, 1892–1895*. Edited by T. D. Nostwich, 239–49. Philadelphia: University of Pennsylvania Press, 1988.

Gould's St. Louis Directory, 1872–1952.

Gould's St. Louis Red-Blue Book, 1918–29.

Haines St. Louis City and County Criss-Cross Directory, 1973–97.

Hyde, William, and Howard L. Conard. *Encyclopedia of the History of St. Louis, A Compendium of History and Biography for Ready Reference.* 3 Vols. St. Louis: The Southern History Company, 1899.

Immigration and Naturalization Service (INS). *Annual Report*, 1940–98.

—— Cable sent to all the U.S. INS field offices on 4 December 1989.

Immigration and Naturalization Service Records. 1787–1954. 959 cu. ft. and 11,476 microfilm reels. National Archives and Records Service, Washington, D.C.

International Institute of Metro St. Louis (IIMS). *Annual Report*, 1998.

Letter of Richard and Evelyn Ho to Melissa M. Szeto, 24 July 2001. In the author's possession.

Letter of Claudia Rhodes to Huping Ling, 18 February 2002. In the author's possession.

Letter of Orville Spreen to Miss Douglas, 6 January 1951, Orville Spreen, Missouri Historical Society, St. Louis.

League of Chinese Americans. *News Letter*. St. Louis, October 1975, Missouri Historical Society, St. Louis.

National Archives and Records Service, Washington, D.C. Contains records of general immigration, Chinese immigration, passenger arrival, Americanization, naturalization, field offices, and alien internment camps.

National Archives–Pacific Sierra Region, San Bruno, California. Holds records on Chinese exclusion and immigration.

National Archives–Central Plains Region, Kansas City, Missouri. Two records are related to Chinese: Chinese Exclusion Cases Habeas Corpus Petitions: 1857–1965, and Criminal Records, 1871–1918, U.S. District Court for Eastern District of Missouri. The former involves Chinese in Iowa, Kansas, Minnesota, Missouri, Nebraska, North Dakota, and South Dakota. The latter contains cases related to Chinese in Missouri involved in manufacturing, selling, and smoking of opium.

Polk's St. Louis City Directory, 1955–80.

Polk's St. Louis County Directory, 1926–76.

Papers Relating to the Campaign to Save Sam Wah Laundry. Correspondence, 1978–86, 9 Folders, Eliot F. Porter, Jr. Papers, Missouri Historical Society, St. Louis.

Recorder of Deeds of City of St. Louis. Archives Department of the Recorder of Deeds, City Hall, St. Louis, Missouri, 63103.

St. Louis Chinese Academy. *Year Book*, 1998.

St. Louis Chinese Gospel Church. "70th Anniversary, 1924–1994," November 1994.

St. Louis Chinese Yellow Pages, 2000, 2002, 2003.

St. Louis Chinese American Yellow Pages, 2002, 2003.

St. Louis County Directory, 1893–1922.

St. Louis in World War II Casualties Scrapbooks.

St. Louis in World War II Scrapbooks, Vols. 1–4.

St. Louis National Guard: 35th Division WWI Scrapbooks, Vols. 1 and 2.

U.S.A. vs. Chu Dock Yuck. Chinese Exclusion Cases Habeas Corpus, RG 21, National Archives–Central Plains Region, Kansas City, Missouri. (Cases below repeat this citation.)

U.S.A. vs. Jue Lime.

U.S.A. vs. Jeu Seung.

U.S.A. vs. Lam Chow.

U.S.A. vs. Lee Mow Lin.

U.S.A. vs. Lee Suey Nom.

U.S.A. vs. Hop Hing.

U.S.A. vs. How Chun Pong.

U.S.A. vs. Leong Choey.

U.S.A. vs. Lung Fook.

U.S.A. vs. Oong Woo.

U.S.A. vs. Sing Lung.

U.S.A. vs. Wong Lung.

U.S. Bureau of the Census. *The U.S. Census*, 1870–2000.

U.S. Congress. "Bush Veto of Chinese Immigration Relief." *Congressional Quarterly Weekly Report* 47 (2 December 1989): 3331.

U.S. Congress. "Chinese Students Win Waiver." *Congressional Quarterly Weekly Report* 47 (25 November 1989): 3245.

U.S. Department of Labor, Bureau of Immigration. *Treaties, Laws, and Rules Governing the Admission of Chinese*. Washington, D.C.: Government Printing Office, 1917.

U.S. Department of State. *Consular Reports: 1979–1986*. Visa Office, U.S. Department of State, Washington, D.C., 1987.

William Carlson Smith Documents. Special Collection, Main Library, University of Oregon.

Yin, Liangwu. *A Summary of the Preliminary Findings of the Chinese Community in the St. Louis Area*. St. Louis, MO: s.n., 1989. Photocopies of articles, etc., found in area libraries.

NEWSPAPERS AND MAGAZINES

Abbreviations

Missouri Republican (M-R), 1876–88.
St. Louis Chinese American News (C-N), 1990–.
St. Louis Chinese Journal (C-J), 1996–.
St. Louis Daily Times (D-T), 1873–77.
St. Louis Globe-Democrat (G-D), 1875–1986.
St. Louis Post-Dispatch (P-D), 1879–.
The St. Louis Republic (S-R), 1888–1919.
St. Louis Republican (S-R), 1873–76.
The St. Louis Stars and Times (S-T), 1932–51.
St. Louis Times (S-T), 1869–73.
St. Louisan.
The World Journal (W-J).

Citations (listed without authors if any)

"Act of Congress Lets Chinese Women Stay with Family Here," *G-D*, 28 December 1942.
"All Limousines in City Hired for Mourners," *G-D*, 23 December 1947.
"Americanization is Easy for Chinese Children in St. Louis Public Schools," *G-D*, 4 September 1927.
"Bones of Chinese to Be Sent Home," *P-D*, 17 November 1928.
"C. H. Quin Chu Dies; Chinese Leader Here," *P-D*, 1 February 1976.
"Charles Quinn New Mayor of Chinatown," *G-D*, 1 February 1948.
"Chinatown Changes Quarters," *G-D*, 4 August 1966.
"Chinatown Going Down—Maybe Chop Chop," *G-D*, 25 January 1963.
"Chinatown Granted a Reprieve until May 1," *G-D*, 25 January 1979.
"Chinatown Just a Memory," *G-D*, 1 February 1978.
"Chinatown Mayor Speaks at Dinner Marking New Year," *G-D*, 11 February 1948.
"Chinese Celebration Planned," *P-D*, 27 January 1976.
"Chinese Change Festivities of the New Year to Jan. 1," *Star*, 27 December 1912.
"Chinese Community Mourns Passing of Its Traditions," *P-D*, 14 February 1965.
"Chinese Congregation Remodeling Webster Church," *P-D*, 25 June 1969.
"Chinese Cook Up Tasty Convention," *G-D*, 19 April 1962.
"The Chinese Colony of St. Louis," *S-R*, 29 July 1900 (Mag. Sec.), 2.

"Chinese Girl Student Talks," *G-D*, 27 May 1934.
"Chinese Group Buys a $100,000 Building Here," *G-D*, 12 September 1948.
"Chinese Here Aiding Homeland," *G-D*, 14 October 1937.
"Chinese Here Search for 'Kung Hsi Fa Tsai'," *G-D*, 27 January 1957.
"Chinese Here Welcome 4650th New Year," *G-D*, 28 January 1952.
"Chinese in St. Louis," *S-R*, 10 January 1880.
"The Chinese in St. Louis," *S-R*, 14 January 1894, 15.
"Chinese in St. Louis Contribute to China's War Effort," *G-D*, 11 August 1939.
"Chinese Nationalists here Split on House Government," *St. Louis Times*, 12 March 1930.
"The Chinese New Year," *G-D*, 2 February 1886.
"Chinese New Year Celebrated in St. Louis," *S-R*, 10 February 1880.
"Chinese Pay $100,000 for Building Here," *P-D*, 12 September 1948.
"Chinese Restaurant, Ho Choy," *P-D*, 26 May 1969.
"The Chinese Speak," *G-D*, 6 November 1943.
"Chinese to Vacate Old Quarters as New Year Begins," *G-D*, 21 January 1966.
"City's Chinatown Must Move again," *G-D*, 19 September 1978.
"Daughter of Mayor of Chinatown Weds," *G-D*, 14 June 1949.
"Demise of Old Chinatown," *G-D*, 20–21 August 1966.
"Does St. Louis Still Have a Chinatown?" *St. Louis Post-Dispatch Magazine*, 19 May 1996, 20.
"50 Years Ago–Saturday, Dec. 15, 1917," *G-D*, 15 December 1967.
"Fire-breathing Dragon to Lead Chinese New Year Parade," *G-D*, 8 February 1979.
"4-year Chinese Language Class Popular at St. Louis U. High," *G-D*, 20 October 1972.
"14-Course Chinese Banquet Served Tong Parley Delegates," *G-D*, 3 April 1949.
"General Notice to the Public," *St. Louis Star-Times*, 13 December 1950.
"Gradual Disappearance of the Chinatown of St. Louis," *P-D*, 25 September 1902.
"Hop Alley," *S-R*, 29 January 1905, 8 (pt. 2).
"Hop Alley Census Adds 300," *S-R*, 2 May 1910, 14.
"Hop Alley Makee Feast Like B. M. L.," *S-R*, 11 October 1914.
"Hop Alley to be Invaded," *S-R*, 1 May 1910 (II), 16.
"Housekeeping in St. Louis Chinatown," *S-R*, 14 August 1910 (Mag. Sec.), 4.
"A Little bit of China Joins Folks 'Down by Der Gravois,' " *G-D*, 6 September 1979.
"More Chinese," *M-R*, 2 January 1870.
"National Convention of On Leong Tong Opens Here Monday," *G-D*, 1 April 1949.
"New Chinatown Here Opens With a Bang," *G-D*, 26 September 1966.
"New Chinatown Springing Up in the 1500 Block of Delmar," *P-D*, 21 July 1966.
"Noisy New Year," *G-D*, 2 February 1976.
"Only Four Chinese Women in St. Louis," *S-R*, 4 October 1908, 4 (pt. 5).
"Pageantry Absent as Chinese Here Celebrate Arrival of Year 4639," *G-D*, 16 February 1942.
"75 Years Ago—Thursday, June 9, 1892," *G-D*, 9 June 1967.

"75 Years Ago—Monday, Feb. 1, 1897," *G-D*, 1 February 1972.
"75 Years Ago—Wednesday, Aug. 25, 1897," *G-D*, 25 August 1972.
"St. Louis Chinatown," *St. Louis Post-Dispatch Magazine*, Sunday, 23 July 1995, 13.
"St. Louis Chinese," *P-D*, 14 November 1971.
"St. Louis Chinese Denounce the Reds," *P-D*, 14 December 1950.
"St. Louis Chinese Mark New Year with Ceremony," *P-D*, 9 February 1967.
"St. Louis Chinese Run Ad Opposing Red's Regime," *St. Louis Star*, 13 December 1950.
"St. Louis Chinese Will Celebrate Historic Day of the Double Tens," *St. Louis Star-Times*, 6 October 1938.
"St Louis Chinese Wishing You 'Kung Hsi Fa Tsai,'" *G-D*, 8 February 1959.
"Their Background is Chinese, But Now They're St. Louisans," *G-D*, 14 February 1972.
"Traditional Chinese Parade Feb. 26," *G-D*, 17 February 1977.
"250 Attend St. Louis Tea for Benefit of Chinese," *P-D*, 18 June 1938.
"2 Sisters Arrested in Chop Suey Raid," *S-R*, 22 August 1910.
"200 Million Queues Will Be Removed," *The St. Louis Republic*, 13 November 1910.
"Weekend Chinese Festival to Be at Shaw's Garden," *G-D*, 3 October 1984.
"Where Chinese Will Party Here," *G-D*, 1 February 1978.
"'Year of the Sheep' Begins for 450 Here," *G-D*, 9 February 1967.
"Young Chinese Pianist Thrilled by America," *G-D*, 26 April 1935.

Interviews of St. Louis Residents

(All interviews were conducted by Huping Ling unless otherwise noted. The brief description only reflects an interviewee at the time of interview.)
Bounds, Doris. Housewife. 13 April 1999.
Cai, Haiyan. Math professor, UMSL; editor, the *Chinese*. 21 December 1998.
Cai, Kin. Waiter, Chinese restaurant. 22 April 1999.
Mrs. Che, owner, Korean restaurant. 22 January 1999.
Chi, James. Pastor, Taiwanese Presbyterian Church of Greater St. Louis. Telephone interview. 18 May 1999.
Chin, Patti. Biological researcher, Monsanto Chemical Company. Interview by Ryan Hillenbrand under the supervision of Huping Ling. 15 October 1996.
Chiu, Edwin. Owner, Central Trading Company. 22 April 1999.
Chiu, Jean. Owner, Central Trading Company. 22 April 1999.
Chou, Mi. Reporter, the *World Journal*. 13 May 1999.
Chow, Miller. Retired teacher, librarian, Parkway School District. 2 June 1999.
Crosslin, Anna. President, IIMS. 28 May 1999.
Doan, Ngoc. Employee, IIMS; former Vietnamese refugee. Telephone interview. 4 March 1999.
Fung, Hung-Gay. Dr. Y. S. Tsiang Professor, UMSL. Telephone interview. 14 May 1999.
Gao, Tony. Attorney. 18 May 1999.
Ha [pseud.]. Case management coordinator, IIMS; former Vietnamese Chinese refugee. 28 May and 14 June 1999.
Ho, Richard. Old Chinatown resident; retiree. Letters to Huping Ling. 2 March and 3 August 2002.

Hong, Lillie Lee. Retired laundry owner. 2 February 1999.

Hsueh, Mu-lien. Housewife. 23 May 1999.

Huang, Eric. Insurance agent; president, Chinese Chamber of Commerce of Greater St. Louis. 10 May 1999.

Hwang, Wen. Director, *C-J*; community activist. 22 April 1999.

Ko, Ann. Proprietor, Chinese laundry, restaurants, and trading company. 19 October 1998. Telephone interview. 19 February 1999.

Ko, Don. Proprietor, Chinese laundry, restaurants, and trading company; co-president, On Leong. 19 October 1998. Telephone interviews. 11 January and 22 February 1999.

Ko, Lily. Registered nurse, health management administrator; Commissioner, the Missouri Community Service Commission. Biographic note, 26 August 2002.

Ko, Walter. Proprietor, optical business; coordinator, the St. Louis Alliance for Preserving the Truth of Sino-Japanese War (SLAPTSJW). 2 June 2001.

Kwong, Yee M. Owner, Hunan Garden Restaurant. 14 April 1999.

Law, Harold. Founder and president, Decisions & Advanced Technology Associates Inc.; former president, St. Louis OCA. Telephone interview. 17 May 1999.

LeLaurin, Susanne. Director of Social Work, IIMS. Telephone interview. 22 February 1999.

Leong, Annie. Retired proprietor, Chinese restaurant and grocery store; former spokesperson, On Leong. 17 December 1998.

Li, Chung Kok. Owner, Lee's Family Buffet; co-president, On Leong. 12 October 1998.

Li, Jerry. Engineer; owner, Great Chef Garden Restaurant. Telephone interview. 4 May 1999.

Liang, Zhihai. Attorney. 13 May 1999.

Liou, Sherwin. Owner, Mandarin House; president, American Midwest Korean Chinese Association and SLAPTSJW. Telephone interview. 4 March 1999.

Lo, Grace Shen. Biochemist, group director, Ralston Purina Company; former president, St. Louis OCA. Telephone interview. 8 March 1999.

Lo, Grace Yin. Tax and accounting manager, Ralston Purina Company; former president, St. Louis OCA. Telephone interviews. 3 July 1998 and 23 February 1999.

Lu, Andrew. Retired orthopedic surgeon. Telephone interviews. 18 April and 6 November 2002.

Lu, Chris. Insurance agent; president, St. Louis Chinese Association. 1 March 1999.

Lu, Jenny. Owner, manager, Great Chef Garden Restaurant. 19 March 1999.

Moncada, Ed. Metro Minister. 13 April 1999.

Pan, Samuel. Pastor, St. Louis Chinese Christian Church. Telephone interview. 17 February 1999.

Peng, Dachung Pat. Retired engineer, Monsanto Chemical Company; owner, Creve Coeur Florist and Gifts; former president, St. Louis OCA. 24 and 26 April 1999.

Peng, Tzy C. Retired engineer; editor of *Chinese American Forum*; former president of the St. Louis OCA. 25 July 1998.

Porter, Eliot F., Jr. Former reporter, editor, *P-D*; organizer, the campaign to save Sam Wah Laundry. 28 December 1998 and 5 January 1999.

Sit, Hong. Former Hop Alley resident; retired minister. Telephone interview. 19 September 2003.

Sui, Yuan-sheng. Owner, Yen Ching Chinese Restaurant. 26 April 1999.

Mrs. Siu. Owner, Yen Ching Chinese Restaurant. 13 May 1999.

Sun, Bin. Biologist, Monsanto Chemical Company. 10 January 1999.

Tai, Ching-Ling. Teacher, St. Louis U. High School; Commissioner, the Missouri Community Service Commission; former president, St. Louis OCA. Telephone interview. 7 April 2002.

Tao, William K. Y. Retired engineer, founder, formal president, WTA; founding president, St. Louis OCA. 4 February 1999.

Wang, Xia [pseud.]. Graduate student; waitress. 11 October 1998.

Wu, Nelson. Writer, artist, emeritus professor, Washington University. 10 February and 23 and 26 May 1999.

Mr. Yang. Employee, Chinese grocery store. 18 April 1999.

Yang, Hsinyi. Secretary, St. Louis Chinese Christian Church. Telephone interview. 16 February 1999.

Yeh, James. Engineer; president, Gateway International; founder, the St. Louis Chinese Jaycees. 29 December 1998.

Yeh, Patricia L. Vice-president, Gateway International; former president, Zonta International Organization. 12 and 29 December 1998.

Yin, Grace Chen. Pianist. 8 September 1998.

Yu, Guanzheng. Owner, Oriental Ginseng and Gift in South. 19 October 1998.

Yueh, Francis. Computer programmer; director, *C-N*. 16 April 1999.

Yueh, May. General secretary, *C-N*. 16 April 1999.

Zhang, James. Broker, Better House Realty; former president, St. Louis Chinese Association. 16 December 1998.

Zhang, Peter. Employee, Schnucks at Woods Mill. 23 April 1999.

Zhu, Anning. Principal, Modern Chinese Language School. Telephone interview. 12 May 1999.

Zong, Wubing. Editor, *Chinese American Forum*. 28 May 1999.

SECONDARY SOURCES

Anderson, Benedict, *Imagined Communities: Reflections on the Origin and Spread of Nationalism*. London: Verso, 1991.

Anderson, Kay J. *Vancouver's Chinatown: Racial Discourse in Canada, 1875–1980*. Montreal and Kingston: McGill-Queen's University Press, 1991.

Allen, Leslie. *Ellis Island*. Liberty Island, N.Y.: Evelyn Hill Group, 1995.

Ashbury, Herbert. *The Gangs of New York*. New York: Paragon House, 1928.

Bao, Xiaolan. *Holding Up More Than Half the Sky: Chinese Women Garment Workers in New York City, 1948–92*. Urbana: University of Illinois Press, 2001.

Barth, Gunther. *Bitter Strength: A History of the Chinese in the United States, 1850–1870*. Cambridge, Mass.: Harvard University Press, 1964.

Barton, H. Arnold. *A Folk Divided: Homeland Swedes and Swedish Americans*. Carbondale: Southern Illinois University Press, 1994.

Basch, Linda, Nina Glick Schiller, and Cristina Blanc-Szanton, eds. *Nations Unbound: Transnational Projects, Postcolonial Predicaments and Deterritorialized Nation-States*. Langhorne, Pa.: Gordon and Breach, 1994.

Bayor, Ronald. *Neighbors in Conflict: The Irish, Germans, Jews, and Italians of New York City, 1929–1941*. Baltimore, Md.: Johns Hopkins University Press, 1978.

Beesley, David. "From Chinese to Chinese American: Chinese Women and Families in a Sierra Nevada Town." *California History* 67 (September 1988): 168–79.

Bennitt, Mark. Ed. *History of the Louisiana Purchase Exposition*. New York: Arno Press, 1976.

Berthoff, Rowland T. *British Immigrants in Industrial America 1790–1950*. Cambridge, Mass.: Russell and Russell, 1953.

Birchall, R. A. *The San Francisco Irish, 1848–1880*. Berkeley and Los Angeles: University of California Press, 1980.

Blake, C. Fred. "The Chinese of Valhalla: Adaptation and Identity in a Midwestern American Cemetery." In *Markers X: Journal of the Association for Gravestone Studies*, ed. Richard E. Meyer, 53–89. Worcester, Mass.: Association for Gravestone Studies, 1993.

——— "There Ought to be a Monument to Alla Lee," *Chinese American Forum* 15, no. 3 (January 2000): 23–25.

Bodnar, John. *The Transplanted: A History of Immigrants in Urban America*. Bloomington: Indiana University Press, 1985.

Bonus, Rick. *Locating Filipino America: Ethnicity and Cultural Politics of Space*. Philadelphia: Temple University Press, 2000.

Browning, Rufus P., Dale Rogers Marshall, and David H. Tabb. *Protest Is Not Enough*. Berkeley: University of California Press, 1984.

Burnett, Betty. *St. Louis at War: The Story of a City 1941–1945*. St. Louis: The Patrice Press, 1987.

Cardoso, Lawrence. *Mexican Immigrants to the United States, 1897–1931: Socio-economic Patterns*. Tucson: University of Arizona Press, 1980.

Cassel, Susie Lan, ed. *The Chinese in America: A History from Gold Mountain to the New Millennium*. Walnut Creek, Calif.: AltaMira Press, 2002.

Cather, Helen Virginia. *The History of San Francisco Chinatown*. San Francisco: R & E Research Associates, 1974.

Chan, Kwok Bun. *Chinese Business Networks: State, Economy and Culture*. Singapore: Prentice Hall, 2000.

Chan, Sucheng. *Asian Americans: An Interpretive History*. Boston: Twayne Publishers, 1991.

——— *This Bitter-Sweet Soil: The Chinese in California Agriculture, 1860–1910*. Berkeley: University of California Press, 1986.

Chan, Sucheng, ed. *Entry Denied: Exclusion and the Chinese in America, 1882–1943*. Philadelphia: Temple University Press, 1991.

———— *Hmong Means Free: Life in Laos and America*. Philadelphia: Temple University Press, 1994.

Chang, Gordon H., ed. *Asian Americans and Politics: Perspectives, Experiences, Prospects*. Stanford, Calif.: Stanford University Press, 2001.

Chang, Joan Chiung-Heui. *Transforming Chinese American Literature: A Study of History, Sexuality, and Ethnicity*. New York: Peter Lang Publishing, 2000.

Chen, Hsiang-Shui. *Chinatown No More: Taiwan Immigrants in Contemporary New York*. Ithaca, N.Y.: Cornell University Press, 1992.

Chen, Jack. *The Chinese of America*. San Francisco: Harper and Row, 1982.

Chen, Julia I. Hsuan. *The Chinese Community in New York*. San Francisco: R & E Research Associates, 1974.

Chen, Kuo-lin. *Hua Ren Bang Pai* [The Chinatown Gangs]. Taipei: Juliu Publishing House, 1995.

Chen, Pen-ch'ang. *Mei-kuo Hua Ch'iao Ts'an Kuan Kung Yeh* [Chinese American Restaurants]. Taipei: Taiwan Far East Books, 1971.

Chen, Shehong. *Being Chinese, Becoming Chinese American*. Urbana: University of Illinois Press, 2002.

Chen, Yong. *Chinese San Francisco, 1850–1943: A Trans-Pacific Community*. Stanford, Calif.: Stanford University Press, 2000.

Cheng, Lucie, et al. *Linking Our Lives: Chinese American Women of Los Angeles*. San Francisco: Chinese Historical Society of America, 1984.

China Institute in America. *A Survey of Chinese Students in American Colleges and Universities in the Past Hundred Years*. New York: The Institute, 1954.

Chinese American Restaurant Association of Greater New York, ed. *Chinese American Restaurant Association of Greater New York, Inc*. New York: The Association, 1959.

Chinese Historical Society of America, ed. *Chinese America: History and Perspectives, 1990*. San Francisco: The Society, 1990.

Chinn, Thomas W. *Bridging the Pacific: San Francisco Chinatown and Its People*. San Francisco: Chinese Historical Society of America, 1989.

Chiu, Ping. *Chinese Labor in California: An Economic Study*. Madison: University of Wisconsin, 1967.

Choi, Kyung. "The Assimilation of Korean Immigrants in the St. Louis Area." Ph.D. diss., St. Louis University, 1984.

Chou, Jesse Chain. "A Survey of Chinese Students in the United States, 1979–1987." Ph.D. diss., Columbia University, 1989.

Christensen, Lawrence Oland. "Black St. Louis: A Study in Race Relations, 1865–1916." Ph.D. diss., University of Missouri, 1972.

Chu, Yung-Deh Richard. "Chinese Secret Societies in America: A Historical Survey." *Asian Profile* 1, no. 1 (1973): 21–38.

Chung, Sue Fawn. "Between Two Worlds: The Zhigongtang and Chinese American Funerary Rituals." In *The Chinese in America: A History from Gold Mountain to the New Millennium*, ed. Susie Lan Cassel, 217–38. Walnut Creek, Calif.: AltaMira Press, 2002.

Cinel, Dino. *From Italy to San Francisco: The Immigrant Experience*. Stanford, Calif.: Stanford University Press, 1982.

Clark, Dennis. *The Irish in Philadelphia: Ten Generations of Urban Experience.* Philadelphia: Temple University Press, 1974.

Cohen, Lucy M. *Chinese in the Post-Civil War South: A People Without a History.* Baton Rouge: Louisiana State University Press, 1984.

Coolidge, Mary R. *Chinese Immigration.* New York: Henry Holt, 1909; reprint, New York: Arno Press, 1969.

Cortinovis, Irene E. "China at the St. Louis World's Fair." *Missouri Historical Review* 77 (1977–78): 59–66.

Cutler, Irving. *The Jews of Chicago: From Shtetl to Suburb.* Urbana: University of Illinois Press, 1996.

Daniels, Roger. *Asian America: Chinese and Japanese in the United States Since 1850.* Seattle: University of Washington Press, 1988.

——— *Coming to America: A History of Immigration and Ethnicity in American Life.* New York: HarperCollins, 1990.

——— *A History of Indian Immigration to the United States: An Interpretive Essay.* New York: The Asia Society, 1989.

Dicker, Laverne Mau. *The Chinese in San Francisco: A Political History.* New York: Dover, 1979.

Dillon, Richard H. *Images of Chinatown.* San Francisco: Book Club of California, 1976.

Diner, Hasia R. *Erin's Daughters in America: Irish Immigrant Women in the Nineteenth Century.* Baltimore, Md.: Johns Hopkins University Press, 1983.

Do, Hien Duc. *The Vietnamese Americans.* Westport, Conn.: Greenwood Press, 1999.

Dreer, Herman. "Negro Leadership in St. Louis: A Study in Race Relations." Ph.D. diss., University of Chicago, 1955.

Early, Geral. *Ain't But a Place: An Anthology of African American Writings about St. Louis.* Columbia: University of Missouri Press, 1998.

Ehrlich, Walter. *Zion in the Valley: The Jewish Community of St. Louis.* Vol. I, 1807–1907. Columbia: University of Missouri Press, 1997.

Espiritu, Yen Le. *Asian American Panethnicity: Bridging Institutions and Identities.* Philadelphia: Temple University Press, 1992.

Fong, Joe Chung. "Transnational Newspapers: The Making of the Post-1965 Globalized/Localized San Gabriel Valley Chinese Community." *Amerasia Journal* 22, no. 3 (1996): 65–77.

Fong, Timothy P. *The First Suburban Chinatown: The Remaking of Monterey Park, California.* Philadelphia: Temple University Press, 1994.

Freeman, James M. *Hearts of Sorrow: Vietnamese-American Lives.* Stanford, Calif.: Stanford University Press, 1991.

Fujita, Stephen S., and David J. O'Brien. *Japanese American Ethnicity: The Persistence of Community.* Seattle: University of Washington Press, 1991.

Gabaccia, Donna. *From Sicily to Elizabeth Street: Housing and Social Change among Italian Immigrants, 1880–1930.* Albany: State University of New York Press, 1984.

Gjerde, Jon. *Major Problems in American Immigration and Ethnic History.* Boston: Houghton Mifflin, 1998.

Glenn, Evelyn Nakano. *Issei, Nisei, War Bride: Three Generations of Japanese American Women in Domestic Service.* Philadelphia: Temple University Press, 1986.

Glick, Clarence Elmer. *Sojourners and Settlers: Chinese Migrants in Hawaii.* Honolulu: University Press of Hawaii, 1980.

Gong, Eng Ying, and Bruce Grant. *Tong War.* New York: Nicholas L. Brown, 1930.

Gordon, Milton. *Assimilation in American Life.* New York: Oxford University Press, 1964.

Gyory, Andrew. *Closing the Gate: Race, Politics, and the Chinese Exclusion Act.* Chapel Hill: University of North Carolina Press, 1998.

Handlin, Oscar. *Adventure in Freedom: Three Hundred Years of Jewish Life in America.* New York: McGraw-Hill, 1954.

——— *Boston's Immigrants, 1790–1865.* Cambridge: Harvard University Press, 1941.

——— *Race and Nationality in American Life.* Garden City, N.Y.: Doubleday, 1957.

——— *The Uprooted: The Epic Story of the Great Migrations That Made the American People.* Boston: Little, Brown, 1973.

Harper, Fowler V., and Jerome H. Skolnick. *Problems of the Family.* New York: Bobbs-Merrill, 1962.

Hayhoe, Ruth, and Marianne Bastid, eds. *China's Education and the Industrialized World: Studies in Cultural Transfer.* Armonk, N.Y.: M. E. Sharpe, 1987.

Heyer, Virginia. "Patterns of Social Organization in New York City's Chinatown." Ph.D. diss, Columbia University, 1953.

Horton, John. *The Politics of Diversity: Immigration, Resistance, and Change in Monterey Park, California.* Philadelphia: Temple University Press, 1995.

Hoy, William. *The Chinese Six Companies.* San Francisco: California Chinese Historical Society, 1942.

Hsu, Immanuel. *The Rise of Modern China.* New York: Oxford University Press, 1990.

Hsu, Madeline Y. *Dreaming of Gold, Dreaming of Home: Transnationalism and Migration Between the United States and South China, 1882–1943.* Stanford, Calif.: Stanford University Press, 2000.

Hurley, Andrew, ed. *Common Fields: An Environmental History of St. Louis.* St. Louis: Missouri Historical Society Press, 1997.

Iglauer, Henry S. "The Demolition of the Louisiana Purchase Exposition of 1904." *Missouri Historical Society Bulletin* 22, no. 4 (1965–66): 457–67.

Ignatiev, Noel. *How the Irish Became White.* New York: Routledge, 1995.

Inoue, Miyako. "Japanese-Americans in St. Louis: From Internees to Professionals." *City and Society* 3, no. 2 (December 1989): 142–52.

Isaac, Harold R. *Images of Asia: American Views of China and India.* New York: Harper & Row, 1972.

Jacobson, Matthew Frye. *Whiteness of a Different Color: European Immigrants and the Alchemy of Race.* Cambridge: Harvard University Press, 1998.

Jew, Victor. "Broken Windows: Anti-Chinese Violence and Interracial Sexuality in 19th Century Milwaukee." In *Asian Pacific American Genders and Sexualities,* ed. Thomas K. Nakayama, 29–51. Tempe: Arizona State University, 1999.

Kuo, Chia-ling. *Social and Political Change in New York's Chinatown: The Role of Voluntary Associations.* New York: Praeger, 1977.

Kuo, W. H., and Nan Lin. "Assimilation of Chinese Americans in Washington, D.C." *Sociological Quarterly* 18 (1977): 340–52.

Kwong, Peter. *Chinatown, New York: Labor and Politics, 1930–1950.* New York: Monthly Review Press, 1979.

——— *The New Chinatown.* New York: Hill and Wang, 1987.

——— *Forbidden Workers: Illegal Chinese Immigrants and American Labor.* New York: New Press, 1997.

Lai, David Chuenyan. "Socio-economic Structures and the Viability of Chinatown." In *Residential and Neighborhood Studies in Victoria,* ed. C. Forward. Victoria: University of Victoria, Western Geographical Series 5 (1973): 101–29.

——— *Chinatowns: Towns Within Cities in Canada.* Vancouver: University of British Columbia Press, 1988.

Lai, H. Mark. "Historical Development of the Chinese Consolidated Benevolent Association/Huiguan System." In *Chinese America: History & Perspectives, 1987.* San Francisco: Chinese Historical Society of America (1987), 13–51.

——— "The Chinese Press in the United States and Canada Since World War II: A Diversity of Voices." In *Chinese America: History & Perspectives, 1990.* San Francisco: Chinese Historical Society of America (1990), 107–56.

——— "Transmitting the Chinese Heritage: Chinese Schools in the United States Mainland and Hawaii." In *Intercultural Relations, Cultural Transformation, and Identity—The Ethnic Chinese—Selected Papers Presented at the 1998 ISSCO Conference,* ed. Teresita Ang See, 124–58. Manila: Kaisa Para Sa Kaunlaran, 2000.

Lee, Rose Hum. *The Chinese in the United States of America.* Hong Kong: Hong Kong University, 1960.

——— *The Growth and Decline of Chinese Communities in the Rocky Mountain Region.* New York: Arno Press, 1978.

——— "The Recent Immigrant Chinese Families of the San Francisco–Oakland Area." *Marriage and Family Living* 18, no. 1 (1956): 14–24.

Leonard, Karen Isaksen. *Making Ethnic Choices: California's Punjabi Mexican Americans.* Philadelphia: Temple University Press, 1992.

——— *The South Asian Americans.* Westport, Conn.: Greenwood Press, 1997.

Li, Peter S. "Chinese Investment and Business in Canada: Ethnic Entrepreneurship Reconsidered," *Pacific Affairs* 66, no. 2 (Summer 1993): 219–43.

——— "Unneighborly Houses or Unwelcome Chinese: The Social Construction of Race in the Battle over 'Monster Houses' in Vancouver, Canada." *International Journal of Comparative Race & Ethnic Studies* 1, no. 1 (1994): 14–33.

——— "Self-Employment among Visible Minority Immigrants, White Immigrants, and Native-Born Persons in Secondary and Tertiary Industries of Canada." *Canadian Journal of Regional Science* 20, nos. 1, 2 (Spring–Summer 1997): 103–18.

Li, Wei. "Spatial Transformation of an Urban Ethnic Community from Chinatown to Chinese Ethnoburb in Los Angeles." Ph.D. diss., University of Southern California, 1997.

——— "Anatomy of a New Ethnic Settlement: The Chinese Ethnoburb in Los Angeles." *Urban Studies* 35, no. 3 (1998): 479–501.

―――― "Los Angeles' Chinese *Ethnoburb*: From Ethnic Service Center to Global Economy Outpost." *Urban Geography* 19, no. 6 (1998): 502–17.

―――― "Building Ethnoburbia: The Emergence and Manifestation of the Chinese Ethnoburb in Los Angeles' San Gabriel Valley." *Journal of Asian American Studies* 2, no. 2 (February 1999): 1–28.

Li, Yu-ning, ed. *History of Chinese with an American Education: 150 Years of Learning and Achievements.* New York: Outer Sky Press, 1999.

Lien, Pei-te. *The Making of Asian America Through Political Participation.* Philadelphia: Temple University Press, 2001.

Lim, Linda Y.C. "Chinese Economic Activity in Southeast Asia." In *The Chinese in Southeast Asia, Vol. I: Ethnicity and Economic Activity.* Linda Y. C. Lim and L. A. Peter Goaling, eds. Singapore: Maruzen Asia, 1983.

Lin, Jan. *Reconstructing Chinatown Ethnic Enclave, Global Change.* Minneapolis: University of Minnesota Press, 1998.

Ling, Huping. "The Changing Patterns of Taiwanese Students in America and the Modernization in Taiwan." In *Modernity and Cultural Identity in Taiwan,* ed. Hanchao Lu, 179–207. River Edge, N.J.: Global Publishing, 2001.

―――― "Chinese American Professional and Business Women in a Midwest Small Town." In *Ethnic Chinese at Turn of Century,* ed. Guotu Zhuang, 398–421. Fujian: Fujian People's Publishing House, 1998.

―――― "Chinese Female Students and the Sino-US Relations." In *New Studies on Chinese Overseas and China,* ed. Cen Huang, Zhuang Gutu, and Tanaka Kyoko, 103–37. Leiden, the Netherlands: IIAS, 2000.

―――― "Chinese Merchant Wives in the United States, 1840–1945." In *Origins and Destinations: 41 Essays on Chinese America,* ed. the Chinese Historical Society of Southern California, 79–92. Los Angeles: Chinese Historical Society of Southern California and UCLA Asian American Studies Center, 1994.

―――― *Chinese St. Louisans.* A series of 30 thematic articles published in *The St. Louis Chinese American News,* 21 December 2000 to 19 July 2001, www.scanews.com/history.

―――― "Family and Marriage of Late-Nineteenth and Early-Twentieth Century Chinese Immigrant Women." *Journal of American Ethnic History* 19, no. 2 (Winter 2000): 43–63.

―――― "Governing 'Hop Alley': On Leong Chinese Merchants and Laborers Association, 1906–1966." *Journal of American Ethnic History* 23, no. 2 (Winter 2004): 50–84.

―――― "Growing up in 'Hop Alley': The Chinese American Youth in St. Louis during the Early-Twentieth Century." In *Asian American Children,* ed. Benson Tong. Westport, Conn.: Greenwood Press, 2004.

―――― "A History of Chinese Female Students in the United States, 1880s–1990s." *The Journal of American Ethnic History* 16, no. 3 (Spring 1997): 81–109.

―――― "Historiograph and Research Methodolies of Chinese American Women." *Research on Women in Modern Chinese History* 9 (August 2001): 235–53.

―――― "A History and Historiography of Chinese Women in America." *American Studies* 1, no. 1 (1997): 127–46.

——— "Hop Alley: Myth and Reality of the St. Louis Chinatown, 1860s–1930s." *Journal of Urban History* 28, no. 2 (January 2002): 184–219.

——— *Jinshan Yao: A History of Chinese American Women.* Beijing: Chinese Social Sciences Publishing House, 1999.

——— "Lu Qiao Qi Ren." *St. Louis Chinese American Journal,* 19 October 2000.

——— *Ping Piao Meiguo: Xin Yimin Shilu* [New Immigrants in America]. Shanxi, China: Beiyue Literature and Art Publishing House, 2003.

——— "Reconceptualizing Chinese American Community in St. Louis: From Chinatown to Cultural Community." *Journal of American Ethnic History* (Summer 2004).

——— "A Study of the Motives for Immigration of Chinese Women in the Late-Nineteenth and Early-Twentieth Century." *American Studies* 1 (1999): 95–121.

——— "Surviving on the Gold Mountain: A Review of Sources about Chinese American Women." *The History Teacher* 26, no. 4 (August 1993): 459–70.

——— *Surviving on the Gold Mountain: Chinese American Women and Their Lives.* Albany: State University of New York Press, 1998.

——— "Sze-Kew Dun, A Chinese American Woman's Experience in Kirksville, Missouri." *Missouri Historical Review* 41, no. 1 (October 1996): 35–51.

Lipsitz, George. *The Possessive Investment in Whiteness: How White People Profit from Identity Politics.* Philadelphia: Temple University Press, 1988.

——— *The Sidewalks of St. Louis: Places, People, and Politics in an American City.* Columbia: University of Missouri Press, 1991.

Liu, Bo-ji. *Meiguo Huaqiao Shi* [History of the Overseas Chinese in the United States]. Taipei: Li Ming Publishing, 1981.

Liu, Haiming. "The Trans-Pacific Family: A Case Study of Sam Chang's Family History." *Amerasia* 18, no. 2 (1992): 1–34.

Locklear, William R. "The Celestials and the Angels: A Study of the Anti-Chinese Movement in Los Angeles to 1882." *Historical Society of Southern California Quarterly* 42 (1960): 239–56.

Loewen, James W. *The Mississippi Chinese: Between Black and White.* Cambridge, Mass.: Harvard University Press, 1971.

Long, Suzanna Maupin. " 'I Made It Mine Tho the Queen Waz Always Fair': The St. Louis Black Clubwomen Movement, 1931–1946." Thesis, University of Missouri–St. Louis, 1988.

Loo, Chalsa M. *Chinatown: Most Time, Hard Time.* New York: Praeger, 1991.

Lui, Mary Ting Yi. " 'The Chinatown Truck Mystery': The Elsie Sigel Murder Case and the Policing of Interracial Sexual Relations in New York City's Chinatown, 1880–1915." Ph.D. diss., Cornell University, 2000.

Lydon, Sandy. *Chinese Gold: The Chinese in the Monterey Bay Region.* Capitola, Calif.: Capitola Book Co., 1985.

Lyman, Stanford M. *Chinese Americans.* New York: Random House, 1974.

——— "Marriage and the Family Among Chinese Immigrants to America, 1850–1960." *Phylon* 24 (1968): 321–30.

Lynch, Otis G., et al. "Testimony on Child Labor." In *American First Hand*, Vol. II, ed. Robert D. Marcus and David Burner, 79–90. New York: St. Martin's Press, 1983.

McKeown, Adam. *Chinese Migrant Networks and Cultural Change, Peru, Chicago, Hawaii, 1900–1936*. Chicago: The University of Chicago Press, 2001.

Mason, Sarah R. "Family Structure and Acculturation in the Chinese Community in Minnesota." In *Asian and Pacific American Experiences: Women's Perspectives*, ed. Nobuya Tsuchida, 160–71. Minneapolis: Asian/Pacific American Learning Resource Center and General College, University of Minnesota, 1982.

———. "Liang May Seen and the Early Chinese Community in Minneapolis." *Minnesota History* (Spring 1995): 223–33.

McDannald, Thomas A. *California's Chinese Heritage: A Legacy of Places*. Keene, Calif.: Heritage West Books, 2000.

Minnick, Sylvia Sun. *Samfow = Chin-shan San-pu: The San Joaquin Chinese Legacy*. Fresno, Calif.: Panorama West, 1988.

Mormino, Gary Ross. *Immigrants on the Hill: Italian-Americans in St. Louis, 1882–1982*. Urbana and Chicago: University of Illinois Press, 1986.

Nash, Gary B., et al. *The American People: Creating a Nation and a Society*. New York: HarperCollins College Publishers, 1994.

Nee, Victor G., and Brett de Bary. *Longtime Californ': A Documentary Study of an American Chinatown*. New York: Pantheon, 1972.

Ng, Franklin. *The Taiwanese Americans*. Westport, Conn.: Greenwood, 1992.

Okihiro, Gary Y. *Common Ground: Reimagining American History*. Princeton, N.J.: Princeton University Press, 2001.

Olson, Audrey L. *St. Louis Germans, 1850–1920: The Nature of an Immigrant Community and Its Relation to the Assimilation Process*. New York: Arno Press, 1980.

Orleans, Leo A. *Chinese Students in America: Policies, Issues, and Numbers*. Washington, D.C.: National Academy Press, 1988.

Park, Kyeyoung. *The Korean American Dream: Immigrants and Small Business in New York City*. Ithaca, N.Y.: Cornell University Press, 1997.

Park, Robert. "Human Migration and the Marginal Man." *American Journal of Sociology* 33, no. 6 (May 1928): 881–93.

Peffer, George Anthony. *If They Don't Bring Their Women Here: Chinese Female Immigration before Exclusion*. Urbana: University of Illinois Press, 1999.

Pickle, Linda Schelbitzki. *Contented among Strangers: Rural German-Speaking Women and Their Families in the Nineteenth-Century Midwest*. Urbana: University of Illinois Press, 1996.

Primm, James Neal. *Lion of the Valley: St. Louis, Missouri*. Boulder, Col.: Pruett, 1990.

Reid, Anthony, ed. *Sojourners and Settlers: Histories of Southeast Asia and the Chinese*. St. Leonards, NSW: Allen and Unwin, 1996.

Reimers, David M. *Still the Golden Door: The Third World Comes to America*. New York: Columbia University Press, 1985.

Reynolds, C. N. "The Chinese Tongs." *American Journal of Sociology* 40 (March 1935): 612–23.

Riddle, Ronald. *Flying Dragon, Flying Streams: Music in the Life of San Francisco's Chinese.* Westport, Conn.: Greenwood, 1983.

Riggs, Fred Warren. *Pressures on Congress: A Study of the Repeal of Chinese Exclusion.* New York: King's Crown, 1950.

Riordon, William. *Honest Graft: The World of George Washington Plunkitt–Plunkitt of Tammany Hall.* St. James, N.Y.: Brandywine Press, 1993.

Roediger, David R. *The Wages of Whiteness: Race and the Making of the American Working Class.* New York: Verso, 1999.

Rudwick, Elliott M. *Race Riot at East St. Louis July 2, 1917.* Carbondale: Southern Illinois University Press, 1964.

Rynerson, Ann M., and Pamela A. DeVoe. "Refugee Women in a Vertical Village: Lowland Laotians in St. Louis." *Social Thought* 10, no. 3 (Summer 1984): 33–48.

Saito, Leland T. *Race and Politics: Asian Americans, Latinos, and Whites in a Los Angeles Suburb.* Urbana: University of Illinois Press, 1998.

Salyer, Lucy E. *Laws Harsh as Tigers: Chinese Immigrants and the Shaping of Modern Immigration Law.* Chapel Hill: University of North Carolina Press, 1995.

Sandmeyer, Elmer C. *The Anti-Chinese Movement.* Urbana: University of Illinois Press, 1973.

Saxton, Alexander. *The Indispensable Enemy: Labor and the Anti-Chinese Movement in California.* Berkeley: University of California Press, 1971.

Schiller, Nina Glick, Linda Basch, and Cristina Blanc-Szanton, eds. *Towards a Transnational Perspective on Migration: Race, Ethnicity, and Nationalism Reconsidered.* New York: New York Academy of Science, 1992.

Shah, Nayan. *Contagious Divides: Epidemics and Race in San Francisco's Chinatown.* Berkeley: University of California Press, 2001.

Sit, Hong. *My View from a Bridge.* Houston, Tex.: Blessing Books, 1999.

Siu, Paul C. P. "The Sojourner." *American Journal of Sociology* 50 (1952): 34–44.

——— *The Chinese Laundryman: A Study of Social Isolation.* New York: New York University Press, 1987.

Sobel, Irwin, Werner Z. Hirsch, and Harry C. Harris. *The Negro in the St. Louis Economy, 1954.* St. Louis, Mo.: Urban League of St. Louis, 1954.

Spickard, Paul R. *Japanese Americans: The Formation and Transformations of an Ethnic Group.* New York: Twayne, 1996.

Sung, Betty Lee. *The Adjustment Experience of Chinese Immigrant Children in New York City.* New York: Center for Migration Studies, 1987.

——— *Gangs in New York's Chinatown.* New York: Office of Child Development, Dept. of Health, Education, and Welfare, 1977.

——— *A Survey of Chinese-American Manpower and Employment.* New York: Praeger, 1976.

St. Louis Chapter of the Organization of Chinese Americans. *Ironing Out the Fabric of Our Past: An Oral History of Five Chinese Americans in St. Louis, The Early 1900's.* St. Louis, Mo.: The Organization, 1993.

Sullivan, Margaret Lo Piccolo. "Hyphenism in St. Louis, 1900–1921: The View from the Outside." Ph.D. diss., St. Louis University, 1968.

Takaki, Ronald, ed. *From Different Shores: Perspectives on Race and Ethnicity in America*. New York: Oxford University Press, 1987.
——— *Strangers from a Different Shore: A History of Asian Americans*. Boston: Little, Brown, 1989.
Tam, Shirley Sui-Ling. "Police Round-up of Chinese in Cleveland in 1925: A Case Study in a Racist Measure and the Chinese Response." Master's thesis, Case Western Reserve University, 1988.
Tamura, Linda. *The Hood River Issei: An Oral History of Japanese Settlers in Oregon's Hood River Valley*. Urbana: University of Illinois Press, 1993.
Tang, Vincent. "Chinese Women Immigrants and the Two-Edged Sword of Habeas Corpus." In *The Chinese American Experience: Papers from the Second National Conference on Chinese American Studies*, ed. Genny Lim, 48–56. San Francisco: Chinese Historical Society of America and the Chinese Cultural Foundation of San Francisco, 1980.
Tchen, John Kuo Wei. *Genthe's Photographs of San Francisco's Old Chinatown*. New York: Dover, 1984.
——— *New York Before Chinatown: Orientalism and the Shaping of American Culture, 1776–1882*. Baltimore, Md.: Johns Hopkins University Press, 1999.
——— "New York Chinese: The Nineteenth-Century Pre-Chinatown Settlement." *Chinese America: History and Perspectives, 1990*. San Francisco: Chinese Historical Society of America, 1990, 157–92.
Thompson, Richard H. *Toronto's Chinatown: The Changing Social Organization of an Ethnic Community*. New York: AMS, 1987.
Tsai, Shih-shan Henry. *The Chinese Experience in America*. Bloomington: Indiana University Press, 1986.
Tseng, Yen-Fen. "Suburban Ethnic Economy: Chinese Business Communities in Los Angeles." Ph.D. diss., University of California, Los Angeles, 1994.
——— "Chinese Ethnic Economy: San Gabriel Valley, Los Angeles County." *Journal of Urban Affairs* 16, no. 2 (1994): 169–89.
——— "Beyond 'Little Taipei': The Development of Taiwanese Immigrant Business in Los Angeles." *International Migration Review* 29, no. 1 (Spring 1995): 33–58.
Tu, Wei-ming, ed. *The Living Tree: The Changing Meaning of Being Chinese Today*. Stanford, Calif.: Stanford University Press, 1994.
Tung, William L. *The Chinese in America 1820–1973: A Chronology and Fact Book*. Dobbs Ferry, N.Y.: Oceana Publications, 1974.
Underwood, Katherine. "Process and Politics: Multiracial Electoral Coalition Building and Representation in Los Angeles' Ninth District, 1949–1962." Ph.D. diss., University of California, San Diego, 1992.
Võ, Linda Trinh, and Rick Bonus, eds. *Contemporary Asian American Communities: Intersections and Divergences*. Philadelphia: Temple University Press, 2002.
Wang, Gungwu. *Community and Nation: Essays on Southeast Asia and the Chinese*. Kuala Lumpur: Allen and Unwin, 1981.
——— *China and the Chinese Overseas*. Singapore: Times Academic Press, 1992.
——— *The Chinese Overseas: From Earthbound China to the Quest for Autonomy*. Cambridge, Mass.: Harvard University Press, 2000.

Wang, Ling-Chi. "Roots and the Changing Identity of the Chinese in the United States." In *The Living Tree: The Changing Meaning of Being Chinese Today*, ed. Tu Wei-ming, 185–212. Stanford, Calif.: Stanford University Press, 1994.

Wang, Xinyang. *Surviving the City: The Chinese Immigrant Experience in New York City, 1890–1970*. Lanham, Md.: Rowman & Littlefield, 2001.

Wang, Y. C. *Chinese Intellectuals and the West, 1872–1949*. Chapel Hill: University of North Carolina Press, 1966.

Washington University. *A Partial Bibliography of Resources on the History of Saint Louis Ethnic Cultures*. St. Louis: Sociology Department, Washington University (n.d.).

Wing, Yung. *My Life in America*. New York: Henry Holt, 1909.

Wong, Bernard P. *A Chinese American Community: Ethnicity and Survival Strategies*. Singapore: Chopmen Enterprises, 1979.

—— *Chinatown: Ethnic Adaptation and Ethnic Identity of the Chinese*. New York: Holt, Rinehart and Winston, 1982.

—— *Patronage, Brokerage, Entrepreneurship and the Chinese Community of New York*. New York: AMS Press, 1988.

Wong, K. Scott. "The Eagle Seeks a Helpless Quarry": Chinatown, the Police, and the Press: The 1903 Boston Chinatown Raid Revisited." *Amerasia Journal* 22, no. 3 (1996): 81–103.

Wright, John A. *Discovering African-American St. Louis: A Guide to Historic Sites*. St. Louis: Missouri Historical Society Press, 1994.

Wu, Yuan-li, ed. *The Economic Condition of Chinese Americans*. Chicago: Pacific/Asian American Mental Health Research Center, 1980.

Yang, Fenggang. *Chinese Christians in America: Conversion, Assimilation, and Adhesive Identities*. University Park, Penn.: Pennsylvania State University Press, 1999.

Yang, Philip Q. *Ethnic Studies: Issues and Approaches*. Albany: State University of New York Press, 2000.

Yans-McLaughlin, Virginia. *Family and Community: Italian Immigrants in Buffalo 1880–1930*. Urbana: University of Illinois Press, 1982.

Yin, Xiao-huang. *Chinese American Literature Since the 1850s*. Urbana: University of Illinois Press, 2000.

Yu, Connie Young. "The World of Our Grandmothers." In *Making Waves: An Anthology of Writings by and about Asian Women*, ed. Asian Women United of California, 33–42. Boston: Beacon Press, 1989.

Yu, Henry. *Thinking Orientals: Migration, Contact, and Exoticism in Modern America*. Oxford: Oxford University Press, 2001.

Yu, Renqiu. *To Save China, To Save Ourselves: The Chinese Hand Laundry Alliance of New York*. Philadelphia: Temple University Press, 1992.

Zhou, Min. *Chinatown: The Socioeconomic Potential of an Urban Enclave*. Philadelphia: Temple University Press, 1992.

Zhao, Xiaojian. *Remaking Chinese America: Immigration, Family, and Community, 1940–1965*. New Brunswick, N.J.: Rutgers University Press, 2002.

Zhou, Yu. "Ethnic Networks as Transactional Networks: Chinese Networks in the Producer Service Sectors of Los Angeles." Ph.D. diss., University of Minnesota, 1996.

Index

Page numbers in italic refer to photographs.